THE WAR AGAINST POPULATION

JACQUELINE KASUN

THE WAR
AGAINST POPULATION

The Economics and Ideology of
World Population Control

IGNATIUS PRESS   SAN FRANCISCO

Cover Photograph by Jerry Martin/AMWEST
Mother and child, Kenya, Africa
Cover Design by Roxanne Mei Lum and Marcia Ryan

©Ignatius Press, San Francisco, 1988
ISBN 0-89870-191-0
Library of Congress catalogue number 87-83505
Printed in the United States of America

For the sake of the children,
who are like arrows
in the quiver of a mighty man
and speak for us in the gate.

CONTENTS

5. Promoting the New Philosophy: The Sex Education Movement 95

The need to promulgate the philosophy of population control
The stated goals of the sex educators
  — The emphasis on combating "overpopulation"
Organizations promoting sex education
  — Planned Parenthood
  — Agency for International Development
  — World Bank
Nature of sex education programs: affective learning and values clarification:
     excerpts from typical programs
  — Emphasis on smaller families
  — Provision of confidential birth control
  — Explicit sex information
  — Emphasis on alternative life-styles
  — Emphasis on change as the new reality
  — Sex roles
The new orthodoxy of sex education
  — Combating dissent
  — Coalition-building
Government funding of sex education

6. Adolescent Pregnancy: Government Family Planning on the Home Front 115

Federal adolescent pregnancy legislation
  — Background
  — Purposes
Trends in childbearing among women under 20
  — Fertility rates
  — Numbers of births
  — Births out-of-wedlock
  — International comparisons
  — Common distortions of the facts
Alleged problems of adolescent pregnancy and facts
  — Dropping out of school
  — Maternal mortality
  — Toxemia
  — Prematurity
  — Suicide rates
  — Infant mortality
  — Child abuse
  — Welfare dependency

FOREWORD

Surprise is the measure of information content, and scientific work is important in proportion to how surprising its results are, assuming that the facts and theory are sound. Professor Jacqueline Kasun's book *The War against Population* is very surprising, even to someone like me who has for many years been following the literature she draws from. Furthermore, her facts seem to be correct and relevant, and her point of view makes good theoretical sense.

Some examples: (1) Kasun's description of the literature used for sex education and the motivations involved came as an unpleasant shock to me; I had thought that the sex education movement was more benign and less insidious. (2) Many of the materials that she has unearthed from official files about the population activities of the U.S. State Department's Agency for International Development in India, Thailand, and elsewhere document scandalous and illegal policies that have heretofore only been the subject of rumor. (3) The data she presents on trends in teenage pregnancies came as a big surprise; like everyone else, I get brainwashed by the population establishment's huge flow of literature, and by reports about it in the newspapers. Furthermore, her critical analyses of fallacious statements made on the basis of misinterpretation of these data are devastating, and are exceedingly valuable.

The hard work Kasun spent collecting information about the dozens of organizations that make up the population establishment in the United States is a great service to the public. The material she presents is invaluable for reference as well as an eye-opener for those interested in the field. It is sure that I, along with many others, will draw frequently upon these chapters for quotations, as well as for data on the money-flows among these organizations and the U.S. government.

The first three theoretical chapters about the economic consequences of population growth and about the results of planned versus "spontaneous" market economic policies should come as no surprise in 1987, because by now there has grown up a substantial literature underpinning the ideas that she presents there. It is therefore regrettable that these ideas and data will nevertheless be so surprising to most people in Western countries that they will be unable to believe that Kasun is presenting a truthful and sound analysis—which she is. All the more important, then, that the book provides this material in an accessible and readable form.

We should all be grateful to Jacqueline Kasun for having the diligence, skill, and courage to write this book.

Julian L. Simon

PREFACE

To write about any continuing phenomenon inevitably raises the problem of omitting events that occur after the book is finished. The drama pictured in the ensuing pages did not come to an end in the last chapter when the manuscript went to the printer but has continued to unfold. There have been new campaigns and new fronts and new fighting on old fronts in the war against population.

One of the chief combatants, the United Nations Fund for Population Activities, lost its major source of funding, the United States, in 1986 and 1987 because of the Fund's continued support of coercive population control in China. There were heated denials of the charges and vows to secure a reversal of the decision. Congress also denied funding to the London-based International Planned Parenthood Federation because that organization supports abortion as a method of family planning. This did not, however, mean any reduction in the millions of dollars going to local Planned Parenthood clinics in the United States or abroad, since these organizations receive their U.S. grants independently of the international federation.

A battle erupted in the U.S. Health and Human Services bureaucracy in 1987 over whether to continue grants to local Planned Parenthood clinics in the United States in view of the law prohibiting grants to "programs where abortion is a method of family planning". The upshot was the issuance of regulations which, if enforced, were expected to reduce Planned Parenthood's government grants by tens of millions of dollars annually. The organization promptly launched a media blitz to "protect reproductive rights". Planned Parenthood also took a leadership role in the drive against confirmation of Judge Robert Bork to the Supreme Court, on grounds that Bork could not be relied upon to uphold the "right to privacy", the linchpin in the abortion rights cases as well as in right-to-die jurisprudence.

There was a setback in the Philippines, which since 1973 had been one of the laboratories and training grounds for the network of international organizations devoted to population control. The new constitution proposed by the Aquino government and overwhelmingly ratified by the populace deleted the clause in the 1973 constitution that had mandated government population control. It also included a clause requiring the state to "protect the life of the mother and the life of the unborn from conception".

The setbacks were tentative, however, and were by no means certain to be sustained by succeeding administrations and governments. On another front, the trend toward complete population planning moved strongly forward, as predicted

15

in Chapter 8. Court decisions allowing the removal of food and water from patients increased in number and in broadness of coverage in the United States. From aged nursing-home patients to young people incapacitated by accidents, the scope of the new rulings made death control a reality just as birth control had been brought about in an earlier period.

There were some signs of weakening on the philosophical front. A 1986 report by the National Academy of Sciences retreated somewhat from its earlier demand for "real population *control*", described in Chapter 7, and acknowledged that population growth may not cause resource exhaustion and slower population growth may not cause economic improvement. It nevertheless decided that more economic progress would be likely to occur if population growth were slower. At the same time some voices called attention to the possibly undesirable consequences of low or negative rates of population growth. Ben Wattenberg's book *The Birth Dearth* (Pharos, 1987) predicted a loss of economic strength and international stature as a result of low birth rates in the West.

These divergences were exceptional, however. "Overpopulation" alarmism continued to prevail as in the past. Decrying the "unprecedented human and economic devastation resulting from rapid global population growth", the Population Institute organized thirty-nine U.S. governors to proclaim World Population Awareness Week in April 1987, "as a part of the emerging national consensus on the world population crisis". The Institute also organized forty-five heads of state to announce their intention to "stop population growth within the near future", adopting "the necessary policies and programs to do so". The U.S. government-funded Population Reference Bureau continued to distribute school materials likening "human overcrowding" to the multiplication of fruit-flies in bottles.

The U.S. government continued to appropriate hundreds of millions of dollars annually for domestic and foreign birth control, as described in Chapter 7. And when certain recipients, such as the UN and International Planned Parenthood, were denied U.S. grants, increased amounts were given to other recipients. The U.S. Agency for International Development, undaunted by misgivings about coercive population control, continued its programs as described in Chapter 4.

On the teenage pregnancy front, activity was especially intense. The movement to install clinics to dispense birth control in schools gathered steam, with the number of such clinics multiplying rapidly in 1986 and 1987. A National Organization on Adolescent Pregnancy and Parenting—a coalition of Planned Parenthood, the Center for Population Options, and other groups discussed in Chapters 5, 6, and 7—held a series of regional conferences to discuss strategies for mandating the kinds of "family life education" described in Chapter 5, establishing school clinics, "greatly" reducing adolescent pregnancy, and achieving "zero population growth", among other lofty purposes.

In a word, the more things changed, the more they stayed the same. And the U.S. government-funded Association for Voluntary Sterilization, operator of a worldwide network of sterilization clinics and lobbyists to governments, changed its name to the Association for Voluntary Surgical Contraception.

October 1987

ACKNOWLEDGMENTS

The idea for this book grew from an article that I wrote on the foreign population programs of the United States and which the Heritage Foundation published in the Winter 1981 issue of its journal, *Policy Review.* Chapter 6 draws on work that I did in writing a chapter on adolescent pregnancy for *Economics and the Family,* edited by Stephen J. Bahr, and published by Lexington in 1980; it also incorporates material that appears in my chapter in *The American Family and the State,* edited by Joseph R. Peden and Fred R. Glahe, published by the Pacific Institute in 1986. The chapter on sex education grew out of an article of mine which *The Public Interest* published in Spring, 1979.

A number of people have read the manuscript and given helpful suggestions. I am especially indebted to Professor Julian Simon for his comments on an early draft of the manuscript.

I am grateful to Humboldt State University for giving me time to write; to my colleagues in the economics department and my students for friendship and inspiration; to the staff of the Humboldt State University Library, especially to Mr. Erich F. Schimps, for unfailingly efficient and courteous assistance; to my daughter Audrey Kasun Moruza for sharing with me her expertise in demography, the results of her research, and her insights; to my son Walter Joseph Kasun and to Danny Ihara for helping with the statistics; to my daughter Christine Kasun Moruza and all of my children for, in the words of Psalm 127, speaking for me in the gate; to my husband Joseph for his assistance in my research and his unfailing encouragement; to a most talented editor, Mrs. Patricia B. Bozell, and a conscientious and efficient typist, Mrs. Diane Eklund.

Finally, I owe an inestimable debt to many friends who, knowing my interests, send me news items, articles, book notices, and other materials. This book owes its inspiration to them and could not have been written without their help. Among these, I am especially grateful to Mrs. Judie Brown.

If there are mistakes in the work, they are all my own.

CHAPTER ONE

"OVERPOPULATION": THE UNEXAMINED DOGMA

It was a traveling exhibit for schoolchildren. Titled "Population: The Problem Is Us", it toured the country at government expense in the mid-1970s. It consisted of a set of illustrated panels with an accompanying script that stated:

> ... there are too many people in the world. We are running out of space. We are running out of energy. We are running out of food. And, although too few people seem to realize it, we are running out of time.[1]

It told the children that "the birth rate must decrease and/or the death rate must increase" since resources were all but exhausted and mass starvation loomed. It warned that, "driven by starvation, people have been known to eat dogs, cats, bird droppings, and even their own children",[2] and it featured a picture of a dead rat on a dinner plate as an example of future "food sources".[3] Overpopulation, it threatened, would lead not only to starvation and cannibalism but to civil violence and nuclear war.

The exhibit was created at the Smithsonian Institution, the national museum of the U.S. government, using federal funds provided by the National Science Foundation, an agency of the U.S. government.

Concurrently, other American schoolchildren were also being treated to federally funded "population education", instructing them on "the growing pressures on global resources, food, jobs, and political stability".[4] They read Paul Ehrlich's book, *The Population Bomb*. They were taught, falsely, that "world population is increasing at a rate of 2 percent per year whereas the food supply is increasing at a rate of 1 percent per year",[5] and equally falsely, that "population growth and rising affluence have reduced reserves of the world's minerals".[6] They viewed

---

[1] *Projectbook for the Exhibition "Population: The Problem Is Us": A Book of Suggestions for Implementing the Exhibition in Your Own Institution* (Washington: The Smithsonian Institution, undated, circulated in late 1970s), p. 9.

[2] Ibid., pp. 20, 23.

[3] Ibid., p. 51.

[4] *Interchange*, Population Education Newsletter published by the Population Reference Bureau, vol. 9, no. 2, September 1980, p. 1.

[5] John J. Burt and Linda Brower Meeks, *Education for Sexuality: Concepts and Programs for Teaching* (Philadelphia: W. B. Saunders, 1975), p. 408.

[6] Elaine M. Murphy, "Population and Resources: What about Tomorrow?" (Washington: Population Reference Bureau, undated, distributed for classroom use in mid-1970s).

slides of the "biological catastrophes" that would result from overpopulation[7] and held class discussions on "what responsible individuals in a 'crowded world' should or can do about population growth".[8] They learned that the world is like a spaceship[9] or a crowded lifeboat,[10] to deduce the fate of mankind, which faces a "population crisis".[11] And then, closer to home, they learned that families who have children are adding to the problems of overpopulation,[12] and besides, children are a costly burden who "need attention . . . 24 hours a day" and spoil marriages by making their fathers "jealous" and rendering their mothers "depleted".[13] They were told to "say good-bye" to numerous wildlife species doomed to extinction as a result of the human population explosion.[14]

This propaganda campaign in the public schools, which indoctrinated a generation of children, was federally funded, despite the fact that no law had committed the United States to this policy. Nor, indeed, had agreement been reached among informed groups that the problem of "overpopulation" even existed. To the contrary, during the same period the government drive against population was gaining momentum, contrary evidence was proliferating. One of the world's most prominent economic demographers, Colin Clark of Oxford University, published a book titled *Population Growth: The Advantages;*[15] and economists Peter Bauer and Basil Yamey of the London School of Economics discovered that the population scare "relies on misleading statistics . . . misunderstands the determinants of economic progress . . . misinterprets the causalities in changes in fertility and changes in income" and "envisages children exclusively as burdens".[16] Moreover, in his major study of *The Economics of Population Growth,* Julian Simon found that

---

[7] Ibid.

[8] *Interchange,* Population Education Newsletter published by the Population Reference Bureau, vol. 8, no. 3, October 1979, p. 1.

[9] Isaac Asimov, *Earth, Our Crowded Spaceship* (New York: John Day, 1974).

[10] Garrett Hardin, "Living on a Lifeboat", *BioScience,* October 1974, reprinted in *The CoEvolution Quarterly,* Summer 1975, pp. 16–23.

[11] Sue Titus Reid and David L. Lyon, eds., *Population Crisis: An Interdisciplinary Perspective* (Glenview: Scott Foresman, 1972).

[12] *Arcata School District Family Life/Sex Education Curriculum Guide* (Arcata, California, June 1976).

[13] Ferndale Elementary School District and Ferndale Union High School District, *Family Life/Sex Education Curriculum Guide: Kindergarten–Twelfth Grade* (Ferndale, California, July 1978). p. 322; Planned Parenthood-Santa Cruz County, *Sex Education: Teacher's Guide and Resource Manual* (Santa Cruz, 1979), p. 149.

[14] *Say Goodbye* (Wilmette, Illinois: Films, Inc., 1972), film recommended for classroom use by Population Reference Bureau, *Population Education: Sources and Resources,* May 1979, p. 23.

[15] Colin Clark, *Population Growth: The Advantages* (Santa Ana: R. L. Sassone, 1972).

[16] Peter T. Bauer and Basil S. Yamey, "The Third World and the West: An Economic Perspective", in W. Scott Thompson, ed., *The Third World: Premises of U.S. Policy* (San Francisco: Institute for Contemporary Studies, 1978), p. 108.

population growth was economically beneficial.[17] Other economists joined in differing from the official antinatalist position.[18]

Commenting on this body of economic findings, Paul Ehrlich, the biologist-author of *The Population Bomb,* charged that economists "continue to whisper in the ears of politicians all kinds of nonsense".[19] If not on the side of the angels, Ehrlich certainly found himself on the side of the U.S. government, which since the mid-1960s has become increasingly committed to a worldwide drive to reduce the growth of population. It has absorbed rapidly increasing amounts of public money, as well as the energies of a growing number of public agencies and publicly subsidized private organizations.

The spirit of the propaganda has permeated American life at all levels, from the highest reaches of the federal bureaucracy to the chronic reporting of overpopulation problems by the media and the population education being pushed in public schools. It has become so much a part of daily American life that its presuppositions and implications are scarcely examined; though volumes are regularly published on the subject, they rarely do more than restate the assumptions as a prelude to proposing even "better" methods of population planning.

But even more alarming are some neglected features inherent in the proposed needs and the probable results of population planning. The factual errors are egregious, true, and the alarmists err when they claim that world food output per person and world mineral reserves are decreasing—that, indeed, the human economic prospect has been growing worse rather than more secure and prosperous by all available objective standards. But these are not the most significant claims made by the advocates of government population planning. The most fundamental, which is often tacit rather than explicit, is that the world faces an unprecedented problem of "crisis" proportions that defies all familiar methods of solution.

Specifically, it is implied that the familiar human response to scarcity—that of economizing—is inadequate under the "new" conditions. Thus the economist's traditional reliance on the individual's ability to choose in impersonal markets is disqualified. Occasionally it is posited that the market mechanism will fail due to "externalities",[20] but it is more often said that mankind is entering by a quantum leap into a new age in which all traditional methods and values are inapplicable.[21] Sometimes it is implied that the uniqueness of this new age inheres in its new

[17] Julian L. Simon, *The Economics of Population Growth* (Princeton: Princeton University Press, 1977).

[18] See, for example, Mark Perlman, "*Population and Economic Change in Developing Countries:* A Review Article", *The Journal of Economic Literature,* vol. 19, no. 1, March 1981, pp. 74–82; Richard A. Easterlin, "Population", in Neil W. Chamberlain, ed., *Contemporary Economic Issues* (Homewood: Richard D. Irwin, Inc., 1973), pp. 301–352.

[19] *Christian Science Monitor,* July 30, 1980, p. B7.

[20] J. J. Spengler, *Origins of Economic Thought and Justice* (Southern Illinois, 1980), p. 144.

[21] Robert L. Heilbroner, *An Inquiry into the Human Prospect* (New York: W. W. Norton & Company, 1980).

technology, and at other times that human nature itself is changing in fundamental respects.

Whatever the cause of this leap into an unmapped future, the widely held conclusion is that since all familiar human institutions are failing and will continue to fail in the "new" circumstances, they must be abandoned and replaced. First among these supposedly failing institutions is the market mechanism, that congeries of institutions and activities by which individuals and groups carry out production and make decisions about the allocation of resources and the distribution of income. Not only the market, but democratic political institutions as well are held to be manifestly unsuitable for the "new" circumstances. Even the traditional family is labeled for extinction because of its inability to adapt to the evolving situation. The new school family life and sex education programs, for example, stress the supposed decline of the traditional family—heterosexual marriage, blood or adoptive relationships—and its replacement by new, "optional" forms, such as communes and homosexual partnerships.[22] Unsurprisingly, traditional moral and ethical teachings must be abandoned.[23]

The decision to repudiate the market is of interest not only to economists but to both those capitalists and market socialists who have seen how impersonal markets can mediate the innate conflict between consumer desires and resource scarcity. The most elegant models of socialism have incorporated the market mechanism into their fundamental design.[24] Adam Smith's "invisible hand", which leads men to serve one another and to economize in their use of resources as they pursue their own self-interest, is relied upon to a considerable extent in a number of socialist countries. John Maurice Clark called it "our main safeguard against exploitation" because it performs "the simple miracle whereby each one increases his gains by increasing his services rather than by reducing them",[25] and Walter Eucken said it protects individuals by breaking up the great concentrations of economic power.[26] The common element here is, of course, the realization that individual decision-making leads not to chaos but to social harmony.

This view is denied by the population planners and it is here that the debate is, or should be, joined. Why are the advocates of government population planning

---

[22] Mary S. Calderone and Eric W. Johnson, *The Family Book About Sexuality* (New York: Harper & Row, 1981), pp. 132–135; California State Department of Education, *Education for Human Sexuality: A Resource Book and Instructional Guide to Sex Education for Kindergarten Through Grade Twelve* (Sacramento, 1979), pp. 27–28.

[23] California State Department of Education, op. cit., pp. 28, 80, 81; Mary S. Calderone, "Sex Education and the Roles of School and Church", *The Annals of the American Academy of Political and Social Science,* vol. 376, March 1968, pp. 53–60.

[24] See, for example, Oskar Lange and Fred M. Taylor, *On the Economic Theory of Socialism* (New York: McGraw Hill, 1964).

[25] John Maurice Clark, *Alternative to Serfdom* (New York: Alfred A. Knopf, 1948), p. 62.

[26] Walter Eucken, *The Foundations of Economics* (Edinburg: Hodge, 1950).

so sure that the market mechanism cannot handle population growth? Why are they so sure that the market will not respond as it has in the past to resource scarcities—by raising prices so as to induce consumers to economize and producers to provide substitutes? Why can individual families not be trusted to adjust the number of their children to their incomes and thus to the given availability of resources? Why do the advocates of government population control assume that human beings must "overbreed", both to their own detriment and to that of society?

It is occasionally averred that the reason for this hypothetical failure is that individuals do not bear the full costs of their childbearing decisions but transfer a large part to society and therefore tend to have "too many" children. This is a dubious claim, for it overlooks the fact that individual families do not receive all the benefits generated by their childbearing. The lifetime productivity and social contribution of children flows largely to persons other than their parents, which, it might be argued, leads families to have fewer children than would be in the best interests of society. Which of these "externalities" is the more important, or whether they balance one another, is a question that waits not merely for an answer but for a reasoned study.

Another reason commonly given for the alleged failure of personal decisions is that individuals do not know how to control the size of their families. But a deeper look makes it abundantly clear that the underlying reason is that the population planners do not believe that individuals, even if fully informed, can be relied upon to make the proper choice. The emphasis on "outreach" and the incentives that pervade the United States' domestic and foreign population efforts testify to this, as will be shown in more depth shortly.

More important than these arguments, however, is the claim that new advances in technology are not amenable to control by market forces—a traditional argument in favor of socialism. From the time of Saint Simon to that of Veblen and on to our own age, the argument has been advanced that the market forces of supply-and-demand are incapable of controlling the vast powers of modern technology. At the dawn of the nineteenth century Saint Simon called for the redesigning of human society to cope with the new forces being unleashed by science. Only planned organization and control would suffice, he claimed. "Men of business" and the market forces which they represented would have to be replaced by planning "experts".[27] In the middle of the nineteenth century Marx created a theoretical model of the capitalist market that purported to prove that the new technological developments would burst asunder the forms of private property and capitalist markets. Three-quarters of a century later Veblen spoke for the planning mentality when he wrote in 1921:

[27] See Keith Taylor (trans. and ed.), *Henri Saint-Simon (1760–1825): Selected Writings on Science, Industry and Social Organisation* (New York: Holmes & Meier, 1975).

The material welfare of the community is unreservedly bound up with the due working of this industrial system, and therefore with its unreserved control by the engineers, who alone are competent to manage it. To do their work as it should be done these men of the industrial general staff must have a free hand, unhampered by commercial considerations . . . [28]

In our own time, Heilbroner expresses a similar but even more profound distrust of market forces:

. . . the external challenge of the human prospect, with its threats of runaway populations, obliterative war, and potential environmental collapse, can be seen as an extended and growing crisis induced by the advent of a command over natural processes and forces that far exceeds the reach of our present mechanisms of social control. [29]

Heilbroner's position is uniquely modern in its pessimism. Unlike Marx and Veblen, who believed that the profit-seeking aspects of supply-and-demand unduly restricted the new technology from fulfilling its *beneficent* potential, Heilbroner sees the market as incapable of controlling an essentially *destructive* technology. Technology, in Heilbroner's view, brings nuclear arms, industrial pollution, and the reduction in death rates that is responsible for the population "explosion"; all of these stubbornly resist control by the market or by benign technological advance. Heilbroner has little hope that pollution-control technology, for example, will be able to offset the bad effects of industrial pollution.

An additional argument is that mankind is rapidly approaching, or has reached, the "limits to growth" or the "carrying capacity" of an earth with "finite" resources. Far from being a new position, it dates back to Thomas Malthus' *Essay on the Principle of Population* (1798), which held that the growth of population must inevitably outrun the growth of food supply. It must be one of the curiosities of our age that though Malthus' forecast has proved mistaken—that, in fact, the living standards of the average person have reached a level probably unsurpassed in history—doom is still pervasively forecast. The modern literature of "limits" is voluminous, including such works as the much-criticized *Limits to Growth* published by the Club of Rome, [30] and the Carter administration's *Global 2000.* [31] In common, these works predict an impending exhaustion of various world economic resources which are assumed to be absolutely fixed in quantity and for which no substitutes can be found. The world is likened to a "spaceship", as in

---

[28] Thorstein Veblen, "The Captains of Finance and the Engineers", in Wesley C. Mitchell, ed., *What Veblen Taught: Selected Writings of Thorstein Veblen* (New York: The Viking Press, 1947), p. 432.

[29] Heilbroner, op. cit., p. 57.

[30] Donella H. Meadows, Dennis L. Meadows et al., *The Limits to Growth: A Report for the Club of Rome's Project on the Predicament of Mankind* (New York: Universe Books, 1972).

[31] *The Global 2000 Report to the President,* A Report Prepared by the Council on Environmental Quality and the Department of State (Washington: U.S. Government Printing Office, 1980).

Boulding's[32] and Asimov's[33] writings; or, even more pessimistically, an over-loaded "lifeboat", as in Garrett Hardin's articles.[34]

Now, in the first place, as for the common assumption in this literature that the limits are fixed and known (or, as Garrett Hardin puts it, each country's "lifeboat" carries a sign that indicates its "capacity"[35]), no such knowledge does in fact exist — for the earth, or for any individual country, or with regard to any resource. No one knows how much petroleum exists on earth or how many people can earn their living in Illinois. What is known is that the types and quantities of economic resources are continually changing, as is the ability of given areas to support life. In the same territories in which earlier men struggled and starved, much larger populations today support themselves in comfort. The difference, of course, lies in the *knowledge* that human beings bring to the task of discovering and managing resources.

But then, secondly, the literature of limits rules out all such increasing knowledge. Indeed, in adopting the lifeboat or spaceship metaphor, the apostles of limits not only rule out all new knowledge, but the discovery of new resources, and in fact, virtually all production. Clearly, if the world is really a spaceship or a lifeboat, then both technology and resources are absolutely fixed, and beyond a low limit, population growth would be disastrous. Adherents of the view insist that that limit is either being rapidly approached or has been passed, about which more later. Important here is that even this extreme view of the human situation does not rule out the potential of market forces. Most of mankind throughout history has lived under conditions that would be regarded today as extreme, even desperate, deprivation. And over the millennia private decisions and private transactions have played an important, often a dominant, role in economic life. The historical record clearly shows that human beings can act and cooperate on their own in the best interests of survival, even under very difficult conditions. But history notwith-standing, the claims that emergencies of one kind or another require the central-ized direction of economic life have been recurrent, especially during this century, which, ironically, has been the most economically prosperous. Today's advocates of coercion — the proponents of population control — posit the imminent approach of resource exhaustion, a condition wherein human beings will abandon all semblance of rational and civilized behavior.

To ward off their "emergency", the proponents of population control call for the adoption of measures that they admit would not be normally admissible. This

[32] Kenneth E. Boulding, "The Economics of the Coming Spaceship Earth", in Henry Jarrett, ed., *Environmental Quality in a Growing Economy*, (Baltimore: Johns Hopkins, 1966), pp. 3–14.

[33] Asimov, op. cit.

[34] Hardin, op.cit.; see also Harold Hayes, "A Conversation with Garrett Hardin", *The Atlantic Monthly*, vol. 247, no. 5, May 1981, pp. 60–70.

[35] Hayes, op. cit.

is surely ample reason for a thoughtful and thorough examination of measures already being propagated.

Social and economic planning require an administrative bureaucracy with powers of enforcement. Modern economic analysis clearly shows that there are no impersonal, automatic mechanisms in the public sector that can simply and perfectly compensate for private market "failure".[36] The public alternative is fraught with inequity and inefficiency, which can be substantial and exceedingly important. Although the theory of bureaucratic behavior has received less attention than that of private consumer choice, public administrators have also proved subject to greed, which hardly leads to social harmony. Government employees and contractors have the same incentives to avoid competition and form monopolies as private firms.[37] They can increase their incomes by padding their costs and bloating their projects, and excuse it by exaggerating the need for their services and discrediting alternative solutions.

Managers of government projects have no market test to meet since they give away their products, even force them on an unwilling public, while collecting the necessary funds by force through the tax system. They can use their government grants to lobby for still more grants and to finance legal action to increase their power. They can bribe other bureaucrats and grants recipients to back their projects with the promise of reciprocal services. Through intergovernmental grants and "subventions" they can arrange their financial affairs so that apparently no one is accountable for any given decision or program. In short, the record of bureaucratic behavior confirms the statement of the great socialist scholar Oskar Lange, that "the real danger of socialism is that of a bureaucratization of economic life".[38] The danger may well be more serious than we realize—it could be nothing less than totalitarianism.

Finally, proponents of the "population crisis" believe that not only must the *agencies* and *methods* of control be changed under the "new" circumstances but also the *criteria for choice*. Since, they argue, the technological and demographic developments of the modern age render all traditional standards of value and goodness either obsolete or questionable, these must be revised—under the leadership, of course, of those who understand the implications of the new developments.

Above all, they hold that the traditional concept of the value and dignity of the individual human being must be overhauled.[39] The good of the *species,* as understood fully only by the advocates of the new views, must in all cases supersede the good as perceived and sought after by individuals.

[36] Richard B. McKenzie and Gordon Tullock, *Modern Political Economy* (New York: McGraw-Hill, 1978), pp. 385–421.

[37] Ibid.; Charles Wolf, Jr., "A Theory of Non-market Failures", *Public Interest,* no. 55, Spring 1979, pp. 114–133.

[38] Lange and Taylor, op. cit., p. 109.

[39] Hayes, op. cit.

Clearly, in the late twentieth century a worldview has emerged that calls into question not only the presuppositions of much of economics, but some basic political and philosophical thought as well. The history of our age may be determined by the outcome of the confrontation between these views.

It must be emphasized that the essential issue is not birth control or family planning. People have throughout history used various means to determine the size of their families, generating a great deal of discussion and debate. But the critical issue raised by recent history, especially in the United States, is whether government has the right or duty to preside over the reproductive process . . . for what reasons, to what extent?

Recent official action in the United States has proceeded as if the question had already been answered. The fact is, however, that it has been neither explicitly asked nor discussed, even as we rush toward a future shaped by its affirmative answer. It is this question that must be examined.

CHAPTER TWO

SCARCITY OR LIFEBOAT ECONOMICS: WHICH IS RIGHT?

The fact of scarcity is the fundamental concern of economics. As one leading textbook puts it in its opening pages, "wants exceed what is available".[1] It pertains to the rich as well as to the poor, since scarcity is not the same thing as poverty. As another text tells students, "higher production levels seem to bring in their train ever-higher consumption standards. Scarcity remains".[2]

Yet another explains,

> we are not able to produce all of everything that everyone wants free; thus we must "economize" our resources, or use them as efficiently as possible ... human wants, if not infinite, go ... far beyond the ability of our productive resources to satisfy them ...[3]

That scarcity is no less real in affluent societies than in poor ones is explained in more general terms by other economists who stress the need to make *choices* whenever alternatives exist. In the words of McKenzie and Tullock,

> the individual makes *choices* from among an array of alternative options ... in each choice situation, a person must always forgo doing one or more things when doing something else. Since *cost* is the most highly valued alternative forgone, all rational behavior involves a cost.[4]

Clearly, the affluent person or society faces a large list of highly valued alternatives, and is likely to have a difficult choice to make—to be more acutely aware of the scarcity and the need to give up one thing in order to have another. It follows that scarcity does not lessen with affluence but is more likely to increase.

Simply put, economists understand scarcity as the inescapable fact that candy bars and ice cream cannot be made out of the same milk and chocolate. A choice must be made, regardless of how much milk and chocolate there is. And the decision to produce milk and chocolate rather than cheese and coffee is another inescapable choice. And so the list continues, endlessly, constituting the core of

---

[1] Armen A. Alchian and William R. Allen, *University Economics,* 3rd ed. (Belmont: Wadsworth Publishing Co., 1972), p. 7.

[2] Paul A. Samuelson, *Economics,* 11th ed. (New York: McGraw Hill, 1980), p. 17.

[3] George Leland Bach, *Economics: An Introduction to Analysis and Policy,* 10th ed. (Englewood Cliffs: Prentice-Hall, Inc., 1980), p. 3.

[4] Richard B. McKenzie and Gordon Tullock, *Modern Political Economy* (New York: McGraw-Hill, 1978), p. 18.

economics. How to choose what to produce, for whom, and how, is the very stuff of economics.

It is important to notice how different these traditional economic concepts of scarcity and choice are from the notions of "lifeboat economics". In Garrett Hardin's metaphor,[5] the lifeboat's capacity is written on its side. The doomsday literature of limits is shot through with the conceit of absolute capacity, which is alien to economics. Not the least of the differences is that in economics humanity is viewed not only as the *raison d'être* of other forms of wealth but as one of the sources of wealth; human labor and ingenuity are resources, means for creating wealth. In the lifeboat, human beings are pure burdens, straining the capacity of the boat. Which of these views is closer to reality?

Is the earth rapidly approaching or has it surpassed its capacity to support human life? But before delving into the existence and nature of limits, keep in mind that the notion of a limited carrying capacity is not the only argument for population control. The view of people, or at least of more people, as simply a curse or affliction has its adherents. Thus Kingsley Davis writes of the "population plague",[6] and Paul Ehrlich speaks with obvious repugnance of "people, people, people, people".[7] Other writers, both old and new, attribute, if not a negative, at least a zero value to people. Thus John D. Rockefeller III, submitting the final report of the Commission on Population Growth and the American Future, wrote:

> in the long run, no substantial benefits will result from further growth of the Nation's population, rather . . . the gradual stabilization of our population would contribute significantly to the Nation's ability to solve its problems. We have looked for, and have not found, any convincing economic argument for continued population growth. The health of our country does not depend on it, nor does the vitality of business nor the welfare of the average person.[8]

The notion embodied in this statement—that, to validate its claim to existence, a human life should justify itself by contributing to such things as the "vitality of business"—is a perfect example of the utilitarian ethic. Though economics has skirted utilitarianism at times, it was never in this sense, but rather in its belief that human beings could be rational in making choices. Economics has been content to value all things in terms of what they mean to individual human beings; it has never valued human beings in terms of supposedly higher values.

[5] Harold Hayes, "A Conversation with Garrett Hardin", *The Atlantic Monthly,* vol. 247, no. 5, May 1981, pp. 60–70.

[6] Kingsley Davis, "The Climax of Population Growth", *California Medicine,* 113, November, 1970, pp. 33–39.

[7] Paul R. Ehrlich, *The Population Bomb* (New York: Balantine Books, 1968), p. 15.

[8] John D. Rockefeller III, Letter to the President and Congress, transmitting the Final Report of the Commission on Population Growth and the American Future, dated March 27, 1972.

The idea that the earth is incapable of continuing to support human life suffuses United States government publications. The House Select Committee on Population reported in 1978 that

> the four major biological systems that humanity depends upon for food and raw materials—ocean fisheries, grasslands, forests, and croplands—are being strained by rapid population growth to the point where, in some cases, they are actually losing productive capacity.[9]

The Carter administration's *Global 2000* report, which was much criticized by research experts,[10] predicted:

> With the persistence of human poverty and misery, the staggering growth of human population, and ever increasing human demands, the possibilities of further stress and permanent damage to the planet's resource base are very real.[11]

Such statements have been duly broadcast by the media despite the facts, which tell a quite different story.

In the first place, world food production has increased considerably faster than population in recent decades. The increase in per capita food output between 1950 and 1977 amounted to either 28 percent or 37 percent, depending on whether United Nations or United States Department of Agriculture figures are used, as Julian Simon has shown.[12] Clearly, this is a very substantial increase. More recent United Nations and U.S. Department of Agriculture data show that world food output has continued to match or outstrip population growth in the years since 1977.[13] Some of the most dramatic increases have occurred in the poorest countries, those designated for "triage" by the apostles of doom. For example, rice and wheat production in India in 1983 was almost three-and-a-half times as great as in 1950. This was considerably more than twice the percentage increase in the population of India in the same period.[14]

---

[9] Select Committee on Population, Report, "World Population: Myths and Realities", U.S. House of Representatives, 95th Congress, 2nd Session (Washington: U.S. Government Printing Office, 1978), p. 5.

[10] Julian L. Simon, "Global Confusion, 1980: A Hard Look at the Global 2000 Report", *The Public Interest*, no. 62, Winter 1981, pp. 3–20.

[11] *The Global 2000 Report to the President: Global Future: Time to Act,* prepared by the Council on Environmental Quality and the U.S. Department of State (Washington: U.S. Government Printing Office, January 1981), p. ix.

[12] Simon, op. cit., pp. 14–16.

[13] *FAO Production Yearbook 1981;* U.S. Department of Agriculture, *World Indices of Agricultural and Food Production, 1974–1983.*

[14] Based on figures appearing in U.S. Bureau of the Census, *Statistical Abstract of the United States,* 1957, 1960, and 1984 eds. presenting UN and FAO data, and U.S. Department of Agriculture, op. cit.

In a recent article written at the Harvard Center for Population Studies, Nick Eberstadt calls attention to the great increases in the world food supply in recent decades. He points out that only about 2 percent of the world's population suffers from serious hunger, in contrast to the much larger estimates publicized by the Food and Agricultural Organization of the United Nations in its applications for grants to continue its attempts to "solve" the world hunger problem. Eberstadt notes that the improving world food situation is probably reflected by the fact that "in the past thirty years, life expectancy in the less developed countries, excluding China, has risen by more than a third",[15] and that "in the past twenty years in these same nations, death rates for one-to-four-year-olds, the age group most vulnerable to nutritional setback, have dropped by nearly half".[16]

He points out that the much-decried increase in food imports by some less-developed countries is not a cause for alarm, but actually requires a smaller proportion of their export earnings to finance than in 1960.[17]

In 1980, according to Eberstadt, even the poorest of the less-developed countries had to use less than 10 percent of their export earnings to pay for their food imports.[18] The good news is underscored by the fact that these countries have been able to export their manufactured and other nonfood items so much in recent years that it is profitable—it is the efficient choice—for them to export these products in exchange for food, just as developed countries do.

The recent famine in Africa may seem to belie these optimistic findings. Africa, however, is a continent torn by war; farmers cannot cultivate and reap in battle zones, and enemy troops often seize or burn crops. Collectivist governments, also endemic in Africa, often seize crops and farm animals without regard for farmers' needs. War and socialism are two great destroyers of the food supply in Africa, as they have been in other continents.

The impressive increases in food production that have occurred in recent decades have barely scratched the surface of the available food-raising resources, according to the best authorities. Farmers use less than half of the earth's arable land and only a minute part of the water available for irrigation. Indeed, three-fourths of the world's available crop-land requires no irrigation.[19]

How large a population could the world's agricultural resources support using presently known methods of farming? Colin Clark, former director of the Agricultural Economic Institute at Oxford University, classified world land-types by their food-raising capabilities and found that if all farmers were to use the best methods,

[15] Nick Eberstadt, "Hunger and Ideology", *Commentary,* vol. 72, no. 1, July 1981, p. 43.
[16] Ibid.
[17] Ibid., p. 44.
[18] Ibid.
[19] Roger Revelle, "The Resources Available for Agriculture", *Scientific American,* vol. 235, no. 3, September 1976, p. 168.

enough food could be raised to provide an American-type diet for 35.1 billion people, more than seven times the present population.[20] Since the American diet is a very rich one, Clark found that it would be possible to feed three times as many again, or more than twenty-two times as many as now exist, at a Japanese standard of food intake. Clark's estimate assumed that nearly half of the earth's land area would remain in conservation areas, for recreation and the preservation of wildlife.[21]

Roger Revelle, former director of the Harvard Center for Population Studies, estimated that world agricultural resources are capable of providing an adequate diet (2,500 kilocalories per day), as well as fiber, rubber, tobacco, and beverages, for 40 billion people, or eight times the present number.[22] This, he thought, would require the use of less than one-fourth—compared with one-ninth today—of the earth's ice-free land area.[23] He presumed that average yields would be about one-half those presently produced in the United States Midwest.[24] Clearly, better yields and/or the use of a larger share of the land area would support over 40 billion persons.

Revelle has estimated that the less-developed continents, those whose present food supplies are most precarious, are capable of feeding 18 billion people, or six times their present population.[25] He has estimated that the continent of Africa alone is capable of feeding 10 billion people, which is twice the amount of the present world population and more than twenty times the 1980 population of Africa.[26] He sees "no known physical or biological reason" why agricultural yields in Asia should not be greatly increased.[27] In a similar vein, the Indian economist Raj Krishna has written that

> ... the amount of land in India that can be brought under irrigation can still be doubled ... Even in Punjab, the Indian state where agriculture is most advanced, the yield of wheat can be doubled. In other states it can be raised three to seven times. Rice yields in the monsoon season can be raised two to 13 times, rice yields in the dry season two to three-and-a-half times, jowar (Indian millet) yields two to 11 times, maize yields two to 10 times, groundnut yields three-and-

[20] Colin Clark, *Population Growth: The Advantages* (Santa Ana: R. L. Sassone, 1972), p. 44.
[21] Ibid., p. 48.
[22] Revelle, op. cit., p. 177.
[23] Ibid., pp. 174–175.
[24] Ibid., p. 177.
[25] Roger Revelle, "The World Supply of Agricultural Land", in Julian L. Simon and Herman Kahn, eds., *The Resourceful Earth: A Response to Global 2000* (Oxford, England: Basil Blackwell Inc., 1984), p. 186.
[26] Ibid., p. 190.
[27] Ibid., p. 193.

a-half to five-and-a-half times and potato yields one-and-a-half to five-and-a-half times.[28]

What Mr. Krishna is, in fact, saying is that Indian agriculture is potentially capable of feeding not only the people of India but the entire population of the world!

Revelle sums up his conclusions and those of other experts by quoting Dr. David Hopper, another well-known authority on agriculture:

The world's food problem does not arise from any physical limitation on potential output or any danger of unduly stressing the environment. The limitations on abundance are to be found in the social and political structures of nations and in the economic relations among them. The unexploited global food resource is there, between Cancer and Capricorn. The successful husbandry of that resource depends on the will and actions of men.[29]

Obviously, such great expansions of output would require larger inputs of fertilizer, energy, and human labor, as Revelle puts it:

Most of the required capital facilities can be constructed in densely populated poor countries by human labor, with little modern machinery: in the process much rural unemployment and under-employment can be alleviated.[30]

In other words, as Clark has noted, future generations can and will build their own farms and houses, just as in the past.

With regard to fertilizer, Clark has pointed out that the world supply of the basic ingredients, potash and sulphates, is adequate for several centuries, while the third major ingredient, nitrogen, is freely available in the atmosphere, though requiring energy for extraction. Since the world's coal supply is adequate for some 2,000 years, this should pose no great problem.[31] Revelle states that

in principle . . . most—perhaps all—of the energy needed in modern high-yielding agriculture could be provided by the farmers themselves. For every ton of cereal grain there are one to two tons of humanly inedible crop residues with an energy content considerably greater than the food energy in the grain.[32]

Surprisingly, in view of the recurrent alarms about desertification, urban encroachment, and other forces supposedly reducing the amount of world agricultural

[28] Raj Krishna, "The Economic Development of India", *Scientific American*, vol. 243, no. 3, September 1980, pp. 173–174.

[29] Revelle, "The World Supply of Agricultural Land", op. cit., p. 184, quoting W. David Hopper, "The Development of Agriculture in Developing Countries", *Scientific American*, September 1976, p. 197–205.

[30] Revelle, "The Resources Available for Agriculture", op. cit., p. 172.

[31] Clark, op. cit., pp. 8, 10, 17.

[32] Revelle, "The Resources Available for Agriculture", op. cit., p. 168.

land, it is actually increasing. Julian Simon has drawn attention to the data indicating this trend:

> A demographer, Joginder Kumar, found in a study at the University of California at Berkeley that there was 9 percent more total arable land in 1960 than in 1950 in 87 countries for which data were available and which constituted 73 percent of the world's total land area. And United Nations data show a 6 percent rise in the world's arable, permanent cropland from around 1963 to 1977 (the last date for which data are available).[33]

And UN data show a further increase of almost 1 percent between 1977 and 1980.[34] Simon also notes that

> there are a total of 2.3 billion acres in the United States. Urban areas plus highways, nonagricultural roads, railroads, and airports total 61 million acres— just 2.7 percent of the total. Clearly, there is little competition between agriculture and cities and roads.[35]

And that,

> furthermore, between 1.25 million and 1.7 million acres of cropland are being created yearly with irrigation, swamp drainage, and other reclamation techniques. This is a much larger quantity of new farmland than the amount that is converted to cities and highways each year.[36]

Simon's point is significant: a very small share of the total land area is used for urban purposes—less than 3 percent in the United States. This is probably a high percentage by world standards since the United States has a peculiarly sprawling type of development. Doxiadis and Papaioannou have estimated that only three-tenths of 1 percent of the land surface of the earth is used for "human settlements".[37]

Similarly, the biologist Francis P. Felice has shown that all the people in the world could be put into the state of Texas, forming one giant city with a population density less than that of many existing cities, and leaving the rest of the world empty.[38] Each man, woman, and child in the 1984 world population could be given more than 1,500 square feet of land space in such a city (the average home in the United States ranges between 1,400 and 1,800 square feet). If one-third of the space of this city were devoted to parks and one-third to industry, each family could still occupy a single-story dwelling of average U.S. size.

In a like vein, R. L. Sassone has calculated that there would be standing room

[33] Julian L. Simon, "Worldwide, Land for Agriculture Is Increasing, Actually", *New York Times*, October 7, 1980, p. 23.

[34] *FAO Production Yearbook*, 1981, p. 45.

[35] Simon, "Worldwide . . . " op. cit.

[36] Ibid.

[37] C. A. Doxiadis and G. Papaioannou, *Ecumenopolis, the Inevitable City of the Future* (New York: W. W. Norton & Co., 1974), p. 179.

[38] Francis P. Felice, "Population Growth", *The Compass*, 1974.

for the entire population of the world within one-quarter of the area of Jacksonville, Florida.[39]

Evidently, if the people of the world are floating in a lifeboat, it is a mammoth one quite capable of carrying many times its present passengers. An observer, in fact, would get the impression that he was looking at an empty boat, since the present occupants take up only a fraction of 1 percent of the boat's space and use less than one-ninth of its ice-free land area to raise their food and other agricultural products. The feeling of the typical air passenger that he is looking down on a mostly empty earth is correct.

On the extremely unlikely assumption that no improvements take place in technology and that population growth continues at its present rate, it will be more than a century and a quarter before world population will approach the limit of the support capacity estimated by Revelle, and almost two centuries before the limit estimated by Clark is reached. And, again on these wild surmises, what will the world be like then? At least one-half of the world's land area will still be in conservation and wildlife areas; and human settlements will occupy no more than 8 percent of the land. In a word, although by our assumptions, average living standards will no longer be able to rise, the boat will still be mostly empty.

Yet despite the optimism for human life in agriculture, and although most of the people in the less-developed world are still engaged in such work, we do live in the industrial age. Among the roughly one-third of the people who live in industrial countries, only a small proportion are farmers. In the United States, for example, one out of thirty people in the labor force is a farmer.

Even the most superficial view of the industrial economy shows how vastly it differs from the economy of agriculture. It uses a high proportion of fossil fuels and metal inputs; it is relatively independent of climate and seasons; a high proportion of its waste products are "non-biodegradable"; and it requires clustering rather than dispersal of its productive units, which encourages urbanization. While depending on agriculture for much of its resources, including its initial stock of capital, it has contributed greatly to the productivity and security of agriculture by providing energy, labor-saving machinery, and chemical fertilizers. Above all, perhaps, it has provided agriculture with cheap, fast transportation, so that local crop failures no longer mean famine.

It is generally agreed that industrialization has been important in reducing mortality and hence increasing population. And concerns regarding the limits of industry match those over the capacity of agriculture. How far can we go with the industrial process before we run out of the minerals and energy that are essential to it? How much "disruption" of nature does the industrial system create and how much can the earth and its inhabitants endure?

It is quite evident that, with few exceptions, intellectuals have never much liked

---

[39] Robert L. Sassone, *Handbook on Population* (Santa Ana: R. L. Sassone, 1978), p. 99.

the industrial process. Its noise, smoke—its obliteration of natural beauty—have never endeared it to the more genteel classes, or perhaps to anybody. But where its unattractive characteristics were once regarded as an unavoidable cost, given the benefits for human beings, now there is a growing conviction—especially among environmentalists—that these costs are unendurable and could be avoided by simply dispensing with part of the population. This is a simple choice from a set of complex alternatives, which raises much more far-reaching questions than whether we are simply "running out of everything".

First, though, the question: Are we running out of everything? If we are, the industrialization process, as well as all the benefits and problems it creates, will soon be at an end. (For those who dislike industry this should be good news indeed, though they shy away from the argument.)

On this score, the signs are clear. There is very little probability of running out of anything essential to the industrial process at any time in the foreseeable future. Over the past decades there have been recurrent predictions of the imminent exhaustion of all energy and basic metals, none of which has come about. And properly so, because it is a familiar chemical principle that nothing is ever "used up". Materials are merely changed into other forms. Some of these forms make subsequent recycling easier, others less so. It is cheaper to retrieve usable metals from the city dump than from their original ore, but once gasoline has been burned it cannot be reused as gasoline. Economists gauge the availability of basic materials by measuring their price-changes over time. A material whose price has risen over time (allowing for changes in the average value of money) is becoming more scarce, while one whose price has fallen is becoming more abundant, relative to the demand for it. Two major economic studies of the availability of basic metals and fuels found no evidence of increasing scarcity over the period 1870–1972.[40] And in 1984 a group of distinguished resource experts reported that the cost trends of nonfuel minerals for the period 1950–1980 "fail to support the increasing scarcity hypothesis".[41]

Julian Simon has recently noted the trend of decreasing scarcity for all raw materials:

An hour's work in the United States has bought increasingly more of copper, wheat, and oil (representative and important raw materials) from 1800 to the present. And the same trend has almost surely held throughout human history. Calculations of expenditures for raw materials as a proportion of total family budgets make the same point even more strongly. These trends imply that the

[40] H. J. Barnett and C. Morse, *Scarcity and Growth: The Economics of Natural Resource Availability* (Baltimore: John Hopkins Press, 1963); V. Kerry Smith, "Re-Examination of the Trends in the Prices of Natural Resource Commodities, 1870–1972", distributed at the Eighty-Seventh Annual Meeting of the American Economic Association, San Francisco, December 1974.

[41] Harold J. Barnett, Gerard M. Van Muiswinkel, Mordecai Schechter, and John G. Myers, "Global Trends in Non-Fuel Minerals", in Simon and Kahn, op. cit., p. 321.

raw materials have been getting increasingly available and less scarce relative to the most important and most fundamental element of life, human work-time. The prices of raw materials have even been falling relative to consumer goods and the Consumer Price Index. All the items in the Consumer Price Index have been produced with increasing efficiency in terms of labor and capital over the years, but the decrease in cost of raw materials has been even greater than that of other goods, a very strong demonstration of progressively decreasing scarcity and increasing availability of raw materials.[42]

Simon also noted that the real price of electricity had fallen at the end of the 1970s to about one-third its level in the 1920s.[43]

Even the Carter administration's gloomy *Global 2000* report admitted that "the real price of most mineral commodities has been constant or declining for many years",[44] indicating less scarcity. Yet the report, in the face of all the evidence of a historical decline in industrial resource scarcity, trumpets an imminent reversal of the trend and an abrupt increase in the prices and scarcity of raw materials.

Other analysts disagree. As Ansley Coale points out, metals exist in tremendous quantities at lower concentrations. Geologists know that going from a concentration of 6 percent to 5 percent multiplies the available quantities by factors of ten to a thousand, depending on the metal.[45]

Ridker and Cecelski of Resources for the Future are equally reassuring, concluding, "in the long run, most of our metal needs can be supplied by iron, aluminum, and magnesium, all of which are extractable from essentially inexhaustible sources".[46]

Even should scarcities of such materials develop, the economic impact would be small:

> metals . . . are only a small fraction of the cost of finished goods. The same is true with energy. . . . In the United States, for example, non-fuel minerals account for less than one-half of one percent of the total output of goods and services, and energy costs comprise less than one percent.[47]

In the case of fuels, the United States has currently reduced its own sources of low-cost petroleum. This can hardly be described as a "crisis", since higher-cost petroleum supplies are still available here while large reserves of low-cost petroleum remain and are being discovered in other parts of the world, though cartel

[42] Simon, "Global Confusion", op. cit., p. 11.

[43] Ibid., p. 13.

[44] *The Global 2000 Report to the President,* vol. 2, *The Technical Report,* prepared by the Council on Environmental Quality and the U.S. Department of State (Washington: U.S. Government Printing Office, 1980), p. 213.

[45] Ansley J. Coale, "Too Many People?" *Challenge,* vol. 17, no. 4, September–October 1974, p. 32.

[46] Ronald G. Ridker and Elizabeth W. Cecelski, "Resources, Environment, and Population: The Nature of Future Limits", *Population Bulletin,* vol. 34, no. 3, August 1979, p. 29.

[47] Ibid., p. 28.

influences are presently affecting prices. Extremely large deposits of coal remain in the United States and throughout the world, enough for a thousand years, possibly more than twice that, at foreseeable rates of increase in demand.[48]

Summarizing the conclusions of a group of energy experts in 1984, Simon and Kahn wrote:

> Barring extraordinary political problems, we expect the price of oil to go down . . . there is no basis to conclude . . . that humankind will ever face a greater shortage of oil in economic terms than it does now; rather, decreasing shortage is the more likely . . . [49]

Speaking of all kinds of energy, they concluded:

> The prospect of running out of energy is purely a bogeyman. The availability of energy has been increasing, and the meaningful cost has been decreasing, over the entire span of humankind's history. We expect this benign trend to continue at least until our sun ceases to shine in perhaps 7 billion years . . . [50]

Furthermore, the United States has tremendous, unexploited opportunities to economize on energy. Because energy has been so cheap, Americans drive their cars more than any other people and, in some parts of the United States, heat their houses without insulation and even with open windows. A reduction in U.S. energy consumption by one-half would put us on a par with the people of western Europe, whose living standards are as high as ours.

Although history teaches that we can expect great technological changes in the future, the nature of these changes is unknown. To attempt, then, to determine the safe capacity of our lifeboat, it seems the better part of wisdom not to anticipate any miraculous rescues, such as breakthroughs in the use of solar or nuclear power. Old-fashioned as it may seem, the coal on board alone will provide us with energy for at least a millennium, to say nothing of the petroleum and natural gas—and solar and nuclear possibilities—all of which remain substantial.[51]

The message is clear. The boat is extremely well stocked. The industrial system will not grind to a halt for lack of supplies.

But what about the disruption (an obscure term, and so all the more dreaded) supposedly created by population growth and/or industrialization? As Heilbroner puts it: "The sheer scale of our intervention into the fragile biosphere is now so great that we are forced to proceed with great caution lest we inadvertently bring about environmental damage of an intolerable sort."[52]

Man has, of course, been intervening in the biosphere for thousands of years.

[48] Clark, op. cit., p. 10; Ridker and Cecelski, op. cit., p. 26.

[49] Simon and Kahn, op. cit., p. 25.

[50] Ibid.

[51] Ridker and Cecelski, op. cit.

[52] Robert L. Heilbroner, *An Inquiry into the Human Prospect* (New York: W. W. Norton & Co., 1980), p. 73.

Perhaps the most massive human intervention was the invention of agriculture. It is not certain that modern industry, which is confined to much smaller areas, is having even an equal effect. Both humanity and the rest of the biosphere have apparently survived the agricultural intervention rather well; in fact, well enough so that our present anxiety is whether too many of us have survived.

"Too many for what?" springs to mind. The fact that more people are now living longer, healthier, better-fed, and more comfortable lives, and have been for many decades, rather suggests that the interventions have been the very opposite of intolerable. According to a number of authorities, the best overall index of environmental quality is life expectancy, which has been increasing throughout the world during this century.[53] It is precisely because of this increase that population has grown even though birth rates have fallen. It is possible, of course, that what the population alarmists really mean is that there are too many *other* people for their taste, or for those who prefer solitude, which is quite another thing.

Once again, as in the case of food and other resources, those who cry "overpopulation" will admit, when (and only when) pressed, that ecological disaster is not quite upon us, but is imminent. The most frightening threat is "the carbon dioxide problem", which postulates that increased combustion of fossil fuels must within the next century raise global temperatures by 1.5 to 3.0 degrees Celsius, with possible bad effects. Regarding which, Ridker and Cecelski of Resources for the Future disagree:

> But the estimate of a 1.5 to 3.0 degree increase is based on a model that ignores a number of factors. Higher temperatures would increase evaporation and thus cloudiness would block out incoming heat, and other air pollutants such as particulates could also reduce global temperatures.... Taking these factors into account provides a range of possible dates when a 1.5 to 3.0 degree increase in temperature might occur which extends from as early as 1990 to perhaps never. This is hardly a useful basis for policy decisions.[54]

Certainly, if and when it becomes apparent that burning fossil fuel is having a deleterious effect on climate, there will be a strong case for measures—economists favor pollution charges—to discourage the use of such fuels and provide the impetus to develop safer substitutes. But will we have the will to undertake these measures? Perhaps yes, perhaps no. But—and this is the most important point—there is no evidence that the ability of human institutions to act in the best interests of human survival is frustrated by the growth of population. Both large and small populations have been well and badly governed. The ineptitude of the government of India can no more be laid to the size of the Indian population than can the good government of the Netherlands or the bad government of some tiny Latin republics.

---

[53] Simon, "Global Confusion", op. cit., pp. 9–10.
[54] Ridker and Cecelski, op. cit., p. 37.

Still more importantly, the nature and extent of environmental disruption is only indirectly—and tenuously, if at all—related to the size and rate of growth of population. The fault lies with technological development. This has been most dramatically shown by Barry Commoner's major studies of the effects of this century's new technologies. Commoner, professor of plant physiology at Washington University in St. Louis and director of the Center for the Biology of Natural Systems, has shown that between 1947 and 1970 population in the United States increased 40 percent, but pollutants increased 267 percent due to the use of synthetic pesticides; 630 percent due to nitrogen oxides in motor fuel; 648 percent due to inorganic fertilizer nitrogen; and 1,845 percent due to detergent phosphorus.[55] All of these pollutants resulted from shifts away from older, less-polluting technologies. What these figures mean is that the only hope for cleaning up the environment lies in a direct attack on the polluting engines, the indiscriminate dumping of wastes into the common air and water supplies, and the other activities responsible for environmental degradation.

The new technologies have given people a vast new power to intervene in nature. The whaling factory ship, for example, has removed the restraints posed by the difficulty and danger of hunting whales, as has the all-weather offroad vehicle in respect to transportation. Even great reductions in population could not now restore the old restraints. But new restraints can be, and are being, imposed by law. Property rights can be defined so as to prevent the indiscriminate dumping of wastes into the air and water, as well as the destruction without replacement of renewable resources. Public access to the habitat of endangered species can also be limited. The principle, in short, can be established that the users of all resources must pay their full costs, since there is no such thing as a "free lunch".

The logic seems obvious. Which, after all, is the better way to prevent a nuclear disaster: to insist upon safety in power production or to distribute contraceptives to the potential victims? Ah, but nuclear power with its risks would not be "necessary" if population growth were not so rapid, insist the advocates of population control. But do they honestly believe this? Is nuclear power development really a regrettable necessity due to population growth in India, or is it what the late Mrs. Gandhi preferred to have, instead of the houses and schools and farms suitable to a growing population? One of the major charges laid against population growth is that it *retards* industrialization by absorbing, into houses and schools and farms, resources that would otherwise go toward it. As Robert S. McNamara, former director of the World Bank, put it:

more children mean more expenditures on food, on shelter, on clothing, on health, on education, on every essential social service. And it means correspondingly

[55] Barry Commoner, "The Environmental Costs of Economic Growth", in Robert Dorfman and Nancy S. Dorfman, eds., *Economics of the Environment: Selected Readings* (New York: W. W. Norton & Co., 1972), pp. 261–283.

less expenditure on investment to achieve the very economic growth required to finance these services.[56]

But if the concern really is with environmental disruption, and if Mr. McNamara's assessment is correct, one of the best ways to prevent it is to allow population growth to hamper industrialization and its pollution. The doomsayers cannot have it both ways. If population growth is retarding industrialization then it must be helping the environment. If it is increasing pollution then it must be helping industrialization.

But despite Mr. McNamara's claims, it has not been established that population growth retards industrialization. What has been clearly shown is that industrial pollution can be controlled by a direct attack on the polluting technologies— where the will exists; where it does not, control will not occur, no matter the rate of population growth. The thought occurs that the inclination to blame pollution on population growth may be only a symptom of the will not to control it. The dramatic improvements in the quality of the air in London,[57] and the water in the Ruhr Basin[58] and the Great Lakes[59] are cases in point. They have all increased in population and industrial concentration while making strides in controlling pollution.

A great deal of questionable material has appeared about the evil impact of population growth on forest resources and land management in the less-developed countries. The Carter administration's *Global 2000* report arrived at a gloomy— even desperate—forecast of the world forest situation in 2000—by assuming, quite arbitrarily, that "deforestation" over the next two decades would occur at a rate almost twice as high as the highest estimate of current rates. They proceeded to apply this fictitious rate from 1973 (not 1980) forward to the year 2000. Statistical manipulations can, of course, guarantee any results sought.[60]

Economic theory posits no simple relationship between population growth and environmental impact. The common assumption is that the larger the population, the more "pressure" on land and other resources. But, in fact, it is usually the most densely settled areas that tend to practice the best land management. Economic theory suggests the reason. When the population is small relative to the land resource, as with our frontier and now in much of Africa and South America, land management and forest practices that would be intolerable if the population were larger can, and even should, be used. The long periods of rotations permit natural recovery, and the "external" effects, such as erosion, affect relatively few other people, if any.

---

[56] *Christian Science Monitor,* July 5, 1977, p. 21.

[57] *Newsweek,* November 16, 1970, p. 67.

[58] Allen V. Kneese, "Water Quality Management by Regional Authorities in the Ruhr Area", in Marshall I. Goldman, ed., *Controlling Pollution: The Economics of a Cleaner America* (Englewood Cliffs: Prentice-Hall, Inc., 1967), pp. 109–129.

[59] Simon, "Global Confusion", op. cit., pp. 8–9.

[60] *The Global 2000 Report,* op. cit., vol. 2, p. 318.

History validates the theory. West Germany is fourteen times as densely settled as Brazil. (Europe is more than six times as densely populated as South America, while the forest resources per capita of South America are sixteen times as large as those of Europe.) The land management and forest practices that are followed in Brazil would be intolerable in Germany, just as the farming and logging practices of our homesteading great-grandfathers would be intolerable today in the United States. Though environmentalists insist that controls will come too late, economic history shows that they come as they are needed, through the swings of the relative prices of land, labor, and other productive resources.

Similarly, the external costs—those, such as erosion, that are transferred to persons other than those who incur them—also bring about social controls when they begin to impinge on enough people. There are numerous examples, from the strict social controls on land and forest management found throughout Europe to the antismoking regulations in many parts of the United States.

The theory also applies to "common property" resources, such as the salmon in northern California and the firewood-producing land of some less-developed countries. Free public access to these resources invites overexploitation, but if a larger population increases the exploitation, the point comes where the negative impact is felt and controls are brought to bear. Thus the restrictions on salmon fishing in California are increasing, and some less-developed countries are assigning private property rights to wood lots, which gives the owners an incentive to manage the lots for sustained yield.

Another myth of the antinatalists has it that population growth diminishes the aesthetic qualities of the human condition. Yet some of the world's most beautiful and most livable cities are the most densely settled. Assorted problems, such as traffic congestion and crime, have also been attributed to overpopulation, and with equal lack of evidence. Quite to the contrary, some urban problems become easier to solve as populations grow and become more densely settled. Traffic congestion, for example, tends to be more severe in sparsely settled cities like Los Angeles, which rely primarily on personal automobiles for transportation, than in more densely inhabited cities where walking, bicycles, and public transport are common.[61]

Experience suggests that it is not population growth, nor the behavior of private business that pose the big threat to environmental quality. It is the government, with its bottomless tax funds and its incentives to enlarge its activities no matter the benefit-cost relationships; witness the many dams and freeways in the United States. And because foreign aid programs so often finance

[61] Jacqueline R. Kasun, "The Love Affair Was a Forced Marriage", *America*, vol. 129, no. 18, December 1, 1973, pp. 418–421. As this article shows, modern traffic jams greatly enhance the perception of crowding and apparent "overpopulation" but in fact are more reflective of public policy than of the size or rate of growth of the human population.

public projects of this nature, enabling foreign governments to ignore the market signals that restrain the private sector, they are open to destructive environmental effects.

But perhaps the main reason why people find it easy to believe in overpopulation is that most of mankind now live, as in ages past, under crowded conditions. Human beings crowd together not because of lack of space on the planet but because of the need to work together, to buy and sell, to give and receive services from one another, to exchange goods and services. Our cities and towns have always thronged with people and traffic—horses, donkeys, and camels in ages past, motor vehicles today.

It accounts for the recurring theme throughout history of overpopulation. Plato and Aristotle worried about it half a millennium before Christ;[62] Athens was a great center of commerce and culture, and a very crowded city. Chinese cities were crowded centers for the exchange of products and ideas; and Confucius and other Chinese thinkers worried about "excessive" population growth.[63] Tertullian, writing in crowded Carthage in the second century after Christ, said,

> What most frequently meets our view (and occasions complaint), is our teeming population. Our numbers are burdensome to the world, which can hardly support us...In very deed, pestilence, and famine, and wars, and earthquakes have to be regarded as a remedy for nations, as the means of pruning the luxuriance of the human race.[64]

Saint Jerome in the fourth century wrote that "the world is already full, and the population is too large for the soil". Monasteries, he believed, might solve the problem.[65]

None of these earlier city-dwelling philosophers could soar over the earth and see that outside of their immediate view there were almost no people at all. And so it is with us. We spend our daily lives amid crowds of people and vehicles, thronging together to conduct our mutual affairs, to trade goods and ideas, and to reap the benefits of specialization and exchange. Given the immediate impact, common to the human condition in all ages, it is easy to suppose, along with Tertullian, that "our numbers are burdensome to the world".

Granted, at last, that the boat has ample supplies and can speed ahead in a healthy way when the will exists, could it still be that slower rates of population growth would help? When pressed, the more rational opponents of population

---

[62] Plato, *Laws,* and Aristotle, *Politica,* cited in the Population Division, United Nations, "History of Population Theories", in Joseph J. Spengler and Otis Dudley Duncan, eds., *Population Theory and Policy: Selected Readings* (Glencoe, Illinois: The Free Press, 1956), pp. 6–7.

[63] Population Division, United Nations, op. cit., p. 6.

[64] Tertullian, *De Anima: A Treatise on the Soul,* cited in Jacob Viner, *Religious Thought and Economic Society* (Durham: Duke University Press, 1978), p. 34.

[65] Jerome, *The Principal Works,* cited in Viner, op. cit., pp. 33–34.

growth admit that resources and environmental problems are not as acute as their more ardent brethren charge but that other kinds of problems are exacerbated by people. For example, the House Select Committee on Population claimed that

> by impeding social and economic progress in an era of rising expectations, further rapid population growth may undermine the internal stability of some developing countries. Internal instability in these countries may, in turn, provide a catalyst for the rejection of established social, economic and political systems, leading to increasing domestic unrest and upheavals and unstable international conditions.[66]

Does population growth really impede "social and economic progress"? From the mid-1960s to 1984, U.S. official statements and policy were based on the assumption that the answer to this question was yes. (Not until the 1984 International Conference on Population did this country, in an official statement, admit the possibility that population growth may not retard economic growth.) The antinatalist argument was, and is, simple: the more mouths there are to feed, the less food for each mouth. For those who suggest that extra mouths come with extra hands to produce food, the argument proceeds to a slightly higher level of sophistication: rapid population growth limits investment and thus acts as a drag on per capita income growth. As Nancy Birdsall, who writes antinatalist materials for the World Bank and other organizations, puts it,

> The idea that rapid population growth slows per capita income growth rests chiefly on two assumptions. First, it is assumed that with rapid increases in the number of workers, each worker produces less in relation to the land and capital each has to work with ... Second, as the number of dependent children per worker increases, it is assumed that a country's total savings will go down, restricting the money available for investments in education and in physical capital like housing, roads, and factories.[67]

Notice that Miss Birdsall, in using the word "assumed", means it quite literally. The astonishing fact is that these assumptions have been neither verified nor questioned by official policymakers; they have simply been taken on faith, with no resort to the means for testing them, which have been and are readily available.

One would suppose that a major policy of the United States and the international lending agencies, such as the World Bank—a policy extending over many years, costing billions of dollars, and involving significant risks in terms of economic welfare and international good will—would be based on thorough investigation of the relevant facts. Population policy, however, has not. It has, as Miss Birdsall makes clear, been based on assumptions—an astonishing fact, not only

[66] Select Committee on Population, op. cit., pp. 5–6.

[67] Nancy Birdsall, "Population Growth and Poverty in the Developing World", *Population Bulletin*, vol. 35, no. 5, December 1980, p. 14.

because the data exist for testing these assumptions, but because the agencies involved spend millions of dollars annually on research. Why then have they not delved into *these* questions?

More to the point, what *does* the available evidence show about the relationship between population growth and economic growth? Though the official agencies and their subsidized researchers have remained resolutely silent on this point, economists have been studying the question for years. Their results are both clear and surprising, in view of all that has been said and done on the assumption that population growth is harmful: *the economic studies have failed to demonstrate that population growth has bad economic effects*. Even more startling, the statistical evidence indicates that among *developing* countries more rapid population growth may be associated with more rapid growth of per capita output.

In an exhaustive study of many countries, Goran Ohlin, a distinguished economic demographer of the University of Uppsala, failed to find any significant relationship between rates of population growth and rates of economic growth. He concluded that "the more rigorous the analysis and the more scrupulous the examination of the evidence, the smaller is the role attributed to population as an independent source of economic problems".[68]

Similarly, in a major review of statistical studies by many scholars, Richard Franke found that the rate of population growth is not a critical factor in economic growth.[69]

Chart 2-1 shows the relationship between the average annual rate of growth of population and the average annual rate of growth in per capita real gross national product for 106 countries in both the developed and less-developed world for the period 1960–1982. The belief pressed by the proponents of population control, including the U.S. foreign aid establishment, would lead us to expect a strong negative relationship in these data, with high rates of population growth associated with low, or negative, rates of output growth. In fact, nothing of the kind is evident—there is hardly any relationship at all. Many countries with high rates of population growth have high rates of per capita output growth, while the converse is also true. The coefficient of determination for these data is .05, indicating a very low degree of statistical relationship.

When the investigation is confined to the developing countries, a clearer relationship emerges from some studies, but it is the opposite of the one posited by proponents of population control. Colin Clark, former director of the Agricultural Economic Institute at Oxford University, studied a large number of developing countries during the 1950–1969 period and found that in general those with the *highest* rates of population growth had the highest rates of growth in

---

[68] Goran Ohlin, "Economic Theory Confronts Population Growth", in Ansley J. Coale, ed., *Economic Factors in Population Growth* (New York: John Wiley, 1976), p. 1.

[69] Richard Franke, "Critical Factors in the Post-War Economic Growth of Nations," in E. Pusic, ed., *Participation and Self-Management* (Zagreb: The Institute for Social Research, 1973), vol. 5.

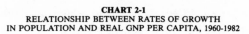

CHART 2-1
RELATIONSHIP BETWEEN RATES OF GROWTH
IN POPULATION AND REAL GNP PER CAPITA, 1960-1982

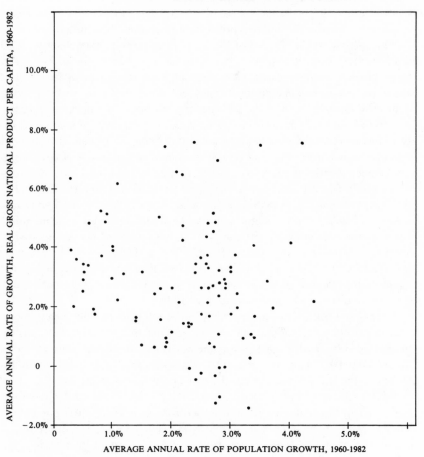

AVERAGE ANNUAL RATE OF POPULATION GROWTH, 1960-1982

Source: Based on data appearing in World Bank, World Development Report, 1984

product per person.[70] Clark, along with other economists, points out that the costs per head to society for a modern infrastructure of transportation and other facilities declines as population grows, thus facilitating an increase in net income per person[71]—the familiar business principle of "spreading the overhead".

Table 2-1 repeats Clark's comparison for a larger number of developing countries over the period 1960–1982. It shows the same relationship noted by Clark: the developing countries with *higher* rates of population growth have *higher* median rates of growth in output per capita. This, of course, is the exact opposite of the relationship claimed by the proponents of government population control.

Other studies have similarly failed to substantiate the antipopulation thesis. In a 1981 study conducted for the U.S. Department of State, Nick Eberstadt found no significant statistical correlation between demographic and economic growth in low-income countries and industrial market economies and only a slight negative correlation in middle-income countries. He concluded that "the economic case against rapid population growth . . . [is] . . . seriously flawed".[72] In a study directed by Richard Franke in 1981, Antonio Celia and Henry Mandelbaum found insignificant or positive relationships between population growth and economic growth in twenty Latin American countries for the decades since 1950.[73] Also directed by Franke, Da-hai Ding in 1982 studied the statistical correlation between population growth and industrial growth per capita in twenty-nine provinces of China, obtaining results that indicated no clear relationship.[74]

There is no evidence that more densely settled populations tend to have lower levels of per capita income and output, despite what antinatalists claim. Some of the most densely settled countries in the world—such as West Germany, the Netherlands, and Japan—have very high levels of per capita income and output. In Asia, the most densely settled regions—Japan, Singapore, Hong Kong, and Taiwan—have the highest output per capita, as Table 2-2 indicates. (Troubled Bangladesh is an exception.) China and India, on the other hand, with much lower population densities (similar to those of Pennsylvania and the United Kingdom, respectively) also have much lower levels of per capita output. Taiwan, with a population

[70] Clark, op. cit., p. 84.

[71] Clark, op. cit.; also Colin Clark, *Conditions of Economic Progress* (New York: Macmillan, 1957); Julian L. Simon, *The Economics of Population Growth* (Princeton: Princeton University Press, 1977), ch. 12.

[72] Nick Eberstadt, " 'Population Control' and the Wealth of Nations: The Implications for American Policy", prepared for the Undersecretary of State for Security Assistance, Science and Technology, Washington, D.C., November 24, 1981, p. 21.

[73] Antonio Celia and Henry Mandelbaum, "Economic Growth in 20 Latin American Countries", submitted to the faculty of Worcester Polytechnic Institute, Worcester, Massachusetts, March 31, 1981.

[74] Da-hai Ding, "Economic Development and Population Control in China", submitted to Worcester Polytechnic Institute, Worcester, Massachusetts, May 21, 1982.

Table 2-1
Growth of Real Gross National Product Per Capita, 1960–1982
Percent per Year

Countries with Population Growth Under 2% per Year GNP Growth*		Countries with Population Growth 2–2.4% per Year GNP Growth*		Countries with Population Growth 2.5–2.9% per Year GNP Growth*		Countries with Population Growth 3% per year or more GNP Growth*	
Haiti	0.6	Chad	−2.8	Ghana	−1.3	Niger	−1.5
Central African		Madagascar	−0.5	Uganda	−1.1	Nicaragua	0.2
Republic	0.6	Nepal	−0.1	Sudan	−0.4	El Salvador	0.9
Chile	0.6	Upper Volta	1.1	Zaire	−0.3	Liberia	0.9
Jamaica	0.7	Burma	1.3	Zambia	−0.1	Honduras	1.0
Guinea	1.5	India	1.3	Somalia	−0.1	Zimbabwe	1.5
Burundi	2.5	Ethiopia	1.4	Bangladesh	0.3	Rwanda	1.7
Portugal	4.8	Mauritania	1.4	Benin	0.6	Tanzania	1.9
China	5.0	Papua New		Peru	1.0	Ivory Coast	2.1
		Guinea	2.1	Mali	1.6	Guatemala	2.4
MEDIAN		Sri Lanka	2.6	Bolivia	1.7	Kenya	2.8
RATE*	1.1	Colombia	3.1	Togo	2.3	Dominican	
		Turkey	3.4	Malawi	2.6	Republic	3.2
		Indonesia	4.2	Cameroon	2.6	Mexico	3.7
		Lesotho	6.5	Morocco	2.6	Syria	4.0
		Republic of		Congo, PR	2.7		
		Korea	6.6	Pakistan	2.8	MEDIAN	
				Philippines	2.8	RATE*	1.8
		MEDIAN		Costa Rica	2.8		
		RATE*	1.4	Algeria	3.2		
				Nigeria	3.3		
				Panama	3.4		
				Egypt	3.6		
				Paraguay	3.7		
				Malaysia	4.3		
				Thailand	4.5		
				Brazil	4.8		
				MEDIAN			
				RATE*	2.6		

SOURCE: Based on World Bank, *World Development Report 1984.* All countries shown had per capita GNP under $2500 in 1982.
*Average annual rate of growth of GNP per person in constant prices

density five times as great as China's, produces more than eight times as much per capita and has as large or a larger volume of trade. The Republic of Korea, with a population density four times as great as China's, has a per capita output almost seven times as great.

On the other hand, low population density (as is found in the United States,

Table 2-2
Population Density and Per Capita GNP, Selected Countries in Asia

Country	Population Per Square Mile, 1985	GNP Per Capita 1985
Bangladesh	1,824	$ 150
Nepal	313	160
Burma	141	190
India	606	270
China	280	310
Sri Lanka	645	380
Pakistan	320	380
Indonesia	235	530
Thailand	260	800
Philippines	490	580
Malaysia	121	2,000
Republic of Korea	1,121	2,150
Taiwan	1,393	2,663*
Hong Kong	13,437	6,230
Singapore	11,411	7,420
Japan	840	11,300

SOURCE: Based on World Bank, *World Development Report 1987,* and *Statistical Abstract of the United States,* 1986.
*1983 from *Statistical Abstract of the United States,* 1987.

which has only sixty-seven persons per square mile) need not be a barrier to high income. Within all countries, however, the most densely settled areas—the cities— have the highest levels of per capita output and income. Economists have long explained these relationships on the grounds mentioned above—the more densely settled populations make better use of their transportation and communications systems as well as other parts of their economic infrastructure. They also have more opportunities for the face-to-face contacts that encourage innovation and productivity.

Nor is there evidence to support the population controllers' assumption that population growth inhibits investment. If this were true, countries with rapidly growing populations would show lower proportions of their total output devoted to investment. But this is not the case, as shown in Chart 2-2, which shows that high rates of investment are just as likely to be achieved in countries with high rates of population growth as in countries with low rates. Currently the less-developed countries with rapidly growing populations are investing a higher share of their gross domestic product (GDP) than are the industrialized economies of North America and Western Europe, which have stable or slowly growing populations. Malaysia, for example, with a population growing at a 2.3 percent per year clip (compared with 1 percent for the United States) achieved investment

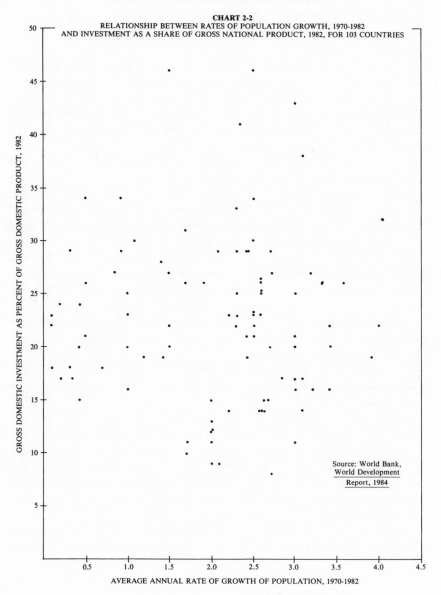

CHART 2-2
RELATIONSHIP BETWEEN RATES OF POPULATION GROWTH, 1970-1982
AND INVESTMENT AS A SHARE OF GROSS NATIONAL PRODUCT, 1982, FOR 103 COUNTRIES

GROSS DOMESTIC INVESTMENT AS PERCENT OF GROSS DOMESTIC PRODUCT, 1982

Source: World Bank,
World Development
Report, 1984

AVERAGE ANNUAL RATE OF GROWTH OF POPULATION, 1970-1982

in 1985 amounting to 28 percent of its gross domestic product, compared with 19 percent for the United States. Mexico, growing at 2.6 percent per year, invested an amount equal to 21 percent of its GDP.[75]

The economic reasoning here is straightforward—voluntary investment depends primarily on expected profitability, which is a function of the efficiency of resource use, not the birth rate. Economics shows that industries and countries that allow investors opportunities to make gains from the efficient use of resources will attract investment capital either at home or from abroad regardless of their rate of population growth or their domestic wealth. The birth rate is simply irrelevant to these considerations. Other economists have similarly noted the lack of evidence that population growth inhibits investment.[76]

Thus speaks the statistical evidence. But what about the theoretical reasoning, the computer models? In their case the results depend on the *assumptions* programmed into the computerized calculations. The computer model most quoted by devotees of population control—the famous Coale-Hoover model[77]—incorporates the assumptions that economic growth depends on the rate of investment and that investment cannot keep up with population growth. Given its built-in assumptions, it necessarily demonstrates that population growth inhibits economic growth, and never mind that its assumptions are not in accord with the observed facts.

The much-reported *Global 2000* computer model, developed under the Carter administration, achieved its gloomy forecast by simply assuming, without any basis in fact, that the earth is rapidly running out of essential resources. Why bother to run such material through computers? Using similar assumptions, Chicken Little arrived at similar conclusions. But computers are mesmerizing modern audiences.

On the other hand, Julian Simon's sophisticated computer model is properly used. It incorporates reasonable assumptions based on observed economic facts, and it demonstrates the long-run *benefits* of population growth in both developing and developed countries.[78] This model incorporates not only the assumption that additional people "dilute" the capital stock (i.e., reduce the ratio of tools to workers), as assumed in the Coale-Hoover model, but also the counteracting observed facts that larger populations acquire and use the economic "infrastructure" with greater ease and efficiency and that larger numbers of workers generate a faster rate of technological improvement because of their creative interaction with each other. For the less-developed countries Simon's model also incorporates the

[75] World Bank, *World Development Report 1984.*

[76] Simon, *The Economics of Population Growth,* op. cit., chaps. 4, 10; Julian L. Simon, *The Ultimate Resource* (Princeton: Princeton University Press, 1981), chap. 13; Eberstadt, " 'Population Control' ", op. cit., pp. 22–23.

[77] Ansley J. Coale and Edgar M. Hoover, *Population Growth and Economic Development in Low-Income Countries* (Princeton: Princeton University Press, 1958).

[78] Simon, *The Economics of Population Growth,* op. cit., chaps. 6 and 13.

observed facts that the demands of a larger population stimulate investment, people devote more hours to work as their family size increases, and labor shifts from agriculture to industry as development proceeds.

Summing up what economists know about the relationship between population and economic growth, Mark Perlman of the University of Pittsburgh put it bluntly in 1975: "If we use antinatalist programs, we do so for reasons other than those simply offered by what we as economists now *know*".[79]

In the article, which reviewed the history of the antinatalist position, Perlman pointed out that Malthus himself retreated significantly from his earlier opinion of the bad effects of population growth; in Perlman's words, "in a nutshell, Malthus was at the end a somewhat dubious Malthusian".[80] (In a 1981 review of recent demographic research, Perlman reiterated his earlier position.)[81]

Facts notwithstanding, a number of economists embrace the early Malthus in coupling population growth with bad effects. Regarding their influence, Perlman says, "as a profession we are riding with policy preferences that are not scientifically based and indeed are in no probabilistic sense all that likely . . . "[82]

The well-known development economist P. T. Bauer has trenchantly criticized the view that population growth retards economic growth. Finding that "rapid population growth has not been an obstacle to sustained economic advance either in the Third World or in the West",[83] he documents his conclusion with a wealth of case studies and statistical evidence gathered from all continents.

In 1960 the distinguished economist Simon Kuznets stressed the advantages of population growth to economic development in a complex analysis. It emphasized that large numbers of people mean larger numbers of able and talented people who, by interacting with each other, discover and disseminate improvements in technology.[84]

Other economists have criticized the assumption that population growth retards economic growth. Easterlin of the University of Pennsylvania has written: "There is little evidence of any significant association, positive or negative, between the income and population growth rates."[85] Fred R. Glahe of the University of

[79] Mark Perlman, "Some Economic Growth Problems and the Part Population Policy Plays", *Quarterly Journal of Economics,* vol. 89, no. 2, May 1975, pp. 247–256.

[80] Ibid., p. 249.

[81] Mark Perlman, *"Population and Economic Change in Developing Countries:* A Review Article", *The Journal of Economic Literature,* vol. 19, no. 1, March 1981, pp. 74–82.

[82] Ibid., p. 81.

[83] P. T. Bauer, *Equality, the Third World, and Economic Delusion* (Cambridge: Harvard University Press, 1981), p. 43. See his entire chap. 3. on "The Population Explosion: Myths and Realities".

[84] Simon Kuznets, "Population Change and Aggregate Output", in *Demographic and Economic Change in Developing Countries, A Conference of the Universities* (Princeton: Princeton University Press for the National Bureau of Economic Research, 1960), pp. 324–340.

[85] Richard A. Easterlin, "Population", in Neil W. Chamberlain, ed., *Contemporary Economic Issues* (Homewood: Richard D. Irwin, 1973), pp. 337–347.

Colorado, commenting on the evidence that the developing nations with the highest population growth rates have achieved the highest economic growth, has said, "It should be pointed out that there is no law of diminishing returns with respect to technology."[86]

These and other economists have spelled out the case against the assumptions and teachings of the population-bombers: population growth permits the easier acquisition as well as the more efficient use of the economic infrastructure—the modern transportation and communications systems, and the education, electrification, irrigation, and waste disposal systems. Population growth encourages agricultural investment—clearing and draining land, building barns and fences, improving the water supply. Population growth increases the size of the market, encouraging producers to specialize and use cost-saving methods of large-scale production. Population growth encourages governments, as well as parents, philanthropists, and taxpayers, to devote more resources to education. If wisely directed, these efforts can result in higher levels of competence in the labor force. Larger populations not only inspire more ideas but more *exchanges,* or improvements, of ideas among people, in a ratio that is necessarily more than proportional to the number of additional people. (For example, if one person joins an existing couple, the possible number of exchanges does not increase by one-third but triples.) One of the advantages of cities, as well as of large universities, is that they are mentally stimulating, that they foster creativity.

The arguments and evidence that population growth does not lead to resource exhaustion, starvation, and environmental catastrophe, fail to persuade the true believers in the population bomb. They have, after all, other rationalizations for their fears of doom. Another recurring theme of the doomsdayers is, in the words of a public affairs statement by the U.S. Department of State, that population growth increases the size of the "politically volatile age group—those 15–24 years",[87] which contributes to political unrest. Ambassador Richard Elliot Benedick, coordinator of population affairs in the U.S. State Department, spelled out the concern for the Senate Foreign Relations Committee in 1980:

> Rapid population growth . . . creates a large proportion of youth in the population. Recent experience, in Iran and other countries, shows that this younger age group—frequently unemployed and crowded into urban slums—is particularly susceptible to extremism, terrorism, and violence as outlets for frustration.[88]

---

[86] Fred R. Glahe and Dwight R. Lee, *Microeconomics: Theory and Applications* (New York: Harcourt Brace Jovanovich, 1981), p. 189.

[87] U.S. Department of State, Bureau of Public Affairs, "World Population Problem", *Gist,* April 1978.

[88] Richard Elliot Benedick, Statement before the Senate Foreign Relations Committee, April 29, 1980, reprinted in *Department of State Bulletin,* vol. 80, no. 2042, September 1980, p. 58.

The ambassador went on to enumerate a long list of countries of economic and strategic importance for the United States where, he claimed, population growth was encouraging "political instability". The list included Turkey, Egypt, Iran, Pakistan, Indonesia, Mexico, Venezuela, Nigeria, Bolivia, Brazil, Morocco, the Philippines, Zimbabwe, and Thailand—countries of special importance to the United States because of their "strategic location, provision of military bases or support, and supply of oil or other critical raw materials".[89] While he admitted that it is "difficult to be analytically precise in pinpointing exact causes of a given historical breakdown in domestic or international order", he nevertheless insisted that "unprecedented demographic pressures" were of great significance.[90]

No results of scientific research support Benedick's belief; it is simply another one of those unverified *assumptions* that advocates of population control rely upon to make their case. It may be, of course, that Ambassador Benedick is right: that the young tend to be more revolutionary and that public bureaucracies who want to stay in power would be wise to encourage the aging of the population through lower birth rates. As public bureaucracies increase their power in this age of growth of government, we may see an increasing manipulation of the population so as to ensure an older and more docile citizenry. However, putting aside the ethical implications and the welfare of society, and speaking only of the self-interest of the ruling bureaucracy, the risks are obvious. Such policy could arouse a deep antagonism among those on the check list, especially if they are the citizens of countries who perceive the policy as a tool of outside interference in their most intimate national affairs.

The question, then, is resolved in favor of the economic notion of scarcity rather than the lifeboat model of absolute limits being the more nearly correct. While resources are always scarce relative to the demands that human beings place upon them, there is no indication of imminent, absolute limits. The limits are so far beyond the levels of our present use of resources as to be nearly invisible, and are actually receding as new knowledge develops. Ironically, though, the perception of economic scarcity may increase along with increasing wealth and income. There is no evidence whatsoever that slower rates of population growth encourage economic growth or economic welfare; on the contrary, the developing countries with *higher* rates of population growth have had higher average rates of per-capita-output growth in the period since 1950. It may, of course, be in the interests of a ruling bureaucracy to rid itself of those people it finds troublesome, but the policy can hardly promote the general welfare, and it would prove very costly, even to the ruling elites.

[89] Ibid.
[90] Ibid.

CHAPTER THREE

PLAN VS. MARKET IN POPULATION CONTROL

Two facts stand out with regard to the world population today: it is becoming more urbanized and it is growing more slowly than it was a decade or so ago. How large it is relative to a century or a millennium ago can only be conjectured since there are no firm facts available. The best population estimates focus on the developed and industrialized countries, which hold only about a third of the world's people. And in these, zero population growth is either already at hand or rapidly approaching.

In the less-developed world, population is probably growing, but less rapidly than in the recent past. Although birth rates have declined, the reduction of major diseases has resulted in death rates that are lower than birth rates. Estimates of the size, distribution, and rates of growth of world population appear in Table 3-1. The table shows that Africa was the only continent in which the rate of population growth did not decline between 1970 and 1986, since a decline in the death rate exceeded that of the birth rate. Worldwide declines in the death rate mean that people everywhere are living longer, healthier lives. And, as Table 3-2 shows, output has grown remarkably more rapidly than population since 1965, so that average world income levels have risen significantly; Table 3-3 shows that per capita output, as well as population, has grown more rapidly in the developing regions than in the industrialized countries since 1966.

Economists and other social scientists have been interested in the determinants of population growth for a long time. The last chapter explored the question of whether population growth threatens to swamp economic growth, as Malthus (at least in his earlier career) and others feared. The answer was that the limits of resource capacity are so far beyond the levels of present use that they can barely be perceived. But in theory, at least, high rates of population growth can increase absolute numbers by large amounts in a relatively short time. What, then, are the determinants of these increases, and what is the probability that they will outrun the capacity of the earth to support them?

Economists and others have advanced a number of theories to explain the different rates of population growth that have occurred in different regions at various times. But do these theories and the historical record reflect rational and socially harmonious behavior on the part of people? Do families act sensibly in adjusting their childbearing to available resources? And do these personal decisions harmonize with the good of the whole, or do families, as the popu-

Table 3-1
Estimated Population and Population Growth Rates
in the World and Selected Regions and Countries

	Estimated Population 1986 (Millions)	Estimated Rate of Population Growth*	
		1970	1986
World	4,942	2.0	1.7
North America	267	1.1	0.7
United States	241	1.0	0.7
Western Europe	155	0.8	0.1
Austria	8	0.4	0.0
West Germany	61	0.6	−0.2
Northern Europe	83	0.6	0.2
Sweden	8	0.8	0.0
United Kingdom	57	0.5	0.2
Eastern Europe	112	0.8	0.4
Southern Europe	143	0.9	0.4
Asia	2,876	2.3	1.8
India	785	2.6	2.3
P.R. China	1,050	1.8	1.0
Japan	122	1.1	0.7
Africa	583	2.6	2.8
Latin America	419	2.9	2.3

SOURCE: Population Reference Bureau, *1970 World Population Data Sheet* and *1986 World Population Data Sheet*, based on UN, World Bank, and U.S. Bureau of Census data.
*Annual rate of natural increase.

lation alarmists charge, selfishly go "too far", reproductively speaking?

Many studies from various times and places throughout the world have found that families in both developed and developing countries do limit their procreation in accordance with their wealth and income. Typical of the literature is this excerpt from the summary of a recent article on the choice of family size in Africa:

> The majority of respondents stressed the financial strain of raising a large number of children, especially of educating them, as their reason for limiting family size.[1]

In a study of rural India, Djurfeldt and Lindberg found that

> family size is less a result of blind sexual urges than most neo-Malthusians tend to think, and more a result of planning and foresight. Thaiyur families

[1] John C. Caldwell and Pat Caldwell, "The Achieved Small Family: Early Fertility Transition in an African City", *Studies in Family Planning*, vol. 9, no. 1, January 1978, p. 1.

Table 3-2
Rate of Growth in Real Gross National Product Per Person,
1965–1985, for Selected Regions and Countries

	Average Annual Growth in Real GNP Per Person (Percent)
Low-Income Countries	2.9
India	1.7
Middle-Income Countries	3.0
Colombia	2.9
Philippines	2.3
Malaysia	4.4
Industrialized Market Economies	2.4
Japan	4.7
West Germany	2.7
United Kingdom	1.6
United States	1.7

SOURCE: World Bank, *World Development Report 1987*

Table 3-3
Rate of Growth in Real Gross National Product Per Person,
1966–1980, for Selected Regions

		Average Annual Growth in Real GNP Per Person (percent)
All Developing Regions		3.4
Africa south of the Sahara	1.8	
East Asia and Pacific	5.3	
Latin America and the Caribbean	3.0	
North Africa and Middle East	5.4	
South Asia	1.7	
More advanced Mediterranean countries	3.7	
Industrial Countries		3.1

SOURCE: World Bank, *Report,* September-October 1981, p. 4.

are, as a matter of fact, to a large extent "planned" ... The poor have less children ... [2]

Another study of family size in Africa concluded that "the great majority of women (87 percent) were keenly aware of the economic disadvantages of a large

[2] Goran Djurfeldt and Staffan Lindberg, "Family Planning in a Tamil Village", in Lars Bondestam and Staffan Bergstrom, eds., *Poverty and Population Control* (London: Academic Press, 1980), p. 108.

family, especially the difficulty of meeting school fees".[3]

A study of rural Guatemala discovered that local attitudes toward family size were "based on economic motives . . . "[4]

Other studies have found the same limiting of family size to fit income and wealth constraints in such diverse times and places as rural Ireland, southern Italy, eighteenth-century Sweden, Polynesia, the United States, tropical Africa, and elsewhere.[5]

To the extent that families do make mistakes in forecasting the future, there is no reason to suppose they always lead to having "too many" children. Common sense and the law of probability point to mistakes being made equally on the side of having "too few" children, when viewed retrospectively.

Families have understood and used methods of birth regulation for thousands of years;[6] and these traditional methods, as well as the more modern variety, are in wide use today in such far-flung places as India,[7] the South Pacific,[8] Latin America,[9] and Africa.[10]

The simple reason why people in the less-developed countries have larger families than people in the more-developed world is that they want them, for excellent social and economic reasons. A recent study in rural Bangladesh found that 82 percent of the women hoped for a family of five to seven;[11] and among women surveyed in one Nigerian study, more than three-fourths wanted at least six children.[12] The major fertility problem of a very large number of people in less-

---

[3] Thomas E. Dow, Jr., and Linda H. Werner, "Family Size and Family Planning in Kenya: Continuity and Change in Metropolitan and Rural Attitudes", *Studies in Family Planning,* vol. 12, no. 6/7, June/July 1981, p. 273.

[4] Jane T. Bertrand et al., "Ethnic Differences in Family Planning Acceptance in Rural Guatemala", *Studies in Family Planning,* vol. 10, no. 8/9, August/September 1979, p. 243.

[5] Julian L. Simon, *The Economics of Population Growth* (Princeton: Princeton University Press, 1977), ch. 14.

[6] John T. Noonan, Jr., *Contraception: A History of Its Treatment by the Catholic Theologians and Canonists* (Cambridge: Harvard University Press, 1965), pp. 9–29, 200–231, 387–394.

[7] Djurfeldt and Lindberg, op. cit., p. 107.

[8] David Lucas and Helen Ware, "Fertility and Family Planning in the South Pacific", *Studies in Family Planning,* vol. 12, no. 8/9, August/September 1981, pp. 303–315.

[9] Michele Goldzieher Shedlin and Paula E. Hollerbach, "Modern and Traditional Fertility Regulation in a Mexican Community: The Process of Decision Making", *Studies in Family Planning,* vol. 12, no. 6/7, June/July 1981, pp. 278–296.

[10] Eugene Weiss and A. A. Udo, "The Calabar Rural Maternal and Child Health/Family Planning Project", *Studies in Family Planning,* vol. 12, no. 2, February 1981, pp. 47–57.

[11] Nilufer R. Ahmed, "Family Size and Sex Preferences among Women in Rural Bangladesh", *Studies in Family Planning,* vol. 12, no. 3, March 1981, pp. 100–109.

[12] Weiss and Udo, op. cit.

developed countries is that they do not have *as many* children as they would like.[13]

There is no good evidence that people in any country are having significantly more children than they want. The widely reported studies of "unwanted" births are defective because they fail to distinguish between the terms "unwanted" and "unplanned". Most births are probably always unplanned.[14] But if the precise timing of births is not easily managed, the size of the family is, and the evidence indicates that families in all countries have no more children than they want.[15]

Our very willingness to believe in "the-problem-of-overpopulation" may be evidence of our paired belief that too many children cause poverty. From this we fall into the logical error of supposing that people who are poor must have too many children. But it is not necessarily true. Even though too many children can cause poverty, poverty can have many other causes as well. There is no evidence that poverty is usually the result of too many children. As we learn in elementary logic, the fact that *a* implies *b* does not necessarily mean that *b* implies *a*. The very keenness with which people view the possible dangers of having too many children and our attempts to guard against the danger suggests that this is not the real threat. Real threats come mostly from dangers that are unperceived and uncontrolled.

It is common knowledge that population growth tends to slow down as the modern economy develops. In the initial stage of development, however, population growth may accelerate, because the increases in income and security make it easier for more children to survive.[16] But as the process continues, higher levels of family income mean higher levels of education for women. These in turn mean higher earnings for women and higher losses of family earnings when the wife leaves the paid labor force to bear and raise children. So it happens that children become progressively more costly in the industrialized urban society.[17]

If children are beloved in all societies, as they are, the economic circumstances surrounding them vary greatly. In societies where children begin to work at a

[13] Joseph A. McFalls, Jr., "Frustrated Fertility: A Population Paradox", *Population Bulletin,* vol. 34, no. 2, May 1979; Anne Bamisaiye et al., "Developing a Clinic Strategy Appropriate to Community Family Planning Needs and Practices: An Experience in Lagos, Nigeria", *Studies in Family Planning,* vol. 9, nos. 2–3, February/March 1978, p. 47.

[14] For a discussion of these problems, see Jacqueline R. Kasun, "Adolescent Pregnancy in the United States: An Evaluation of Recent Federal Action", in Stephen J. Bahr, ed., *Economics and the Family* (Lexington, Massachusetts: Lexington Books, 1980), p. 132; James Ford, M.D., Testimony before United States Senate Committee on Labor and Human Resources, March 31, 1981, Part II, p. 5.

[15] Elise F. Jones et al., "Contraceptive Efficacy: The Significance of Method and Motivation", *Studies in Family Planning,* vol. 11, no. 2, February 1980, pp. 39–50; N. K. Nair and L. P. Chow, "Fertility Intentions and Behavior: Some Findings from Taiwan", *Studies in Family Planning,* vol. 11, no. 7/8, July/August 1980, pp. 255–263.

[16] Simon, op. cit., pp. 362–363.

[17] Ibid., p. 351; Mark Perlman, "Population and Economic Change in Developing Countries: A Review Article", *The Journal of Economic Literature,* vol. 19, no. 1, March 1981, pp. 74–82.

young age, where their mothers do not work, and where they do not receive long, expensive educations, big families cost relatively little. Large families even add to the welfare of the whole. Economies of scale, familiar enough in industry, apply equally to families. And, in the absence of public social security systems, larger numbers of children can take care of their aging parents with less individual sacrifice.

But in the developed, urbanized, industrial society all this changes. Children do not work; they require long, expensive education; bearing and raising them means large losses of earnings by their mothers; and social security retirement income depends on the parents' earnings, not on their children. The costs of children rise disproportionately to the increases in income that development brings; and the average family size falls. Unsurprisingly, in the industrialized countries population growth rates are now below replacement levels and population is declining in several of them.[18]

Summed up, it is clear that there are constraints on population growth and that families do respond rationally to these constraints. But two further questions spring up: do initial increases in income stimulate too great an increase in population before the constraints begin to operate; and do families transfer enough of the costs of their children to society as to lead them to have more children than they "should" have?

In response, recall that output has quite remarkably outstripped population growth during the period for which these data are available, even in the regions where population has grown most rapidly. In the period from 1960 to 1982, among 106 countries enumerated by the World Bank, there were only twelve in which population growth exceeded output growth. Two of these—oil-rich Kuwait and the United Arab Emirates—have the highest per capita incomes in the world. All of the other ten experienced that most serious disruption of economic life— external and/or civil conflict—during the period. The evidence for the past two decades, therefore, does not support the notion that people have been producing "too many" children relative to their ability to provide for them.

Regarding the "external costs" of childbearing, these are most important in economies where high levels of "free" public health care, "free" education, and other public services are provided. Few such services, however, are provided in the less-developed countries where population growth rates are highest—high levels of these services characterize the rich countries where population growth rates are generally below replacement levels. In other words, the opportunity to transfer part of the costs of children is not available to encourage childbearing in the less-developed countries; and, where it is available in the developed economies, it is not offsetting the high cost of children to the families.

[18] See Table 3-1; U.S. Bureau of the Census, *Statistical Abstract of the United States, 1984*, pp. 857–859; Charles F. Westoff, "Marriage and Fertility in the Developed Countries", *Scientific American*, vol. 239, no. 6, December 1978, pp. 51–57.

Keep in mind too that the so-called free services for children are paid for with taxes. Since public agencies, in their own self-interest, have an incentive to provide more services at a higher cost than consumers would voluntarily buy, the "free" services reduce the real income of the family and its ability to support children—and the inclination to have them. In a word, "free" public services, far from transferring part of the costs of unproductive children to society, actually transfer the costs of unproductive bureaucrats to families.

Furthermore, if children put "external costs" on society, they extend external benefits as well. Each child born will not only consume public services, such as education, public health care, and military defense, but will also contribute to the support of these services. In the United States, for example, each child born in 1983 is expected to spend forty-seven years in the labor force, earn more than two-thirds of a million dollars over his lifetime, and pay more than a quarter of a million dollars in taxes. The discounted net present value in 1983 of the typical child's future earnings, over and above the cost of his own maintenance, amounted to $70,000.[19] This sum would be available to support public services and add to society's capital. It is precisely because children who have been born have also grown and contributed so much more than their own costs that the social wealth and income have increased so greatly.

It does not appear, therefore, that families are led to have "too many" children by reason of any ability to transfer net real costs to society. On the contrary, because the large social benefits created by children do not bless their own families, externalities must often lead families to have fewer children—to the detriment of society.

It may be argued that if population is not outrunning economic growth it is due to the vigor of international population control programs in recent decades. The programs have most certainly been forceful and may have reduced fertility. But it is not at all certain whether their net effect was to increase or reduce per capita income in the countries where they were implemented. Though U.S. aid programmers such as R. T. Ravenholt are certain that "resources divided by population equals well-being" and reducing population always and everywhere increases per capita income,[20] economists are not so certain. The size of the population determines not only the number of consumers but also the number of producers and therefore affects total output, the "top" of the ratio the population planners aspire to improve. Adding to the complexity, the rate of population growth also affects the rates of saving, investment, and new technological improvements, again with complex effects on the "top" of the ratio. And, largely ignored, forceful methods of population control can affect morale, with consequences for the level of output. It all means that the effects of recent forceful

[19] Based on average earnings, average life expectancy, and average cost of living. See discussion in chapter 6.

[20] St. Louis Dispatch, April 22, 1977.

methods of fertility control on per capita output cannot be known. What *is* known, based on reason and worldwide observation, is that families do adjust their procreation to their resources.

Still another argument has it that, while families may adjust their procreation to their resources, they lack the foreknowledge to make good decisions. True, no one has perfect, or even very good, foreknowledge. All human decisions, whether made by private individuals or by professional planners, involve risk. Actual events are usually better or worse than expected. But in forecasting the future, as well as in coping with the present, the family has more reason to make a correct decision than professional planners because it has far less opportunity to transfer the cost of its mistakes to third parties. If the family's decisions turn out to be wrong, the family will suffer. Planners neither use nor risk the loss of their own resources but those of others.

But surely planners have better information about the future than families? Information, perhaps. But facts must lead somewhere. And while all kinds of planners, forecasters, fortune tellers, and soothsayers need to impress their publics with their powers, the record of their actual forecasts is dreary. History is littered with the wreckage of sophisticated economic forecasts gone wrong. What is astonishing is that anyone still listens. The only reason we do, of course, is that we cannot avoid making decisions, we have to try to forecast the unknowable future, and we keep looking to the self-proclaimed prophets.

George Gilder has written about the dismal track record of the forecasts made by experts:

> In the fifteenth century the longbow—with its unlimited supplies of ammunition, its rapid-firing capacity (twelve shots per minute), and its long range of some two hundred yards—was regarded as the ultimate weapon. Leading seventeenth-century intellectuals imagined that all the available inventions were already behind us. In the eighteenth century even Adam Smith himself envisaged the eventual decline of capitalism into a stationary state. Sismondi thought economic development was all over in 1815 and John Stuart Mill supposed that we had reached the end of the line in 1830. In 1843 the U.S. Commissioner of Patents thought that the onrush of inventions might "presage [a time] when human improvement must end". Alvin Hansen and scores of other economists predicted socialist stagnation as the likely human prospect after World War II. Even Thomas Edison believed that the major inventions had all been accomplished during his own lifetime.[21]

It goes on. Consider a few recent forecasts made by experts. In 1949 the United Nations Scientific Conference on the Conservation and Utilization of Resources estimated world reserves of important metals and fuels. As Colin Clark has pointed out, at the rates of use of these estimated reserves in the 1950s and 1960s,

[21] George Gilder, *Wealth and Poverty* (New York: Basic Books, Inc., 1981), p. 256.

the world should have run out of lead, chromium, zinc, and copper by 1975.[22] Not only did nothing of the kind occur, but their reserves increased enormously, despite unprecedented (and unpredicted) rates of use. The reason, of course, is that companies do not and cannot know the size or location of all mineral deposits; they only explore what is economically optimal, in view of their rate of extraction, which for many minerals is a ten to thirty years supply.

In 1967 the Council of Economic Advisors, commenting on the 3 percent increase in the price level for the preceding year, wrote " . . . inflationary forces set in motion during the period of overly rapid expansion are still alive, although their strength is waning".[23] As everyone now knows, those forces did not wane but waxed mightily in subsequent years. In 1968 well-known biologist Paul Ehrlich forecast that, "In the 1970s the world will undergo famines—hundreds of millions of people are going to starve to death."[24] Nothing of the sort happened. In 1972 Dennis L. Meadows in his famous *The Limits to Growth* predicted that if current consumption trends continued, reserves of copper, gold, lead, petroleum, silver, tin, zinc, and mercury would be exhausted within the next two decades.[25] Now more than a decade into the countdown for these minerals, exhaustion is about as imminent as when Meadows spoke his warning.

Why are the experts so pessimistic in their forecasts of everything except the future good of their own policies? Gilder suggests: "Because human beings become exhausted and decline as they grow older, they are inclined to believe that societies do as well."[26] But he thinks the problem goes deeper, amounting to a "profound incomprehension of the human situation" with its inherent risks and opportunities.[27] And surely pride plays a part: the experts' unshakable belief that they have the prevision, the wisdom—and therefore the right—to manage other people's affairs.

To have a child always means to accept a risk—the risk of unforeseeable future disasters. The fact that per capita income, wealth, and security have risen in recent decades throughout the world, is fair proof that families have been more right in accepting the risks than the counselors of despair who were clamoring to deter them.

Then what about the charge made by people like Robert S. McNamara, former director of the World Bank, that population growth, by nurturing children, "drains away" resources that might "better" be invested in industry?[28] The answer is simple—Mr. McNamara has his preferences and the world's families have acted upon theirs. Mr. McNamara defends himself by claiming that "excessive"

[22] Colin Clark, *Population Growth: The Advantages* (Santa Ana: R. L. Sassone, 1972), pp. 8–9.

[23] *Economic Report of the President, 1967* (Washington: U.S. Government Printing Office, 1967), p. 38.

[24] Paul R. Ehrlich, *The Population Bomb* (New York: Ballantine Books, 1968), Prologue.

[25] Donella H. Meadows, Dennis L. Meadows, et al., *The Limits to Growth: A Report for the Club of Rome's Project on the Predicament of Mankind* (New York: Universe Books, 1972), pp. 56–59.

[26] Gilder, op. cit., p. 256.

[27] Ibid.

[28] *Christian Science Monitor,* July 5, 1977, pp. 20–21.

births—children—in the underdeveloped countries block investments from creating jobs to prevent unemployment.[29] But as the last chapter shows, government family planners simply *assume*, with no evidence at all, that high birth rates discourage investment. Countries with high birth rates do in *fact* achieve just as high levels of savings and investment as countries with low birth rates. It is nevertheless also a fact that many of the developing economies do have unacceptably high levels of unemployment. This has an explanation that is quite different from the one offered by Mr. McNamara and other proponents of government population control. Many development economists believe that the government-sponsored strategies for development themselves create unemployment by taxing agriculture and subsidizing a highly automated, capital-intensive industrial development that requires little labor.[30] The effect of these plans, which have been encouraged by Mr. McNamara's own World Bank, has been to reduce relative incomes in agriculture and increase them in urban industry, but only for a privileged few, and at the expense of those who remain in agriculture. The result is to label relatively large segments of the population as "surplus" in the modern economy. The next small step is to get rid of such "surplus" people, to cry "overpopulation".

If Mr. McNamara were correct in his belief that unemployment springs from underinvestment, we would surely find the scarce industrial equipment in full use in the less-developed countries, even overly used. But this is not the case. Industrial equipment in many of the less-developed countries is often used at only a fraction of its capacity, suggesting not too little investment but too much, in excess of the economies' abilities to provide other inputs and markets for industrial products.[31] The problem, as White explains, is that

> the relative prices of capital and labor are frequently badly out of line with their true social worth: A wide variety of government policies have made capital artificially cheap in capital-short economies, while labor has been made artificially expensive in many of these same economies. Capital is made cheaper through government-subsidized low-interest loans, favorable exchange rates or low tariffs for imported capital goods, tax holidays on new investments, and accelerated depreciation on capital goods . . . Labor in urban manufacturing has been made more expensive through minimum wage legislation, mandated fringe benefits, restrictions on the ability to lay off workers, and government-encouraged union pressures. These labor provisions are most likely to be enforced in the government sector, in large firms and in MNCs [multi-national corporations] . . . they are a major factor in encouraging high urban unemployment. Real urban wages are frequently two or more times rural wages . . . In a number of

[29] Ibid.

[30] See Derek T. Healey, "Development Policy: New Thinking about an Interpretation", *Journal of Economic Literature*, vol. 10, no. 3, September 1972, pp. 757–797.

[31] Healey, op. cit.; Lawrence J. White, "The Evidence on Appropriate Factor Proportions for Manufacturing in Less Developed Countries: A Survey", *Economic Development and Cultural Change*, vol. 27, no. 1, October 1978, pp. 27–59.

countries, the relative distortion of labor and capital prices, rather than getting better, has become worse during the years since the Second World War . . . [32]

White's analysis sheds light not only on the high unemployment but on the much-decried migration to urban areas in the less-developed countries. The problems exist, but they have been created not by overpopulation, or lack of capital, as McNamara claims, but by the policies of the development planners themselves.

In addition to inappropriate prices for capital and labor, White faults "the strong tendency for entrepreneurs and especially engineers to think in terms of developed-country mechanized technology as the ideal", the "confusion between high labor productivity and efficiency", and "badly conceived, capital-intensive public projects", all of which lead to excessive investment and mechanization and the underuse of labor.[33] These problems, White notes, become progressively more severe whenever decision-makers are able to escape the constraints imposed by free market competition.[34]

The economic mistakes of the development planners have ranged from the ludicrous to the tragic. The British government lavished 35 million pounds on a groundnut (peanut) development scheme in East Africa, which produced no groundnuts.[35] In the late 1970s Indian planners, after having subsidized heavy industry for decades, went on a small-is-beautiful kick and forced large textile plants to produce yarn for handweaving, which raised their costs.[36] Hirschman describes "the spectacle, frequently on display in underdeveloped countries, of half-finished structures in reinforced concrete which were intended to become government buildings, hospitals, stadiums, etc."[37] The U.S. Peace Corps poured money into rabbit production in the Philippines, where rabbit meat is regarded as unclean, and the rabbits ended up in speculative breeding.[38] The World Bank under Robert S. McNamara financed, and thus kept in power, the government of Tanzania while it coercively collectivized farms and compelled a mass migration of its people, with devastating effects on food output.[39] During the Great Leap Forward, Chinese development planners compelled the people to build water projects and tackle new methods of cultivation, which reduced the quality of the land; they forced a misallocation of industrial resources that idled a significant part

[32] Ibid., pp. 47–48.

[33] Ibid., pp. 49–50.

[34] Ibid.

[35] Peter T. Bauer, "The 'English Sickness' Is Getting the Wrong Diagnosis", *Fortune*, vol. 94, no. 3, September 1976, pp. 160–164.

[36] *Far Eastern Economic Review*, December 22, 1978.

[37] Albert O. Hirschman, *A Bias for Hope* (New Haven: Yale University Press, 1971), p. 259.

[38] Personal letter to Jacqueline Kasun.

[39] P. T. Bauer, *Equality, the Third World, and Economic Delusion* (Cambridge: Harvard University Press, 1981), p. 106.

of their industrial capacity and overworked the rest.[40] The result of this debacle was starvation for millions.[41]

Throughout Africa socialist governments have taxed farmers to subsidize privileged city activities, thus diminishing their ability to supply food. They have collectivized land ownership, thus inviting overgrazing and destruction of trees, and their aftermath—desertification and famine.

Variations on the same theme appear in the recent economic experience of Mexico, the Philippines, Central America—in fact, with a few bright exceptions, the entire developing world. Hence their inability to pay off their development loans.

The common thread that runs through these assorted horrors is that the mistakes were not borne by their makers. No matter their intent they knew from the outset that they would not be responsible for the costs. This cannot help but encourage experimentation and innovation, as it is admiringly called. The much-criticized reluctance of small farmers and businessmen in the less-developed countries to "innovate" stems from their knowledge that they cannot escape from their mistakes. Families have the same excellent reason to manage their affairs prudently, including their reproductive affairs. All of them—farmers, small businessmen, families—not only bear the costs of their own mistakes, but also those made by their planners, a further and powerful restraint against any rash action.

In other words, it is not families, but development planners, who behave irrationally with respect to economic constraints, being largely free from them. They can command, through taxation and intergovernmental grants, resources that would not have come to them voluntarily. They can dispose of resources without meeting the market tests that restrain families and private businesses. And they can use their tax-supported power over the media to propagandize the world into believing that it is overpopulation and not their own misuse of economic resources that threatens world prosperity and peace.

This state of affairs could only come about in a milieu of planning. It could not occur in a market economy in which the users of resources have to pay the full cost, bidding against other users, and recovering those costs by offering, in competition with others, goods and services that the public *wants* to buy. The development planners, like all governmental bureaucracies, can dispense with the voluntarism of the market.

Economic theory shows that under these circumstances, planners have both the incentive and the opportunity to maximize their own welfare by maximizing their

[40] Arthur G. Ashbrook, "Main Lines of Chinese Communist Economic Policy", in *An Economic Profile of Mainland China,* Studies Prepared for the Joint Economic Committee, Congress of the United States (Washington: U.S. Government Printing Office, 1967), pp. 15–44.

[41] "The Human Cost of Communism in China", Report to Subcommittee to Investigate the Administration of the Internal Security Act, Committee on the Judiciary, U.S. Senate, 92d Congress, 1st Session, 1971, pp. 13–16.

projects in complete disregard of market tests. They exaggerate the "need" for their projects and the "benefits" that will result, and they understate the direct costs and the harmful side-effects. They also form mutually beneficial alliances with private businesses and with bureaucrats in other public agencies to promote their plans.

Obviously, these plans do not harmonize with those of other groups in the economy. Unlike the market economy, in which all participants are both restrained and motivated by each other's preferences, planning is by its nature autarchic. Sellers in the market economy must please or lose their customers. Buyers cannot command resources, but must compete for them.

Market prices mediate between buyers and sellers, simultaneously reflecting the preferences of customers and the scarcity of resources in all related markets throughout the economy. And all free markets are related to one another by virtue of the relationships between inputs and outputs, substitutes and complementary goods.

This kinship imposes a natural harmony on the prices that send economic messages to the market-oriented economic society. For example, any difficulty in obtaining a given resource—say, oil—raises the price of the resource, which induces consumers to economize in its use and rewards businesses that create substitutes. Smaller cars, gasohol, the coal boom, the new wood-stove industry, fireplace converters, heavier sweaters and winter underwear, and high demand for wool blankets and down comforters are only some of the more visible of the waves and ripples radiating infinitely outward from the change in the price of oil.

There are, on the other hand, no forces to bring a natural social harmony out of the activities of public planners. These plans are by definition arbitrary, substituting the force of authority for the freedom of the market. Though the remaining free markets will try to fit their actions to those of the planners, their adjustments will probably be as unacceptable to the planners as the original situation they felt constrained to "correct". And they will feel obliged to intervene still further. A case in point is the attempt by the U.S. government to raise agricultural prices that stimulated a series of further interventions, ranging from selling surpluses on foreign markets to pulling farmland out of production.

Far from surprising, it should be expected that public planners produce economic dislocations—unemployment, inflation, poverty, and more. The remedy in the view of the development planners is not, of course, to abandon planning but to intensify it. And so, inevitably, population planning, which is population control, becomes an integral part of development planning. The planners need to know and control the size, composition, rate of growth, location, skills, and level of consumption of the population. Otherwise, comprehensive economic planning is impossible because too many of the variables are out of the planners' control.

For its part, the market economy provides restraints on its participants—restraints that prevent them from overpopulating or overinvesting or any excessive behavior detrimental to society. Public central planning becomes comprehensive planning that results in population control—not because people overbreed but because planners have to expand their activities.

The performance of planned economies has been one of the chief failures of our century. They have been riddled by flagrant waste, misallocation of resources, and economic injustice. The recent economic history of China is a case in point. Though commonly described as "overpopulated", China has in fact about the same population density as the state of Pennsylvania, as Table 3-4 indicates.

Table 3-4
How Bad Is the So-Called "Population Problem" in China?
Many countries are more crowded than China, but few produce as little per person, as the following table shows:

Country or State	Persons per square mile 1985	GNP per capita, dollars, 1985
Taiwan	1,393	2,663*
Rep. of Korea	1,121	2,150
Japan	840	11,300
West Germany	635	10,940
India	606	270
United Kingdom	599	8,460
Switzerland	405	16,370
China	280	310
France	261	9,540
United States	67	16,690
Pennsylvania	264	n.a.
Maryland	447	n.a.
New York	375	n.a.

SOURCE: Population densities from *Statistical Abstract of the United States,* 1986, 1987; GNP figures from World Bank, *World Development Report 1987.*
*1983 from *Statistical Abstract of the United States,* 1987.

Nevertheless, after more than three decades of economic mismanagement by their central planners, the Chinese people have realized one of the slowest rates of development and lowest standards of living on earth. Though they have vast industrial and agricultural resources and are an industrious and intelligent people, their output in 1985 amounted to only $300 per person, barely enough for survival. Most of their economic resources are unused. For example, less than a third of their agricultural land is in crops.[42] As discussed earlier, far more densely populated nations around them in Asia have forged ahead of them in economic development. Taiwan, with a population density five times as great as China's,

---

[42] Food and Agriculture Organization of the United Nations, *FAO Production Yearbook,* 1980.

produces eight times as much per capita and has an as large or larger volume of trade.[43] The Republic of Korea, with a population density four times as great as China's, has a per capita output seven times as great.[44]

The fact that China is now belatedly experimenting with some free-enterprise incentives is testimony to the superior efficiency of the market economy with its free-price system. Similar testimony is found in the Yugoslav and Hungarian espousal of the market economy and in the aborted recommendation of Soviet economists in 1965 that a profit system be substituted for central planning.[45] The contrast between free market West Germany and socially planned United Kingdom after World War II is another case in point.[46] More evidence exists in the successful development experience of Hong Kong, Korea, Japan, and Taiwan. Similarly, the rapid recovery and development during 1921–1928 of the Soviet economy under Lenin's New Economic Policy, which relied on market principles, can be compared with the economic and human devastation created by the ensuing Five-Year Plans.[47]

Such examples do not, of course, settle all questions as to the precise role of government in the economy, but they do clearly show that it must be strictly limited, and that central planning is an economic and human disaster. That governments so often resort to central planning during war indicates not that planning achieves greater efficiency or justice, but that it gives the rulers the control they want, regardless of the cost to the populace. The planned economy is, in fact, as Lange observed of the Soviet system, *"sui generis* a wartime economy".[48] It is the economic posture of a government at war, either with an external enemy or, as is so often the case, with its own people.

Nor is it true, as some authoritarian government officials claim, that the market economy requires a higher level of economic development than pertains in most third-world countries. The propensity to "truck, barter, and exchange" is, as Adam Smith observed,[49] deeply rooted in human nature—as any American parent who observes his children exchanging their Trick-or-Treat loot can testify. Trade and traders appear throughout ancient literature. Throughout history, rulers have devoted great energies to controlling in their own interests the markets and trade by which their subjects increased their economic welfare.

---

[43] See Table 3-4.

[44] Ibid.

[45] Alexander Birman, "The Reform in a Nutshell", *Soviet Life,* February 1970.

[46] Andrew Shonfield, *Modern Capitalism: The Changing Balance of Public and Private Power* (London: Oxford University Press, 1965), pp. 88–120, 239–297; Bauer, "The 'English Sickness' Is Getting the Wrong Diagnosis", op. cit.

[47] See Howard J. Sherman, *The Soviet Economy* (Boston: Little, Brown and Company, 1969), chaps. 3, 4.

[48] Oskar Lange, *The Political Economy of Socialism* (Warsaw, 1957), p. 16.

[49] Adam Smith, *An Inquiry into the Nature and Causes of the Wealth of Nations,* 5th ed. (London, 1789; reprint ed., New York: Modern Library, 1937), p. 13.

Modern development economists have written fascinating descriptions of the "penny capitalism" found in the less-industrialized economies.[50]

Recent experience has also shown that planning, once begun, perpetuates and extends itself. The Soviet Union, of course, never intended to turn back, but the abortive experience with the 1965 economic "reforms" shows the difficulty of reducing even the smallest part of the bureaucratic overlay in the planned economy once it is in place.

It could be countered that the Soviet Union is not a good example of economic planning burgeoning into population control since, in keeping with Marxist dogma, it has never explicitly espoused an antinatalist policy and has even criticized the capitalist countries for their Malthusian leanings.[51] But the Soviet antinatalist policy never had to be explicit because it was built into the foundations of Soviet planning, with its low wages and consumption, and restricted housing. More blatantly, free abortion plays its part in the population controls operated by the Soviet government. The controls are themselves controlled, adjusted from time to time in furtherance of the planners' goals, as when abortion was restricted from 1936 to 1955 when it appeared that manpower shortages might hamper industry and the armed services.[52] On the whole, the manipulation is efficient. The comprehensive internal and external passport system, compulsory military service, and the restraints on civilian labor give the government direct command over the location of the population and indirect control over its rate of growth.

This spotlights the paradox — that the most fervent antinatalism is voiced in the United States, which is, or claims to be, the world headquarters of free enterprise. If it is true that the free market imposes natural constraints so that people tend not to overdo anything, then the free-market society should militate against antinatalism.

There are several possible explanations for this apparent contradiction. First, the United States not only espouses free-market economics but also the free market in ideas; and the ideas of socialist planning have been widely taught in the country, leading inexorably to population planning. Secondly, largely as a result of the Great Depression, the belief has grown that the free market can operate well only under the aegis of government. Hand in hand with this idea is the notion that "experts" can help — are in fact necessary — in the affairs of all human institutions, including the family. The very success and wealth of the free-market economy make it possible for a large part of the labor force to indulge in these expert-oriented activities rather than in the production of food and other basics of consumption.

[50] Peter T. Bauer and Basil S. Yamey, *The Economics of Under-developed Countries* (Chicago: The University of Chicago Press, 1957), pp. 38–40.

[51] Audrey Kasun, "The Orthodox Soviet View of Demographic Policy as Compared to the Policies in Hungary, Romania, and Bulgaria", unpublished manuscript written at the University of California at Berkeley, March 1979.

[52] Ibid., pp. 11–12.

A further reason is that participants in the free-market economy do not necessarily enjoy or support its constraints, especially as they apply to themselves. From the time of Adam Smith businessmen have spent great energy sidestepping the rigors of competition, trying to insulate themselves from the test of the market. Efforts to monopolize markets, erect walls of tariff protection, obtain government subsidies, and transfer costs to third parties are perennial. To the extent that these efforts have succeeded, it is inaccurate to speak of the United States as a free-market economy, despite all the rhetoric.

Total government receipts in the United States grew from 34 percent of the national income in 1960 to 40 percent in 1986,[53] which is a higher fraction than in some avowedly socialist countries. The logical extension of the drive toward central planning, which has been so prominent a feature of our recent economic life, could account for the antinatalism of the country. It is striking that in the mid-1960s the federal government began its family planning program along with its War on Poverty, the comprehensive federal plan to abolish not only poverty but all manner of social problems.

More recently, Congressman Richard L. Ottinger has justified his bill to control the growth of the population of the United States on the grounds that it is necessary for "the Federal Government [to have] the capacity to more accurately forecast and effectively respond to short-term and long-term trends in the relationships between population, resources, and the environment, both at home and abroad . . . "[54] Obviously, such power is only necessary to a government that plans to control its people's economic destiny rather than allow them to work it out for themselves.

The issue of population control is an inescapable part of the dispute over planning versus free markets. The free-market economy, with its system of built-in restraints and incentives, does not need population control. The planned economy, which views such control as an integral part of its administrative controls, does. The planners can no more allow population to take care of itself than they can allow investment to take care of itself. They may not need to articulate any particular population policy—they may even articulate one they do not follow—but they must control the growth, location, and major attributes of the population.

As the central government expands its economic role by taxing and borrowing to increase its share of total spending, the appetites of special interests also grow. Government grants for "family planning" serve as an incentive for special-interest groups to work to increase the size of those grants and the economic and political power of their recipients. The growth of government feeds on itself, as does the influence of special-interest groups, such as the antinatalists.

There are reasons too why the United States has been more aggressively

---

[53] Based on U.S. Department of Commerce figures reproduced in *Economic Report of the President, 1987* (Washington: U.S. Government Printing Office, 1987), pp. 270, 336.

[54] *Congressional Record*, vol. 127, no. 9, January 19, 1981.

antinatalist in its foreign policy rather than at home. In the first place, although there is no doubt that the policy has aroused antagonism in foreign countries, it has been promoted as a condition for receiving foreign aid, which tends to quiet objections. In return for large flows of American aid, pragmatic foreign rulers consider the demands a small price to pay, especially if democratic elections are not an important factor in their politics. A policy that would arouse instant outrage and serious political repercussions in the United States is, through a form of blackmail, made possible in a foreign country. Americans, themselves, are willing to tolerate foreign policy schemes that they would spurn if applied to themselves. The rationale is that "as long as we're feeding them, we should have something to say". The fact is, of course, that U.S. aid does not feed the people of any country and adds only a relatively small share to the self-support of any people. But the amounts are large enough to induce the foreign ruling elites who receive them to accept U.S. meddling (perhaps because the elites get the aid and other persons experience the meddling) and to persuade Americans that they should "have something to say".

In addition, the aid program calls for plans to allocate and use the funds: though the United States sometimes tries in marginal ways to encourage free-market activities, the very nature of the aid program means that resources are being plied by governments in nonmarket ways. The foreign aid program requires central planning and its logical extension, population planning and control. Congressman Ottinger, in calling for a domestic policy of population control, rightly states, "we are not asking for anything which we do not already advocate to the less-developed nations of the world."[55]

One of the grounds most commonly offered for economic and social planning is that justice requires it—that the profit motive in the market economy results in such gross inequities that only large-scale public intervention can correct them. Similarly, one of the perennial arguments for publicly supported family planning is that otherwise the poor would not be able to afford it.

To which there is a twofold answer. In the first place, there is no evidence at all that the planned economies achieve a higher degree of economic justice than does the free market. Even if we assume that there is a consensus on the need to redistribute purchasing power, it can be done without destroying the freedom of choice and efficiency of the market economy. Those who want the poor to have more birth control could voluntarily support the services on a private charitable basis without destroying anyone's freedom of choice. Alternatively, the poor might be given money that was donated by the more well-to-do. Those who think the poor are too poor can offer them birth control services or money that the poor themselves can spend on birth control or something else they might choose. But those who espouse any kind of planning in the interests of justice and fairness to

[55] *Congressional Record*, Extensions of Remarks, August 2, 1979.

the poor, never favor voluntary solutions to the problems they perceive in the distribution of income or property. When given the opportunity, the public-planning advocates have invariably accumulated as much power as possible over income and property. Stripped of their masks, what they really want is not justice but control over other people's lives.

To conclude: the dynamics of the market as compared with those of the planned economy show that the market imposes constraints on its participants so that they have strong incentives not to do anything to excess. As a result, in the free-market economy, there is no need for public efforts to restrain, or encourage, reproduction.

Economic interventions by public planners are not in any case self-limiting; they produce conditions that inspire or require still further interventions, leading almost inevitably to the control of reproduction. It follows that the drive for population control in our time is a natural outgrowth of the trend toward governmental economic and social planning, which has been so prominent a feature of twentieth-century history here and in many other countries.

CHAPTER FOUR

UNITED STATES FOREIGN AID
AND POPULATION CONTROL

There is no question but that the United States' antinatalism has, for a number of reasons, been projected more frankly in foreign than in domestic policy. No one who follows the congressional hearings on foreign aid can fail to be startled by the depth of the official U.S. commitment to population control abroad. Paul Ehrlich's "population bomb" and Kingsley Davis's "population plague"[1] have seduced official aid circles.

In his 1978 testimony on foreign aid, Secretary of State Cyrus Vance ranked "population planning" the "second major focus of AID [U.S. Agency for International Development] funding", second only to "global problems of hunger and malnutrition",[2] and he linked the latter so closely to "population pressure" as to give them equal importance in the design of U.S. aid programs, a view amply reinforced by other features of the program.

Since 1965 the United States has contributed more to foreign population-control programs than all other countries combined and has pressured other countries and international agencies to back the programs.[3] In addition to more than 2 billion dollars in explicit AID "population assistance" appropriations to various countries and international organizations such as the United Nations Fund for Population Activities, the United States has made donations to the World Bank and to United Nations organizations—including the World Health Organization, the Food and Agriculture Organization, UNESCO, UNICEF, and the International Labor Organization—that have been used for population control, with a degree of enthusiasm and dedication equal to that of the AID bureaucracy.

Early in the 1970s the United States' foreign aid bureaucracy spelled out its plan to bring world population growth to a halt. In a classified document prepared in 1974 and not declassified until 1980, the aid planners voiced their intent to bring about "a two-child family on the average" throughout the world by the year

---

[1] Kingsley Davis, "The Climax of Population Growth", *California Medicine,* vol. 113, no. 5, November 1970, pp. 33–39.

[2] *Hearings* before the Committee on International Relations, House of Representatives, on Foreign Assistance Legislation for Fiscal Year 1979, Part 1, pp. 13–14.

[3] Based on Population Reference Bureau, *World Population Growth and Response: 1965–1975—A Decade of Global Action* (Washington: The Population Reference Bureau, April 1976), pp. 226–227; and Agency for International Development, *Rationale for AID Support of Population Programs,* January 1982, p. 24; and World Bank, *World Development Report 1984,* pp. 148, 180–181.

2000.[4] The plan called for the announcement, "after suitable preparation", of a goal of "near stability" for the U.S. population.[5] As for the world, it envisioned a "far larger, high-level effort" to "bring population growth under control"[6] and named the countries where the planners would concentrate their efforts—India, Bangladesh, Pakistan, Ethiopia, Mexico, Indonesia, Brazil, the Philippines, Thailand, Egypt, Turkey, Nigeria, and Colombia.[7] It suggested specific measures to persuade people to have smaller families and warned that "mandatory population control measures" might be necessary.[8]

As a step toward the realization of their plan, AID officials initiated and Congress enacted Section 104(d) of the International Development and Food Assistance Act of 1978, which provides that American foreign aid "shall be administered so as to give particular attention to . . . the impact of all programs, projects, and activities on population growth. All . . . activities proposed for financing . . . shall be designed to build motivation for smaller families . . . in programs such as education . . . , nutrition, disease control, maternal and child health services, improvements in the status and employment of women, agricultural production, rural development, and assistance to the urban poor."

In its Section 102 on "Development Assistance Policy", the 1978 act said that U.S. aid would be "concentrated" in countries that demonstrate their "commitment and progress" by their "control of population growth", along with other indications of serious intent. An explanatory footnote in the Report on Population and Development Assistance by the House Select Committee on Population states that "the whole of AID's development assistance effort" was intended to be included within the population-control provisions of Section 104.[9]

Thus, although (or perhaps because) U.S. birth-controllers had met with a disappointing "absence of widespread public demand"[10] and a lack of "clear and vigorous support"[11] by foreign governments for population control, and an "under-utilization of . . . outreach",[12] not to mention the fact that "attitudes of men are still anti-vasectory",[13] the machinery was stepped up. Statements by the foreign aid

---

[4] U.S. Government Document, NSSM 200, "Implications of Worldwide Population Growth for U.S. Security and Overseas Interests", December 10, 1974, declassified December 31, 1980, p. 14.

[5] Ibid., p. 19.

[6] Ibid., p. 194.

[7] Ibid., p. 15.

[8] Ibid., pp. 118–194.

[9] Select Committee on Population, Report, "Population and Development Assistance", U.S. House of Representatives, 95th Congress, 2nd Session (Washington: U.S. Government Printing Office, 1978), p. 111.

[10] Ibid., p. 55.

[11] Ibid., p. 59.

[12] Ibid.

[13] Ibid., p. 55.

bureaucracy show the zeal of their commitment. For example, Dr. Reimert T. Ravenholt, director of AID's Office of Population since its formation, was quoted in a 1977 interview with the *St. Louis Post-Dispatch* as demanding the sterilization of one-quarter of the fertile women of the world to meet U.S. goals of population control and to maintain "the normal operation of U.S. commercial interests around the world".[14]   Dr. Ravenholt was reported to believe that only such extreme measures could counteract the "population explosion" that would otherwise so reduce living standards that foreign rebellions would spring up "against the strong U.S. commercial presence".

In the same vein, Robert S. McNamara, as executive director of the World Bank that channels a major portion of U.S. aid to foreign countries, predicted that continued population growth would result in "poverty, hunger, stress, crowding, and frustration", which would threaten social, economic, and military stability. Declaring that this would not be "a world that anyone wants" in an interview published by the *Christian Science Monitor* on July 5, 1977, Mr. McNamara warned that if present methods of population control "fail, and population pressures become too great, nations will be driven to more coercive methods". That the failure of ill-conceived government programs could be blamed on "population pressures" seems not to have occurred to Mr. McNamara, who visited India at the height of the compulsory sterilization campaign in 1976 to congratulate the government for its "political will and determination" in the campaign.[15]

John J. Gilligan, administrator of AID, described in 1978 congressional hearings how the agency is "stressing the importance of population impact" in its programs.[16] He reported to the House Select Committee on Population that "Country Development Strategy Statements" were being prepared for each country to incorporate American population concerns into the plans for economic development. And he spoke of his hope that development projects in Pakistan, El Salvador, the Sahel, Morocco, Nepal, Nicaragua, Indonesia, India, and Tanzania would either reduce fertility directly, as by educating and employing women, or would discover the "determinants of fertility".[17]

Months before Congress enacted Section 104 (d), with its comprehensive design for foreign population control, into U.S. foreign aid law, impatient officials at AID were taking steps to implement the law with little regard for the congressional stamp of approval. An AID cable to its foreign missions in early 1977 described how the agency intended to encourage "female education" and "female employment", support "laws . . . to increase the age of marriage", bolster "integrated

---

[14] *St. Louis Post-Dispatch,* April 22, 1977, p. 1.

[15] Peter T. Bauer and Basil S. Yamey, "The Third World and the West: An Economic Perspective", in W. Scott Thompson, ed., *The Third World: Premises of U.S. Policy* (San Francisco: Institute for Contemporary Studies, 1978), p. 302.

[16] *Hearings,* op. cit., p. 210.

[17] Select Committee on Population, *Report,* op. cit., pp. 119–120.

health, nutrition, and family planning services", and encourage "cohesive village organization linked to federal structures (e.g. in Indonesia), which has plainly encouraged family planning", by "reducing parental reliance on children for old-age support", and by offering "direct rewards for smaller families" including "rewards for communities or individuals who limit fertility . . . "[18]

The list was startling not only for the degree of American interference in the national and personal affairs of foreign citizens, but for the appended statement averring that already "most missions include such projects among their total mix of projects". Then "why", the agency asked itself in its cable, "has the agency initiated [Section 104 (d)] now?" Why indeed, since such legislative enactments are apparently unnecessary for the operations of the agency? AID answered its own question: "to demonstrate . . . that the agency puts very high priority on reducing population growth".[19]

Subsequent Carter administration foreign policy statements only reaffirmed the determination to control foreign population, despite acknowledged "resistance" in some countries. The Department of State *Bulletin* for March 1980, for example, noted the opposition in Africa to population control programs;[20] but countered with an admonition by Secretary of State Cyrus Vance on the "tension between spiraling global population growth and finite resources"[21] and a promise from Thomas Ehrlich, director of the newly created U.S. International Development Cooperation Agency, that the United States would direct an "accelerated attack" on the population-control front.[22] In May 1980, the new Secretary of State Edmund S. Muskie, known for his espousal of the "Club of Rome, zero-growth, Malthusian perspective",[23] promised to make what he called the "environmental arm" of the state department even "more visible".[24]

In his January 14, 1981, Farewell Address, President Jimmy Carter reemphasized the overriding importance his administration had attached to the problem of "overpopulation". He called for "courage and foresight" to meet this grave problem.[25] And on April 1, 1981, Mr. Peter McPherson, administrator of AID, appeared before the Senate Foreign Relations Committee to request on behalf of the Reagan administration $253 million for "Population Planning programs" for fiscal year 1982, a 33 percent increase over the amount spent in 1981. In making his request Mr. McPherson reiterated the same concerns that had animated the preced-

---

[18] Ibid., pp. 112–120.
[19] Ibid., p. 118.
[20] *Department of State Bulletin,* vol. 80, no. 2036, March 1980, p. 13.
[21] Ibid., p. 40.
[22] Ibid., p. 54.
[23] *Department of State Bulletin,* vol. 80, no. 2039, June 1980, p. D.
[24] Ibid.
[25] Jimmy Carter, "Farewell Address: Major Issues Facing the Nation", *Vital Speeches of the Day,* vol. XLVII, no. 8, February 1, 1981, p. 227.

ing administration: "Rapid population growth in the developing countries is one of the primary obstacles to the expansion of food production, reduction and [sic] malnutrition and chronic disease, and conservation of dwindling non-renewable resources."[26]

Congress gave McPherson less than he asked for that year, and the following year the administration initially suggested that no money be given for population assistance. It was quickly shouted down, however, by members of the population lobby within the administration and Congress.[27] By 1986 the appropriation for AID population assistance amounted to $238 million, which, although it was 20 percent greater in money terms than during the last year of the Carter administration, was actually a bit smaller in real terms.[28]

Descriptions of AID projects embodying the strategies enumerated above appear throughout the development literature. The conviction prevails that, as AID put it in its 1976 policy paper on "U.S. Population Related Assistance", family planning by itself "may not suffice" to bring world birth rates down to two children per woman. Or, as the National Security Council, which has gotten into the population-control act, stated in its first Annual Report in 1976, " . . . family planning services and information alone will not bring birth rates down to . . . an average family of slightly more than two children."[29]

It is not enough, in the prevailing wisdom, to provide a setting within which people can choose voluntarily the number of children they wish to have in the light of the costs and benefits. The official view decrees that the U.S. government has the right and the duty to set a worldwide target of an average of two children per family, and, in the explicit words of U.S. law, to funnel its aid to foreign countries so as to "build motivation for smaller families through modification of economic and social conditions supportive of the desire for large families . . . "[30] By law and regulation, U.S. funds may not be used to provide compulsory contraception or sterilization, or to pay for abortions, or to provide "incentives designed to induce acceptance of any one method of contraception over another".[31]

---

[26] Statement of Honorable M. Peter McPherson, Administrator, Agency for International Development Before the Senate Foreign Relations Committee, April 1, 1981.

[27] The Population Crisis Committee/Draper Fund, *Report of Activities 1980–81*, p. 6.

[28] *Budget of the United States Government*, 1981, 1985, 1988; *Congressional Quarterly*, September 1, 1984.

[29] Select Committee on Population, *Report*, op. cit., p. 100.

[30] International Development and Food Assistance Act of 1978, Section 104(d).

[31] *Hearings*, op. cit., p. 280. In 1973 the Helms Amendment to the Foreign Assistance Act of 1961 forbade using U.S. foreign aid funds to pay for abortions; AID, however, decided that this did not prohibit the use of U.S. tax dollars to equip abortion clinics or to train doctors to perform abortions or to finance abortion research. Thus AID virtually nullified the Helms Amendment. See Patrick A. Trueman, "Abortion and American Foreign Policy", *AUL Studies in Law and Medicine*, no. 9 (Chicago: Americans United for Life, 1980).

But the United States is officially committed to circumventing individual choice, and the law, through "motivation".

In its campaign to change the hearts and minds of mankind and to limit the family size of the world to suit U.S. foreign affairs officials, the foreign aid bureaucracy increasingly relies on the "village system" of population control. Much touted by former U.S. Ambassador for Population Affairs Marshall Green and other officials,[32] this system combines all known fertility-reducing strategies that impinge most intimately on the lives of villagers, or roughly one-half or so of mankind. When, as AID cable 017208 said, the village is linked to a demanding "federal structure" or central government, the results can be amazingly effective.

AID has been instrumental in developing the system in Indonesia, where the central government supports a network of some 30,000 village "family planning" units.[33] The local units extract and transmit information on the contraceptive habits of village couples, as in the province of Bali where, according to a World Bank report, the monthly village council meeting "begins with a roll call; each man responds by saying whether he and his wife are using contraceptives. Replies are plotted on a village map—prominently displayed."[34] Local fieldworkers receive bonuses for "recruiting" citizens for contraceptive services, and the central government sets "targets" for the number of "new acceptors" of contraception and launches special recruitment "drives".[35] The government provides group rewards to villages that reach the targets. These rewards consist of increased food supplements, health services, and other benefits.[36]

In general, the foreign aid establishment prefers group incentives because they avoid the appearance of paying individuals to use birth control or to have themselves sterilized (which, though listed among the options of AID's cable 017208 and actually in use, attracts criticism); and in any case, they embody the even stronger goad of group pressure. The woman who volunteers for IUD insertion in Indonesia will not only enjoy the village's food bonus but will earn her neighbors' gratitude for their share in the booty. Conversely, those who refuse this "service" will be depriving their neighbors as well as themselves of food.[37] The Indonesian program points up the significance of the increasing emphasis given by aid planners to "integration" of family planning with food programs and other

[32] Ambassador Marshall Green, Coordinator of Population Affairs, U.S. Department of State, Speech, "United States Perspectives on World Population Issues", to The Conference Board's Conference on Population Trends and Implications, Dallas, Texas, March 30, 1977.

[33] The Population Council, *Studies in Family Planning*, vol. 9, no. 9, September 1978, pp. 235–237.

[34] The World Bank, *World Development Report 1980* (Washington, 1980), p. 80.

[35] The Population Council, *Studies in Family Planning*, vol. 5, no. 5, May 1974, pp. 148–151, and vol. 7, no. 7, July 1976, pp. 188–196.

[36] The Population Council, *Studies in Family Planning*, September 1978, op. cit.; Select Committee on Population, *Report*, op. cit., p. 70.

[37] See Robert M. Veatch, "Governmental Population Incentives: Ethical Issues at Stake", *Studies in Family Planning*, vol. 8, no. 4, April 1977, pp. 100–108.

services. Such integration does a thorough job of building the proper "motivation for smaller families".

Enthusiasm abounded over the success of the program in Indonesia that made the country "a textbook illustration of what can be done through enlightened and vigorous government programs", in the glowing words of John J. Gilligan, administrator of AID in the Carter administration.[38] Noting the 15 percent fertility drop in the area during the 1965–1976 period, the House Select Committee on Population reported with unconscious irony that somehow these "improvements occurred in the absence of significant gains in the social and economic conditions of the vast majority of Indonesians".[39] But that concern—whether things will ever improve for the Indonesians—did not seem to ruffle the committee. The primary object is, after all, being achieved; population growth is shrinking. In an emotional speech to the committee, Dr. Haryono Suyono, Deputy Chairman Number Three of the Indonesian National Family Planning Coordinating Board, expressed his government's gratitude to AID for its "spiritual and moral support for our efforts to which we cannot attach a price tag".[40]

AID and its companion organizations have extended this same spiritual and moral support to other programs to induce population control. In one case, villagers in India were offered cash payments on condition that 75 percent of all men in the village submit to vasectomy;[41] and in another Indian village, "100 percent of the eligible couples" accepted family planning, mostly vasectomy, in exchange for a new village well.[42] Though the next step, the compulsory sterilization campaign, gave Indian family planning a rather bad press, with 3 million sterilized within six months in 1976 over the protests of numerous killed or wounded,[43] the principle of "motivation" stands unchallenged in foreign aid circles. In Taiwan, families having no more than two or three children have been awarded annual bank deposits, redeemable to pay educational expenses.[44] In Singapore, the government charged higher hospital delivery fees for each additional child, abolished paid maternity leave, abolished the priority for large families in the allocation of subsidized housing, and abolished the income tax relief for the fourth child and subsequent children in a family.[45] The government of Singapore has subsequently reversed some of these controls.

India has long been a laboratory for experiments in population control, in

---

[38] *Hearings,* op. cit., p. 238.
[39] Select Committee on Population, *Report,* op. cit., p. 68.
[40] Ibid., p. 71.
[41] Veatch, op. cit.
[42] Ibid.
[43] Population Reference Bureau, *Intercom,* vol. 4, no. 12, December 1976, p. 3.
[44] The Population Council, *Studies in Family Planning,* vol. 7, no. 1, January 1976, p. 31.
[45] Ibid.

which AID is heavily involved. According to Joseph Califano, President Johnson, "an ardent proponent of birth control at home and abroad",

> ... repeatedly rejected the unanimous pleas of his advisors from Secretary of State Dean Rusk to National Security Advisor Walt Rostow to ship wheat to the starving Indians during their 1966 famine. He demanded that the Indian government first agree to mount a massive birth control program. The Indians finally moved and Johnson released the wheat over a sufficiently extended period to make certain the birth control program was off the ground.[46]

In his book, *How to Kill Population*, Edward Pohlman describes the incentive payoffs for vasectomies performed in public places such as railroad stations, often in filthy surroundings, with up to 20 sterilizations an hour.[47] Based on his experience as a U.S.-supported "population expert" in India, Pohlman has thought up new ways of improving population control. Since "India has a terrible unemployment problem", Pohlman suggests that "bright, educated, unemployed Indians" be trained as vasectomy specialists.[48] He admits, though, that despite the pressure, the incentives, and the efficiency of the program, "people are somewhat reluctant to have the operation".[49] Unfazed, Pohlman relates that in many parts of India men have been promised, falsely, that vasectomy is "easily and certainly reversible".[50]

Pohlman also mentions the "terrible problems" created by IUDs in India: how Indian women go to the village midwives who "rip out the IUD for 1 or 2 rupees".[51] Not surprisingly, he reports that in India "there is some anger with an America that can interfere with Indian affairs because of financial power".[52] In fact, he confesses that some Indians regard this foreign control of their population as a form of "genocide".[53] And he does not hesitate to admit that local people often go along with the programs, not because they believe in them, but because they provide income and numerous local jobs (as they do in the United States).[54] He suggests that nonmonetary incentives—food, health care, and education—may be more effective than money and have "great public relations value".[55]

---

[46] Joseph Califano, *Governing America* (New York: Simon & Schuster, 1981), p. 52.
[47] Edward Pohlman, *How to Kill Population* (Philadelphia: The Westminster Press, 1971), p. 114.
[48] Ibid., p. 115.
[49] Ibid., p. 116.
[50] Ibid., p. 138.
[51] Ibid., p. 118.
[52] Ibid., p. 135.
[53] Ibid., p. 161.
[54] Ibid., p. 137.
[55] Ibid., p. 148. Whether such "public relations value" is positive or negative for the United States, is open to question. Dr. Marie Mignon Mascarenhas, a World Health Organization investigator in Bangalore, India, reports that a U.S.-sponsored offer of a nutrition program in her hospital for women who would consent to undergo abortion or sterilization created bitterness. See Marie Mignon Mascarenhas, "Aid for an Alternative Strategy to Population Control in India", address sponsored by American Family Institute, Washington, D.C., July 3, 1981.

One of Pohlman's major arguments in favor of incentive payments to people who consent to sterilization is eugenic—because money is more valuable to poor people, "incentives may have their greatest impact on birth rates in the lower classes".[56] Society, he proclaims, has the "right to force family size limits";[57] it is "only a matter of time until massive incentives become accepted as a necessity in population control".[58]

Pohlman's ringing conclusion is a call for "a war against population",[59] financed by "massive programs of foreign aid for population control incentives"[60] and by the assurance that U.S. AID specialists are now (1971) "studying the economic angles" involved.[61] He was right: incentive programs have increasingly consumed the energies of U.S. planners in the years since.

One of the most enthusiastic supporters of incentives is Ambassador Richard Elliot Benedick, coordinator of Population Affairs in the Department of State in both the Carter and Reagan administrations. Ambassador Benedick, who believes that "insistence on the 'right' to multiply indiscriminately represents a misplaced morality",[62] has said that while "it would be inappropriate for the U.S. to appear in a position of attempting to coerce other governments into limiting their populations . . . [I] would wholeheartedly endorse all means short of an inflexible aid linkage."[63]

Appropriate incentives can also, of course, be used to "motivate" reluctant governments. In Thailand, for example, a World Bank mission in 1958–1959 impressed on the government the "adverse effects" of population growth. The Thais were unpersuaded but permitted the Population Council, a private American organization created by John D. Rockefeller III, to enter the country with $1.5 million in 1963 to drum up support for population control among the country's leadership. By 1968 the Thai government was committed to "family planning" and received $3.5 million from AID for this purpose. The World Bank followed up with an increase in loans—more than $700 million for the years 1969–1977—and Thailand began to receive about $100 million a year in U.S. economic and military assistance, far larger than the amounts prior to 1969.[64]

---

[56] Edward Pohlman, *Incentives and Compensations in Birth Planning* (Chapel Hill: Carolina Population Center, Monograph 11, 1971), p. 5.

[57] Ibid., p. 7.

[58] Ibid.

[59] Pohlman, *How to Kill Population*, op. cit., p. 134.

[60] Ibid., p. 132.

[61] Ibid., p. 134.

[62] Prepared Statement of Ambassador Richard Elliot Benedick before the Subcommittee on International Economic Policy and Trade Committee on Foreign Affairs, U.S. House of Representatives, February 29, 1980.

[63] Ibid.

[64] The Population Council, *Studies in Family Planning*, vol. 4, no. 9, September 1973; The Population Council, "Thailand", *Country Profiles*, March 1972; World Bank, *Annual Reports: Statistical Abstract of the United States*, 1975, p. 319.

The Thai government in its turn has not only behaved, it has become a model of cooperation. It operates programs to train, not only midwives and other health workers, but even teachers and border patrol police in techniques of family planning.[65] According to the Population Council, a number of new methods are being used to popularize birth control in Thailand, including "special motivational and educational efforts" in the labor rooms of hospitals "with all hospital staff taking part in these efforts". The results have been remarkable: 43 percent of all obstetrical patients at one hospital accepted sterilization,[66] and between 1965 and 1975 the crude birth rate fell 23 percent. In September 1978 the Thai government reported its "increasing program emphasis on sterilization" as an indication of its "concern for providing the most efficient means of achieving a significant impact on the nation's growth rate". This particular motivation resulted in an "encouraging response to vasectomy" that prompted a revision of the "demographic achievements targets" to even lower levels of population growth than had been thought possible.[67]

Thailand has been helped in its family planning program not only by AID and the World Bank, but by almost all of the leading lights of international population control—UNICEF, UNFPA (the United Nations Fund for Population Activities), the Population Council, the International Planned Parenthood Federation, the University of North Carolina, the Rockefeller Foundation, the Ford Foundation, World Education, Inc., the Pathfinder Fund, and Church World Service.[68] And these organizations receive solid amounts, in some cases most or all, of their support from AID.[69] According to the House Select Committee on Population, the advantages of nongovernmental organizations is in their "flexibility", their ability to "provide a wide range of services".[70] Some critics have charged that such agencies violate congressional restrictions on the funding of coercive population control measures and abortions. Lending some credibility to the charge, Dr. Daniel Weintraub, director of Family Planning International Assistance (one of the international arms of Planned Parenthood and an "intermediary" funded almost exclusively by AID to give subgrants to like-minded organizations), reported to the House Select Committee on Population that if his subgrantees were subjected to U.S. government audit, "we would lose our ... ability to operate effectively".[71]

For those who might be tempted to believe that family planning somehow wins friends for the United States or forestalls "social unrest", as claimed by its

[65] The Population Council, *Studies in Family Planning,* vol. 9, no. 9, September 1978, p. 251.

[66] The Population Council, "Thailand", *Country Profiles,* op. cit., pp. 10–11.

[67] The Population Council, *Studies in Family Planning,* September 1978, op. cit., pp. 251–252.

[68] The Population Council, "Thailand", *Country Profiles,* op. cit., pp. 16–17.

[69] Select Committee on Population, *Report,* op. cit., p. 22; Population Reference Bureau, *World Population Growth and Response,* op.cit., p. 228.

[70] Select Committee on Population, *Report,* op. cit., p. 23.

[71] Ibid., p. 24.

promoters, consider the case of Iran. With the support of the control system—AID, International Planned Parenthood, the Pathfinder Fund, the Universities of North Carolina and Chicago, and the Ford Foundation—the Shah and his sister became enthusiastic proponents of family planning, urging other less-developed countries to follow their lead. Per capita public expenditures on birth control were among the highest in the developing world in Iran, and the government trained thousands of highly paid health corps workers to serve as physicians, nurses, and motivators. The ministries of health and education redesigned the school curriculum, rewrote the textbooks, and retrained thousands of teachers to emphasize "population education" and sex education.[72]

The "Isfahan Model Family Planning Project" attracted worldwide attention for its mobilization of "educational and recruiting activities . . . mass media, mobile units, and doctors".[73] All methods of reducing births were legalized, including abortion and sterilization.

Upon seizing power, the new government threw out the family planning apparatus, threw out the law allowing abortion and sterilization, and, in short order, threw out the United States.[74] (Interestingly, the Iranian birth rate, one of the highest in the world, showed little decline during the family planning years.[75])

Nor is Iran an isolated case. Antagonism toward the U.S. concept of population control has surfaced in numerous countries.[76] Ambassador Richard Benedick, a staunch supporter of foreign population control, has reported frankly to Congress on the "sensitivity" of the programs,[77] the "lack of . . . commitment"[78] and "opposition"[79] to them by foreign peoples. The Agency for International Development has admitted that the "sensitivity of population programs" is so great in foreign countries that "it has been more acceptable to many countries to receive support through multilateral agencies such as the UNFPA [United Nations Fund for Population Activities] or the large private and voluntary organizations" that are supported by AID rather than from AID directly, and most programs are

[72] The Population Council, "Iran", *Country Profiles,* October 1972.

[73] The Population Council, *Studies in Family Planning,* vol. 7, no. 11, November 1976, pp. 308–321.

[74] Population Reference Bureau, *Intercom,* vol. 7, no. 3, March 1979, p. 13.

[75] The Population Council, *Studies in Family Planning,* vol. 9, no. 4, April 1978, p. 77.

[76] See, for example, John C. Caldwell, "The Containment of World Population Growth", *Studies in Family Planning,* vol. 6, no. 12, December 1975, pp. 429–436; also see Paul Singer, text of address, World Population Conference, Bucharest, 1974, reported in *Studies in Family Planning,* vol. 5, no. 12, December 1974, pp. 368–369; see also the National Reports of P.L.A.N.—Protect Life in All Nations, Inc., available from the American Life Lobby, Washington, D.C.

[77] Prepared Statement of Ambassador Richard Elliot Benedick before the Subcommittee on International Economic Policy and Trade, Committee on Foreign Affairs, U.S. House of Representatives, February 29, 1980.

[78] Ibid.

[79] Ibid.

financed and conducted in this manner.[80] (One of the first acts of the Sandinista government in Nicaragua was to close the AID-financed birth control clinics.[81]) An AID memorandum of 1982 strongly implied that all support for foreign population control programs would collapse if the United States stopped financing them and making them a condition for receiving American foreign aid.[82]

The inescapable conclusion is that AID's population control programs create antagonism where the United States needs friendship, and increase the costs of achieving the nation's legitimate foreign policy objectives. Needless to say, as long as the United States is willing to supply hundreds of millions of dollars for foreign population control there will be no lack of eager applicants to furnish AID with the "requests for population assistance" that AID then uses to justify its budgets.

As the seventies turned into the eighties there were increasing reports of "incentives" as well as outright coercion being used in foreign population control programs. There was, of course, the one-child-family program of forced abortion, sterilization, and infanticide in the People's Republic of China. The Agency for International Development disclaimed direct involvement in the program, although it was a major contributor to the International Planned Parenthood Federation and the UN Fund for Population Activities, both of which supplied funds to the Chinese program.[83] China and the United States also exchanged researchers to study population policy.[84]

China was indeed a rich field for study. Christopher Wren reported in the *New York Times* that thousands of Chinese women were being "rounded up and forced to have abortions". He described women "locked in detention cells or hauled before mass rallies and harangued into consenting to abortions". He told of "vigilantes [who] abducted pregnant women on the streets and hauled them off, sometimes handcuffed or trussed, to abortion clinics", and of "aborted babies which were . . . crying when they were born".[85] Michele Vink wrote in the *Wall Street Journal* of women who were "handcuffed, tied with ropes or placed in pig's baskets" for their forced trips to the abortion clinics.[86] According to Steven Mosher, the People's Republic Press was openly speaking of the "butchering,

---

[80] AID Briefing Paper on Population for the Administrator's Retreat, June 20, 1981, pp. 3–4.

[81] Population Reference Bureau, *Intercom,* March 1980, p. 5.

[82] Agency for International Development, "Rationale for AID Support of Population Programs", January 1982.

[83] International Planned Parenthood Federation, *Report to Donors,* 1980, p. 40; UN Fund for Population Activities, *Reports* for 1980, 1981, 1982, 1983.

[84] Population Reference Bureau, *Intercom,* July 1980, p. 4.

[85] Christopher Wren, "Chinese Region Showing Resistance to National Goals for Birth Control", *New York Times,* May 16, 1982.

[86] Michele Vink, "Abortion and Birth Control in Canton, China", *Wall Street Journal,* November 30, 1981.

drowning, and leaving to die of female infants and the maltreating of women who have given birth to girls".[87]

There were disturbing reports from some countries where the U.S. foreign aid bureaucracy was directly involved. An AID-financed sterilization drive in El Salvador was reported as using a quota system to achieve more than 20,000 sterilizations a year without adequate provisions for voluntary consent.[88] In Bangladesh the AID-financed program reportedly set annual sterilization targets, offering money payments to persons recruiting patients for the operation, to the patients themselves, and to those who performed the surgery. Many of the patients were said not to understand the nature of the operation.[89] Also in Bangladesh, an AID project linked birth control with oral rehydration treatment for children with diarrhea.[90] Since the treatment often means the difference between life and death for young children, it serves as a powerful incentive for their mothers to accept the proffered birth control.

The Catholic bishops of the Philippines protested that the one-child-family sterilization drive in that country relied on "pressure" to achieve its goals.[91] The new Aquino constitution, overwhelmingly approved by the electorate in 1987, deleted the clause in the former constitution that mandated government (AID supported) family planning.[92]

A citizens' group in Mexico charged that the International Monetary Fund had required the promise of a drastic reduction in births in return for loans to the Mexican government and that, as a consequence, the Mexican government was promoting a "massive" birth control campaign with "immovable determination".[93]

The head of a Washington auditing firm presented evidence in 1984 that AID was contributing, through the International Planned Parenthood Federation, to programs in India and Korea that were imposing penalties for exceeding birth quotas, and to programs in Sri Lanka, Bangladesh, Nepal, and Korea that were

[87] Steven W. Mosher, "Why Are Baby Girls Being Killed in China?" *Wall Street Journal,* July 25, 1983; also see Steven W. Mosher, *Broken Earth: The Rural Chinese* (New York: The Free Press, 1983).

[88] Chris Hedges, "U.S. Is Key Player in Controversial Birth Control Plan", *Christian Science Monitor,* January 13, 1984, p. 8.

[89] Betsy Hartmann and Jane Hughes, "And the Poor Get Sterilized", *The Nation,* June 30, 1984, pp. 798–800.

[90] James F. Phillips, et al., "Integrating Health Service Components into a Comprehensive Family Planning and Basic MCH Programme: Lessons from the MATLAB Family Planning Health Services Project", paper presented at the National Council for International Health Conference on International Health and Family Planning: Controversy and Consensus, Washington, D.C., June 10 through 13, 1984, reported in Robert G. Marshall, "AID's Carrot Is a Big Stick", reprint by American Life Lobby, Stafford, Virginia, 1984.

[91] The Episcopal Commission on Family Life, "The Philippine Population Control Program", July 20, 1984.

[92] On the Philippines program, see The Population Reference Bureau, *World Population Growth and Response,* op. cit., pp. 96–98.

[93] Statement of Comite Nacional Pro-Vida, A. C., September 15, 1983.

paying people to be sterilized. He also presented evidence that AID was flouting the law by financing abortion.[94]

Simultaneously, the U.S.-funded population control establishment was more openly supporting overt government action to reduce fertility, discarding its earlier pose of helping people achieve their own desired family size. The World Bank's *Development Report 1984* featured a lengthy discussion of "incentives and disincentives", noting that such measures were "indispensable" in those cases where "a private-social gap still exists"—i.e., the people want more children than their government thinks they should have.[95] The bank, which receives a major part of its funds from the United States, reported that programs using incentives and disincentives existed in more than thirty countries in 1984.[96] It insisted that "voluntary" incentives "need be no more objectionable than any other taxes or subsidies",[97] and it described the Chinese program in detail.[98] Other members of the population control establishment commended the Chinese program for its "exceptionally high implementation rate",[99] its "high commitment",[100] and its excellent design.[101]

To make matters even clearer, the bank enumerated the successive "policy steps" by which countries move from the collection of census data and the provision of family planning through voluntary private agencies, to government commitment and programs, which in turn progress from services to "outreach", to incentives and disincentives, and finally to birth quotas.[102] On this scale the bank assigned grades to various countries for their degree of commitment to population control, with China, Colombia, Mexico, Sri Lanka, the Republic of Korea, Indonesia, and Malaysia given a "very strong index" or a "strong index", and other countries ranked as "moderate" or "weak".[103] Apparently, at the time of writing, the report's authors had not yet received word that in 1984 the government of Malaysia decided to abandon its eighteen-year program of population control.[104]

Within the Reagan administration, 1984 heralded a softening on the population control front. In August the administration delivered a message to the International Conference on Population in Mexico City saying that, far from being the

[94] William M. O'Reilly, "U.S. Agency for International Development Funding of Abortion and Sterilization", draft, April 14, 1984.

[95] The World Bank, *World Development Report 1984,* p. 160.

[96] Ibid., p. 123.

[97] Ibid., p. 161.

[98] Ibid., pp. 124, 160.

[99] UN Fund for Population Activities, *1981 Report,* p. 52.

[100] Ibid.

[101] Population Reference Bureau, *Intercom,* March/April 1983, p. 7; Lester Brown, *Worldwatch Paper* #53; International Planned Parenthood Federation, *People,* vol. 10, no. 1, 1983, p. 24.

[102] World Bank, op. cit., pp. 155–162.

[103] Ibid., p. 156.

[104] *The Wall Street Journal,* April 10, 1984.

cause of all economic and social problems, population growth is "of itself a neutral phenomenon. It is not necessarily good or ill." The recent growth in world population, it maintained, had resulted from the spread of life-saving advances in health care and food production, which demonstrated "not poor planning . . . but human progress". It further maintained that there had been an "over-reaction by some" to population, but that the real cause of poverty was "governmental control of economies, a development which effectively constrained economic growth". It blamed the low levels of development on government price-fixing, confiscatory taxation, and the disruption of economic incentives by government planners, and said that for the past three years the administration had been trying to reverse the policy of "demographic over-reaction".[105]

Averring that "attempts to use abortion, involuntary sterilization, or other coercive measures in family planning must be shunned", it stated that the United States would "no longer contribute to separate nongovernmental organizations which perform or actively promote abortion as a method of family planning in other nations". The message was carried to the conference by the former senator from New York, James L. Buckley, known as a firm supporter of the declared views.[106]

The announcement provoked instant fury among advocates of population control. Congressman James Scheuer said, "We do not accept this radical departure from long-established, bipartisan policy."[107] Representative Patricia Schroeder decided that the administration had "gone off the cliff",[108] and former senators Robert Taft, Jr., and Joseph D. Tydings believed the statement "represents the adoption of a 'fundamentalist, know-nothing' political philosophy".[109] The *New York Times* called it "ignorant" and "dangerous",[110] while the *Christian Science Monitor* wrote that it "falls far short of a comprehensive overview of the challenge"[111] and dedicated a featured series of special articles on the "tidal wave of humanity"[112] with its resulting "overcrowding"[113] and problems of "people, people, people".[114]

There were howls of protest from the population agencies funded directly or indirectly by the U.S. government. Peters Willson of the Alan Guttmacher Institute, the U.S. government-funded "research" arm of Planned Parenthood, warned that

---

[105] *Policy Statement of the United States of America at the United Nations International Conference on Population (2nd Session)*, Mexico, D.F., August 6–13, 1984.

[106] *National Review,* August 10, 1984, pp. 15–16.

[107] "Delegates Slam Reagan's Abortion Funds Policy," *Rocky Mountain News,* August 12, 1984.

[108] "Schroeder Fighting Administration Rule on Family Planning", *Rocky Mountain News,* August 12, 1984.

[109] Robert Taft, Jr., and Joseph D. Tydings, Joint Statement, June 6, 1984.

[110] *The New York Times,* June 21, 1984.

[111] August 9, 1984, p. 17.

[112] *Christian Science Monitor,* August 6, 1984.

[113] *Christian Science Monitor,* August 8, 1984.

[114] *Christian Science Monitor,* August 7, 1984.

it "seeks to pre-empt Congress",[115] and Werner Fornos of the Population Institute called it "election year rhetoric on the backs of poor women around the world"[116] and gave a luncheon for the delegates from the People's Republic of China and sympathetic members of Congress.[117]

There were more howls of protest in 1986 and 1987 when the Reagan administration, responding to the Kemp/Kasten Amendment prohibiting U.S. government funding for coercive population control programs, redirected the $25 million annual UN Fund for Population Activities grant to other population agencies because of UNFPA's support of the Chinese program.

The United States has for two decades thrown its massive energies and resources to the task of "motivating" the rest of the world, especially the less-developed world, to limit births. The drive is expanding, using all of the "linkages" of the development process—education, urbanization, industrialization, the female labor force, and modern, life-saving health services—to induce reductions in fertility. Though it retains some semblance of an attempt to improve economic and social conditions, it increasingly takes on all the aspects of a movement promoted for its own sake.

For there is no evidence that this vigorous program has improved economic conditions in the world, or advanced the interests of the United States. Those who imagine that foreign population control serves the cause of American "imperialism" are quite mistaken. On the contrary, the programs, as noted, impose significant costs on the United States, not only of money but of goodwill in sensitive areas. Their existence, however, lends credibility, momentum, and financial power to the population control movement. And they serve as an essential part of the "suitable preparation" that the document said would have to pave the way for the "announcement" of the goal of "near stability" for population in the United States.[118] The foreign programs make it possible for congressmen introducing population-control legislation for the United States to make such statements as Richard Ottinger's in 1979. On introducing his bill to bring about zero population growth in the United States, Ottinger said, "We are not asking for anything which we do not already advocate to the less developed nations of the world."[119] Ottinger repeated these sentiments in 1984 when he again introduced his plan for zero population growth in this country.[120]

[115] *Congressional Record* — Senate, June 18, 1984.

[116] *Washington Times,* August 3, 1984.

[117] *Washington Times,* August 10, 1984.

[118] U.S. Government Document, NSSM 200, op. cit., p. 19.

[119] Hon. Richard L. Ottinger, *Congressional Record,* August 2, 1979.

[120] Hon. Richard L. Ottinger, on HR 2491, *Congressional Record,* August 10, 1984, No. 107.

CHAPTER FIVE

PROMOTING THE NEW PHILOSOPHY:
THE SEX EDUCATION MOVEMENT

As William Ball revealed in his classic 1968 study of population control,[1] the adoption of such a sweeping policy demands a method of promulgating what is no less than a new philosophy. People must be made to believe in the obligation to limit population in order to bow to the restrictions and the invasions of their privacy. To this end, as Ball points out, shortly after the U.S. government initiated its family planning program in 1965, the Department of Health, Education, and Welfare issued a report calling for sex education in the schools.[2] Although President Johnson expressly asked for a program that would only ensure that "all families have access to information and services that will allow freedom to choose the number and spacing of their children within the dictates of individual conscience",[3] the department made it clear that its sights went far beyond mere "access". Young people, through federally funded sex education, must perceive their "responsibilities" in the area of birth control.[4]

The revelation by the department, as Ball notes, had been preceded by congressional hearings[5] and numerous population assemblies held throughout the country to spread the message that the population crisis was of such catastrophic proportions that mere access to information would prove trivial. Speakers at the gatherings urged the need for motivation, and possibly coercion.[6] Since then the federally funded drive for sex education to overturn the old values has, with minor setbacks, plunged ahead.

In 1968, three years after the initiation of the federal family planning program, Mary Steichen Calderone, founder of the Sex Information and Education Council of the United States and former medical director of Planned Parenthood, wrote:

If man as he is, is obsolescent, then what kind do we want to produce in his place

[1] William B. Ball, *Population Control* (Export, Pennsylvania: U.S. Coalition for Life, reprinted from Donald A. Grannella, ed., *Religion and the Public Order,* no. 4, Cornell University Press, 1968).

[2] *HEW Indicators, Family Planning: One Aspect of Freedom to Choose,* June 1966.

[3] Quoted in Population Reference Bureau, *World Population Growth and Response: 1965–1975 — A Decade of Global Action* (Washington: The Population Reference Bureau, April 1976), p. 184.

[4] *HEW Indicators, Family Planning,* op. cit.

[5] *Hearings* on S. 1676, before the Subcommittee on Foreign Expenditures of the Senate Committee on Government Operations, 89th Congress, 1st Session, pts. 1–5 (1965), 2nd Session, pts. 1–5A (1966) (Washington: U.S. Government Printing Office).

[6] Ball, op. cit.

and how do we design the production line? — that is the real question facing
... sex education.[7]

She went on to stipulate that this production process would be "consciously
engineered" by society's "best minds"[8] and would provide the "conditioning" of
attitudes and behavior as deemed desirable by, of course, the leaders of her
movement.[9]

But just what attitudes and behavior would be inculcated was left somewhat
vague in this article. It threw out some stock nebulous phrases: the new program
would "eliminate fears and anxieties", and "develop objective and understanding
attitudes toward sex" so that people could "utilize sexuality effectively".[10]

But Calderone was far more specific in the Preface to her *Manual of Family
Planning and Contraceptive Practice:*

> *family planning practice* and *contraceptive practice* as they are being developed can
> now only be applied with total effectiveness in the service of *population practice*
> ... the stark necessity emerges for a population policy explicitly developed and
> stated by our government and by every government on behalf of its own nation
> as soon as possible [emphasis in original].
> ... control of population growth in both developing and developed coun-
> tries is crucial to socioeconomic evolution and stability and therefore to world
> welfare and world peace.[11]

Calderone's doleful predictions appear again in *The Family Book about Sexuality,* in
which she and Eric Johnson insist that, "if human reproduction is not soon
drastically reduced, our earth will contain more people than its space and resources
can possibly support ... Human fertility must somehow be reduced. If it is not,
disaster is inevitable ... "[12] We have adequate birth control methods, the authors
say, "to keep the world's birth rate, the population of the world, and the number
of children in any family, community, or group within desired limits". But the
problem is "to get that knowledge to people who need to use these methods in
such a way that they will be motivated to use them consistently".[13]

Other prominent sex educators, similarly obsessed with overpopulation, embrace
the propaganda methods in the government sex programs. In their widely used
textbook, *Education for Human Sexuality,* Burt and Meeks tell their readers that

---

[7] Mary S. Calderone, "Sex Education and the Roles of School and Church", *The Annals of the
American Academy of Political and Social Science,* vol. 376, March 1968, p. 57.

[8] Ibid., p. 59.

[9] Ibid., p. 61.

[10] Ibid.

[11] Mary Steichen Calderone, ed., *Manual of Family Planning and Contraceptive Practice,* 2nd ed.
(Baltimore: The Williams & Wilkins Co., 1970), Preface, pp. vii–viii.

[12] Mary S. Calderone and Eric W. Johnson, *The Family Book About Sexuality* (New York:
Harper & Row, 1981), p. 106.

[13] Ibid., p. 83.

"the population explosion" is the "greatest problem in the world today" which, if not brought under control, will result in mass starvation by the year 2000.[14] And in its *Implementing DHEW Policy on Family Planning* the Department of Health, Education, and Welfare touts its sex education projects to reduce fertility, especially among minorities.[15]

Lester Kirkendall, one of the founders of the Sex Information and Education Council, wrote in the *Humanist* magazine in 1965 that "sex education is . . . clearly tied in a socially significant way to family planning and population limitation and policy," and spoke candidly of the special treatment needed for "lower class families" because of their "ineffective" contraceptive practices.[16]

Local curriculum guides for sex education are riddled with the horrors of overpopulation. A typical program for seventh and eighth graders does a thorough job of linking its population and family planning objectives:

Contraception and Population Stabilization

A. The student will develop a knowledge, awareness, and understanding of the need for mature and responsible decisions regarding population stabilization through the use of contraception.
  1. discuss the effects of overpopulation—short and long range.
    a. threat to life—jobs, crowded housing, lack of farmland.
    b. long range—famine and eventual death.
  2. consider future generations and need for wanted child—film and discussion.
  3. contraception—the purpose is to be able to decide the best time to have a child.
    a. explain and discuss the menstrual cycle and ovulation by using charts, stress the importance of pelvic exam, breast check, and pap smear.
    b. tell students resources where family planning is available.
    c. discuss birth control methods—pill, IUD, diaphragm, jelly, condom, foam, douching, withdrawal, rhythm by showing a film and showing a kit with the methods present.
    d. discuss the permanent methods of birth control—vasectomy and tubal ligation.[17]

For years, leading promoters of government population control programs, such as Planned Parenthood and the American Public Health Association, have under-

---

[14] John J. Burt and Linda Brower Meeks, *Education for Sexuality: Concepts and Programs for Teaching* (Philadelphia: W. B. Saunders Company, 1975), pp. 408–409.

[15] Dr. Oscar Harkavy, *Implementing DHEW Policy on Family Planning and Population* (Washington: Department of Health, Education, and Welfare, 1967), p. 16a, attachments B.

[16] Lester Kirkendall, "Sex Education: A Reappraisal", *Humanist,* vol. 25, Special Issue, Spring 1965, p. 78.

[17] Reproduced directly from *Arcata School District Family Life/Sex Education Curriculum Guide* (Arcata, California, June 1976).

stood that sex education is vital to their goals. In its five-year plan for 1976–1980, the Planned Parenthood Federation of America, Inc., called for a "zero rate of natural population increase"[18] hand-in-hand with the requisite sex education to "raise the level of awareness among all persons of family planning, human sexuality, population growth, and health in general".[19] The federation pressed its affiliates to "assert leadership in developing and promoting educational programs in human sexuality in clinics, in local schools, and other organizations".[20]

In its *Federation Declaration of Principles & Purposes: A Planning Document for 1979–1981,* Planned Parenthood called for

> Education and training [to] foster, through population education initiatives, the idea that there is an urgent need to slow population growth and conserve resources worldwide, and that these considerations should be a part of the process of personal choice regarding one's fertility.[21]

And for

> Advocacy and public information [to] raise the level of awareness, both at home and abroad, about the magnitude of the population problem, the role that the United States must play in meeting it, the relationship between population growth and the role of women, and the need for increased support for these programs.[22]

The same proclamation was sounded in the organization's planning document *'Til Victory Is Won: An Action Agenda for 1982–84.*

In 1977 Planned Parenthood and other like groups joined with Zero Population Growth to hammer out a detailed proposal for massive federal grants under the Public Health Services Act, the Social Security Act, and the Elementary and Secondary Education Act to finance "fertility control".[23] Subsequently financed by Congress, it provided for "school-based education programs" and "training of faculty"[24] and a spate of other educational ploys "to be undertaken . . . by health agencies, community groups and the media".[25]

Sex education is vital to the population control programs financed by the Agency for International Development. As, for instance, the model program

---

[18] *A Five Year Plan: 1976–1980 for the Planned Parenthood Federation of America, Inc.,* approved by the PPFA membership, October 22, 1975, Seattle, Washington, p. 3.

[19] Ibid., p. 9.

[20] Ibid.

[21] Planned Parenthood Federation of America, *Federation Declaration of Principles & Purposes: A Planning Document for 1979–1981,* p. 13.

[22] Ibid.

[23] *Planned Births, the Future of the Family and the Quality of American Life* (Planned Parenthood et al., June 1977), pp. 2–3.

[24] Ibid., Table 1, "Proposed 1979–1981 Program for Improving Fertility Regulation".

[25] Ibid., p. 26.

already mentioned, that was designed for Iran, and implemented by the Shah and the Ministries of Health and Education, that redesigned the school curriculum, rewrote the textbooks, and retrained thousands of teachers to emphasize population and sex education.[26]

The World Bank, the leading whip of government population control, understands the potential of education in instilling a "modern" outlook toward family planning,[27] as does the Population Reference Bureau in describing its effectiveness throughout the world.[28] By 1978 there were so many sex education programs for youth in developing countries that the Center for Population Options created a special "clearinghouse" in Washington, D.C., to keep track of them.[29] In 1983 this agency published a list of 102 such programs, of which only eleven were operated by the governments of the countries in which they were located,[30] suggesting, once again, the antagonism that the countries targeted by the population planners have against population control. The International Planned Parenthood Federation, the world's leading promoter of sex education, operated the largest number of programs.[31]

Quite unscrupulously, if understandably, sex education is seldom explicitly promoted to the general public as a measure for population control. More commonly, it is concealed behind lofty sounding phrases such as "total physical, mental, and social well-being",[32] or "a spiral of learning experience to establish sexuality as an entity within healthy interpersonal relationships",[33] or even as a way to create the ideal human beings of the future—"not . . . furtive, exploitive, leering, guilt-ridden, apathetic, compulsive, joyless . . . not like ourselves", but "eager, passionate, caring, unafraid, open, responsible, exultant".[34]

Since the mid-1970s in the United States, the blame on "sexual ignorance" for the supposedly high rates of adolescent pregnancy has made good copy for the sale

[26] The Population Council, "Iran", *Country Profiles,* October 1972, p. 12.

[27] *World Development Report, 1980* (Washington, D.C.: The World Bank, August 1980), p. 47.

[28] Population Reference Bureau, *World Population Growth and Response,* op. cit., pp. 201, 203–223.

[29] International Clearinghouse on Adolescent Fertility/Center for Population Options, "An Analysis of the Nature and Level of Adolescent Fertility Programming in Developing Countries", revised October 1983.

[30] Ibid.

[31] Ibid.

[32] Ferndale Elementary School District and Ferndale Union High School District, *Family Life/Sex Education Curriculum Guide: Kindergarten–Twelfth Grade* (Ferndale, California, July 1978); p. 2.

[33] Ferndale, op. cit., p. 2; the identical language is also found in the "Overall Objectives", *Arcata School District Family Life/Sex Education Curriculum Guide,* op. cit.

[34] Mary S. Calderone, "The Challenge Ahead: In Search of Healthy Sexuality", in Herbert A. Otto, ed., *The New Sex Education: The Sex Educator's Resource Book* (Chicago: Follett Publishing Company, 1978), p. 358.

of the new sex programs.[35] The promotional pitch was thought to have such
wide public appeal that the Alan Guttmacher Institute, the "research" arm of
Planned Parenthood, published two widely disseminated booklets on the so-called
teenage pregnancy "epidemic" and launched a media blitz based on the slogan:
"1 million teenagers are getting pregnant".[36] The scheme backfired, however,
when statistical studies showed not only that virtually all teenagers coming for
pregnancy counseling were already familiar with contraception, but that adolescent
pregnancy actually increased when the new sex programs were introduced, and
mostly in the areas receiving the most lavish expenditures.[37]

But the failure of the avowed purposes notwithstanding, the carefully designed
programs continue relentlessly toward the real demographic goal. By an unremitting insistence on "values clarification" they strive to inculcate "affective learning"
(as opposed to "cognitive learning"),[38] a method that is essential to their success.
The desirability of small families, for both individual and social reasons, is constantly
stressed. A typical curriculum guide asks children to discuss "the problems that
would be eliminated if I were the only child",[39] and to analyze "hostilities"
between brothers and sisters, and family "conflicts".[40] The guide asks children to
decide whether they are "parent material"[41] and offers a list of "reasons for
having children", among them: "to prove your feminity or masculinity (I can do
it!)"; "to make up for your own unhappy childhood"; "to get back at your

---

[35] International Clearinghouse on Adolescent Fertility, op. cit.; California State Department of
Education, *Education for Human Sexuality: A Resource Book and Instructional Guide to Sex Education
for Kindergarten Through Grade Twelve* (Sacramento, 1979), p. 1. The Department of Education
distributed this manual to several thousand local classroom teachers in training sessions held
throughout the state in 1979–80. A major public outcry resulted, and outraged citizens filed
multiple lawsuits against the department over the use of the manual. Sex education became an issue
in the 1982 election of the State Superintendent of Public Instruction. The incumbent, Wilson
Riles, was defeated and replaced by Bill Honig, who pledged to establish higher standards for
public education.

[36] Alan Guttmacher Institute, *11 Million Teenagers: What Can Be Done about the Epidemic of
Adolescent Pregnancies in the United States* (New York: Planned Parenthood Federation of America,
Inc., 1976); *Teenage Pregnancy: The Problem That Hasn't Gone Away* (New York: The Alan
Guttmacher Institute, 1981).

[37] See Hearings of United States Senate Committee on Labor and Human Resources, March
31, 1981, testimony of Susan Roylance, James H. Ford, and Jacqueline Kasun.

[38] California State Department of Education, op. cit., pp. 2–7. That education should be
regarded primarily as a conditioning process, rather than an effort to instill knowledge and
discernment, has been made perfectly clear by Planned Parenthood: "Public education may be
defined as the dissemination of specific information designed for target audiences with the
objective of modifying attitudes, behavior change and or skills".—*A Five Year Plan*, op. cit., p. 9.

[39] Ferndale Elementary School District, op. cit., p. 69.

[40] Ibid., pp. 68–69.

[41] Ibid., p. 290.

parents"[42]; and other motives, all suggesting that persons who want children must, at the least, be socially inadequate, and, more probably, psychologically deranged. The language is not unique; it appears in a number of local guides. Though ostensibly prepared locally and financed under separate state and federal grants, the local curriculum guides duplicate large parts of each other's contents, with entire sections photocopied from a common source.

The programs concentrate on how difficult it is to raise children and how unattractive they really are. "Babies are *not* sweet little things. They wet and dirty themselves, they get sick, they're very expensive to take care of", advises one Planned Parenthood pamphlet.[43] And in the same vein, other guides warn that "it is estimated that it takes $70,000 to $100,000 (not including mother's loss of income) to raise a child these days", and that "babies need attention and care 24 hours a day" and often spoil marriages by making their fathers "jealous" and their mothers "depleted".[44]

The "values clarification strategies" used so extensively in modern sex classes carry out the themes. The following exercise appears in Sidney Simon's widely used *Meeting Yourself Halfway: 31 Values Clarification Strategies for Daily Living:*

> The population problem is very serious and involves every country on this planet. What steps would you encourage to help resolve the problem?
> . . . volunteer to organize birth-control information centers throughout the country
> . . . joint a pro-abortion lobbying group
> . . . encourage the limitation of two children per family and have the parents sterilized to prevent future births[45]

The programs provide for classroom visits, lectures, and distribution of literature by antinatalist groups—Planned Parenthood,[46] Zero Population Growth,[47] and the National Alliance for Optional Parenthood,[48] formerly known as the National Organization of Non-Parents. The sex programs instruct children in all methods of blocking fertility—contraception, sterilization, and abortion. They make children learn the telephone numbers of birth control and abortion clinics

[42] Ibid., p. 321; this page is apparently a photocopy of an identical page in Planned Parenthood–Santa Cruz County, *Sex Education: Teacher's Guide and Resource Manual* (Santa Cruz, 1979), p. 148.

[43] Rocky Mountain Planned Parenthood, *The Perils of Puberty* (Denver, 1974), p. 15, recommended in California State Department of Education, op. cit., p. 97.

[44] Ferndale Elementary School District, op. cit., pp. 321–322; also in Planned Parenthood–Santa Cruz County, op. cit., p. 149.

[45] Sidney B. Simon, *Meeting Yourself Halfway: Thirty-one Values Clarification Strategies for Daily Living* (Niles, Illinois: Argus Communications, 1974), p. 47, recommended in California State Department of Education, op. cit., p. 47, 82, 141.

[46] California State Department of Education, op. cit., p. 133.

[47] Ibid., p. 63.

[48] Ibid., p. 61.

and the bus routes to them.[49] They teach children that all services to arrest fertility are freely available on a "confidential" basis—i.e., no one will tell their parents[50]—and enlighten them on how to become legally "emancipated" from their parents.[51] Children are required to choose among the various options in the event of an unplanned pregnancy,[52] to decide whether it is better to have an abortion or to give birth to an unwanted child.[53] They take care of one of these options by teaching Sol Gordon's commandment: "no one has the right to bring an unwanted child into the world".[54]

Children age twelve take field trips to drug stores, where they check out the availability of contraceptive products,[55] and go through a birth control clinic "from beginning to end", filling out a patient's form.[56] On these trips they may be invited to participate in a group examination of each other's genital organs in order to demonstrate the insertion of a diaphragm.[57]

The school programs also expound on other aspects of the population control agenda. They discuss, in considerable depth, genetic screening and the selective abortion of babies suspected of having Down's syndrome or the like.[58] Though euthanasia is not as yet directly espoused, the California program draws the students' attention to the "aging process" by presenting this tableau for discussion: "Sometimes Grandfather is fine; at other times he takes off his clothes, defecates on the floor—what are you going to do with Grandfather . . . ?"[59]

The sex educators insinuate themselves into the lives of children at early ages, no later than kindergarten and, if possible, at the age of three, either through day nurseries or their own parents (properly trained, of course, in modern "parenting" classes). The goal of these early efforts is to accustom children to "open" and explicit discussions of sex and to bend their attitudes regarding family life, sex— for pleasure rather than for procreation—and their gender identity.[60]

Starting with a "bathroom tour" for a mixed group in kindergarten or nursery school, the process of desensitization begins by naming and explaining the male

[49] Ibid., pp. 125, 135.

[50] Ibid.

[51] Ibid.

[52] Ibid., p. 143.

[53] Kathy McCoy and Charles Wibbelsman, *The Teenage Body Book* (New York: Simon & Schuster, 1978), pp. 190–196, recommended in California State Department of Education, op. cit., p. 77.

[54] Sol Gordon, *You* (New York: Times Books, 1978), p. 79, quoted in California State Department of Education, op. cit., p. 80.

[55] California State Department of Education, op. cit., p. 123.

[56] Ibid., p. 135.

[57] Ruth Bell et al., *Changing Bodies, Changing Lives* (New York: Random House, 1980), p. 175. This is an account of such a field trip to the Feminist Women's Health Center in Los Angeles.

[58] McCoy and Wibbelsman, op. cit., p. 197.

[59] California State Department of Education, op. cit., p. 115.

[60] Calderone and Johnson, op. cit., chap. 1.

and female genital parts and sexual intercourse.[61] The process continues through childhood and adolescence. By the time children are in the seventh grade, they will have mastered ovulation, intercourse, fertilization, anatomy (including ovaries, Fallopian tubes, uterus, vagina, hymen, labia, clitoris, scrotum, penis, testes, prostate, Cowper's glands), erection, ejaculation, orgasm, genetics, embryonic development, the stages of birth, breastfeeding, bottlefeeding, and birth control.[62]

In case the sheer intensity of the program seems startling, remember that sex educators regard the sexual self as the total self. As the "SIECUS/New York University Principles Basic to Education for Sexuality" puts it, "The SIECUS concept of sexuality refers to the totality of being a person . . . as a function of the total personality it is concerned with the biological, psychological, sociological, spiritual, and cultural variables of life which, by their effects on personality development and interpersonal relations can in turn affect social structure."[63]

A typical local curriculum guide says it more simply: "Human Sexuality is everything a person sees as HIMSELF."[64] If the human being is the proper domain of the sex educators, as they insist, the rest follows as the night the day.

In high school the instruction becomes even more personally engrossing. Students work as boy-girl pairs on "physiology definition sheets" in which they define "foreplay", "erection", "ejaculation", and similar privacies.[65] They discuss whether they are satisfied with their "size of sex organs",[66] and take part in mixed-group "body-drawing" in which they draw and label the penis, testicles, scrotum, vagina, clitoris, vulva, labia, and so forth.[67] They fill out questionnaires on the frequency with which they engage in heavy petting, masturbation, and sexual intercourse.[68] They "role play" the parts of young people who have been having intercourse with each other "for a long time".[69]

What is the reason for the unremitting invasion of students' personal privacy? Sometimes they speak of building "trust and sharing", as in the case of the body drawing exercise.[70] Or, among other exalted purposes, they cite the intent to

[61] California State Department of Education, op. cit., pp. 93, 94, 99.

[62] *Arcata School District Family Life/Sex Education,* op. cit.; Burt and Meeks, op. cit., pp. 337–403.

[63] "The Siecus/New York University Principles Basic to Education for Sexuality", reprinted in *The Journal of School Health,* vol. 51, no. 4, April 1981, p. 315.

[64] Ferndale Elementary School District, op. cit., p. 44.

[65] Ibid., pp. 286, 303.

[66] Ibid., p. 293; this classroom exercise also appears in Planned Parenthood–Santa Cruz County, op. cit., p. 135.

[67] Ferndale Elementary School District, op. cit., pp. 285–286; Joan Helmich and Jan Loreen, *Sexuality Education and Training: Theory, Techniques, and Resources,* 2nd ed. (Planned Parenthood of Seattle/King County), p. 102; Planned Parenthood: Santa Cruz County, op. cit., p. 206.

[68] Douglas Kirby, Judith Alter, and Peter Scales, *An Analysis of Sex Education Programs and Evaluation Methods: Questionnaire Kit,* HEW Contract #200-78-0804, July 1979.

[69] Planned Parenthood–Santa Cruz County, op. cit., p. 256.

[70] Ferndale Elementary School District, op. cit., p. 286.

"eliminate fears and anxieties"[71] and to "enlighten a dark antisex dogma based on factual errors and conditions of life that no longer exist".[72] Whatever the aims, one result is certain: if the programs work, they must break down all personal reserve on sexual matters. The authorities no longer have to worry about a populace that regards sexual activities as private. They no longer lack information touching citizens' sexual behavior; and they are no longer barred from citizens' personal counsels. As one article put it, the sex educators want nothing less than to become "the best friends in the adult world that many of these students have ever had".[73] The obvious convenience for purposes of population planning is heady incitement for power-seekers.

In some cases, in response to strong parental pressure, the promoters of classroom sex education have modified their programs, going so far as to include sexual abstinence as a method of preventing pregnancy.[74] But the thrust remains: "overpopulation" is engulfing the planet and "responsible" young people can respond to this threat by becoming more "open" about their sexuality and by obtaining free and confidential birth control services, which are demonstrated in class, from their nearby Planned Parenthood clinic, whose address they learn in class.[75]

Views on family life are a second major preoccupation of sex educators. Like Mark Twain's death, the demise of the traditional family is greatly exaggerated. Calderone and Johnson, for example, present a table showing that the so-called nuclear family has virtually disappeared. They document it by the simple expedient of categorizing married couples whose children have left home, and families with resident grandparents and other relatives as "non-nuclear", more similar to "experimental arrangements" than to traditional forms.[76] Other programs, with similar punctiliousness, teach that the traditional family is disappearing.[77] The key to the methodology is easy: ignore facts that fail to support your theses and create others that do. The fact, for example, that two-thirds of all American children live with both natural parents is never mentioned.[78] Nor is the fact that, although divorce is increasing, the proportion of broken families may be little higher today than in earlier times when widowhood, informal separation, and

---

[71] Calderone, "Sex Education and . . . " op. cit., p. 60.

[72] Calderone and Johnson, op. cit., p. 172.

[73] Edward A. Brann et al., "Strategies for the Prevention of Pregnancy in Adolescents", reprinted by the U.S. Department of Health, Education, and Welfare, Public Health Service, from *Advances in Planned Parenthood*, vol. XIV, no. 2, 1979, p. 75.

[74] Arcata *Union*, October 25, 1984; Six Rivers Planned Parenthood, *Family Life/Sex Education: Curriculum Guide*, revised October 1984.

[75] Six Rivers Planned Parenthood, op. cit.

[76] Calderone and Johnson, op. cit., p. 133.

[77] California State Department of Education, op. cit., pp. 23–32.

[78] Based on U.S. Bureau of the Census data appearing in Paul C. Glick, "Children of Divorced Parents in Demographic Perspective", *Journal of Social Issues*, vol. 35, no. 4, 1979, p. 171.

desertion were more common. Having established that the traditional family is a relic of history, the educators lead children to discuss their own choices among various lifestyles — "intentional communities, the extended family, communes, group marriage, couples living together w/o marriage, single parenthood ... "[79]

Not only do the sex programs encourage students to opt for lifestyles opposed to the traditional monogamous marriage with children, but they discredit the students' own parents' wisdom and authority. Claiming to "improve communication" between parents and children,[80] they encourage children to report their family problems, even asking children as young as age six if their parents molest them or are alcoholic.[81] Young children and adolescents must divulge their grievances and feelings toward their families to their sex classes.[82]

The determined assault on the family serves the double purpose of lessening its attractiveness and discrediting its moral authority. The problem with families, really, is that they produce and nurture children. As Kingsley Davis puts it, "the parent-child bond is peculiarly close" and "in having children an individual is not only creating new human beings but is also creating new and durable bonds for himself."[83]

The most effective way to limit the inconvenient desire of families for what Davis regards as an excessive number of children is to "lessen ... the identity of children with parents, or lessen ... the likelihood that this identity will be satisfying". And he taps one of the best ways to accomplish this — "the school system, one of the main functions of which appears to be to alienate offspring from their parents".[84] He also suggests that childbearing would be discouraged "if males were relieved of responsibility for children and denied identification with them; for, without the daily assistance of a man, few women seem likely to bear and rear two or more children".[85]

Other impediments to births, according to Davis, are "very high divorce rates, homosexuality, pornography, and free sexual unions ... "[86] Davis sees additional hope in "the child welfare services, which have increasingly tended to displace the father as a necessary member of the family, and the health services which have increasingly flouted parental authority with respect to contraception and abortion". And he notes that these public services have the peculiarity of lessening the cost of children to their parents at the same time as they "interpose other authorities

[79] California State Department of Education, op. cit., pp. 27–28.

[80] Ibid., *Teacher Resource Kit,* Goal 4, Concept 4 (no page number).

[81] Ibid., pp. 138–139.

[82] Ibid., *Teacher Resource Kit,* Goal 6, Concept 6, pp. 20, 22, 26, 146.

[83] Kingsley Davis, "Population Policy and the Theory of Reproductive Motivation", *Economic Development and Cultural Change,* vol. 25, Supplement, 1977, p. 176.

[84] Ibid., p. 174.

[85] Ibid., p. 178.

[86] Ibid.

between the parent and the child and thus dilute the parent-child identity".[87]

Clearly, to weaken or destroy the traditional family, which not only produces children but rivals the modern behemoth state as a source of support and authority for individuals, is to strengthen government population control. Calderone and Johnson can hopefully announce that because of the decline of the family, "we may be evolving into an age in which the individual will more and more replace the family as the basic unit of society".[88]

The thought invigorates the new sex educators in their unremitting efforts to stress the individual rather than the interpersonal nature of sexual activity. Burt and Meeks, for example, describe coitus briefly but dwell for pages on the "four phases of sexual response" of the separate individuals. They liken sexual response to a person "jumping off a diving board" and suggest that junior high school teachers discuss in depth "the person's" (singular)—not "the persons'" (plural) —feelings about sexual excitement and orgasm.[89]

In keeping with the focus on the isolated individual, masturbation is the most highly recommended form of sexual expression. Most obviously, of course, as the sex educators readily admit, pregnancy is impossible.[90] But masturbation has other benefits as well. "Sex is too important to glop up with sentiment", a Planned Parenthood pamphlet for teenagers advises. "If you feel sexy, for heaven's sake admit it to yourself. If the feeling and tension bother you, you can masturbate. Masturbation cannot hurt you and it will make you feel more relaxed."[91] The prominent sex educator Peter Scales agrees: "If we were a little more positive about masturbation, we would be helping a lot of people relieve sexual tension and get them away from going into sexual experiences that they really don't want to have and are not ready to handle."[92] Not to be outdone, Calderone and Johnson teach that "masturbation for release of tension and to experience pleasure occurs throughout the lives of most people with only positive effects—unless they are made to feel anxious or guilty about it".[93] They recommend it for babies,[94] children, young people, and adults "well into old age"; and "sometimes in painful situations such as illness of the partner or separation by . . . travel, death, or divorce, but usually as a part of ordinary life".[95]

[87] Ibid., p. 174.

[88] Calderone and Johnson, op. cit., p. 161.

[89] Burt and Meeks, op. cit., pp. 352–356.

[90] Eric W. Johnson, *Love and Sex in Plain Language,* 3rd ed. (New York: Bantam Books, 1979), p. 66, recommended in California State Department of Education, op. cit., p. 79.

[91] Rocky Mountain Planned Parenthood, op.cit.

[92] Peter Scales, Speech, "Adolescent Sexuality Is More Than Sex", sponsored by The Greater Pittsburgh Sexuality Council in cooperation with the Family Planning Council of Western Pennsylvania, Inc., December 7 and 8, 1979.

[93] Calderone and Johnson, op. cit., p. 21.

[94] Ibid.

[95] Ibid., p. 26.

And, most emphatically, it is of great importance "in developing a strong sense of the self".[96]

Since sex educators believe that little girls are less likely than little boys to discover their "organs of pleasure" spontaneously, they give special attention to little girls in locating the clitoris, and castigate parents who withhold this essential information from their daughters.[97]

The stress on the self is carried out in the prevalent "values clarification" exercises. "Who Are All Those Others? And What Are They Doing in My Life?" queries Sidney Simon in his *Meeting Yourself Halfway: Thirty-One Values Clarification Strategies for Daily Living*. A diagram portrays "Me" at the center of the page, surrounded by "parent-guardian", "peer leader", "important teacher", and others (but no brothers or sisters).[98] The importance of "healthy self-concepts", "self-esteem", and "self-acceptance" rules supreme.[99]

The self as the locus of "decision-making skills" receives concentrated attention. Children are taught that they must choose not only their own behavior but their own values, under the direction, of course, of their sex teachers. They encourage them at early ages to criticize their parents' standards as well as those taught by organized religion.[100]

The educators hammer away at standards of truth and goodness, insisting they are not constant and enduring but must be revised by those who are "up-to-date on important facts science has discovered".[101] Calderone quotes Mesthene as saying, "Change is the new reality ... the unchanging ... is unreal, constraining, a false goal." Children must "become familiar with change, feel comfortable with it, understand it, master it, and control it".[102] Human standards—the human material itself—must be altered to accord with the changes in technology created by science, and it is the high duty and privilege of the scientifically trained sex educators, as representatives of society's "best minds", to provide children and their parents with whatever up-to-date information they need to adjust their standards and values.[103]

A smooth transition in logic leads to the ordination of the sex educators as the new high priests of the new orthodoxy. No appeal to a higher law is possible for

[96] Ibid.

[97] Workshop in "Teenage Sexuality", given by Humboldt County Health Department to teachers of Arcata High School, California, March–April 1978.

[98] Simon, op. cit., p. 87.

[99] See California State Department of Education, op. cit., pp. 38–50; also Sylvia S. Hacker, "It Isn't Sex Education Unless ... ", *The Journal of School Health*, vol. 51, no. 4, April 1981, p. 208.

[100] California State Department of Education, op. cit., pp. 19, 33, 39, 45, 141–142; Sidney B. Simon et al., *Values Clarification: A Handbook of Practical Strategies for Teachers and Students* (New York: Hart Publishing, 1972), pp. 43, 51; Johnson, op. cit., pp. 65–66.

[101] Calderone and Johnson, op. cit., p. 1.

[102] Calderone, "Sex Education and ... ," op. cit., p. 57.

[103] Ibid., pp. 57–59.

the masses; for there is no higher law than the most up-to-date facts announced by science. If today's announced facts differ from yesterday's, so much the worse for yesterday. Change is the only reality. Truth is what Calderone and Johnson say it is: "Where religious laws or rules about sex were made on the basis of ignorance of facts now known, laws and rules need to be reexamined and recast to be consonant with these facts."[104]

And no one but those empowered to determine the latest facts will control this constant flux of change, regardless of Mesthene's optimistic statement. Neither children nor their parents will have control; their duty is to comply with a canon over which they have no say whatsoever.

The valuing process, with its elements of "freely choosing", is in consequence not only allowed, but insisted upon by the new elite.[105] The participants, armed with the appropriate "facts" and a list of selected choices by their leaders, can be trusted to arrive at the "clear wisdom of the group"[106] as predesigned by the authorities. And to make doubly sure there are no slip-ups, the values-clarifying procedure makes its participants "publicly affirm" their beliefs and opinions, without secret ballot,[107] in full view of their peers and leaders.

The denigration of traditional religion is of paramount importance in the plans of the new sex education/population control establishment. All rival loyalties and authorities must be destroyed if the individual is to be liberated for his new role vis-à-vis the state and its ruling elites. One avenue of attack is to charge religion with fostering sexual "dysfunction".[108] The instructional materials ridicule Christian practices and ethics, portraying Christians as stupid, ignorant, bigoted, and, of all things, of wearing funny shoes.[109] Some far-sighted people, they are happy to report, no longer blindly follow the antediluvian teachings of the Catholic church, but instead "decide to follow their own consciences without asking the Church what to do".[110] Children exposed to the values-clarification exercises are asked if they would really want to "go to heaven if it meant playing a harp all day",[111] and, "how many of you would be upset if organized religion disappeared?"[112] They implant doubts by suggesting that religious ethics are riddled with insincerity:

---

[104] Calderone and Johnson, op.cit., p. 171.

[105] Simon et al., op. cit.

[106] Calderone and Johnson, op. cit., p. 213.

[107] Simon et al., op. cit., pp. 18–20.

[108] William H. Masters and Virginia E. Johnson, "The Role of Religion in Sexual Dysfunction", in Mary S. Calderone, ed., *Sexuality and Human Values: The Personal Dimension of Sexual Experience* (New York: Association Press, a SIECUS Book, 1974), pp. 86–96.

[109] Judy Blume, *Are You There God? It's Me, Margaret* (New York: Dell, 1970), pp. 128–134, recommended in California State Department of Education, op. cit., p. 77.

[110] Johnson, op. cit., p. 83.

[111] Simon et al., op. cit., p. 43.

[112] Ibid., p. 51.

"A man cheats on his income tax each year, but donates all the money . . . to his church."[113]

But they make exceptions. Those clerics and other churchmen who swim in apologies for the past repressive influence of the churches and join sex educators in their demands for "reform" are eagerly embraced and publicized by the movement.[114] Their deathless sayings are reverently quoted, they become advisors and consultants to the entire network promoting sex education.[115]

Preoccupation with "sex roles" is the final most significant feature of the programs. To undermine or destroy the traditional family and replace it with a "sense of self"—a ploy to reduce birth rates and increase the influence of the state—boys and girls have to learn to reject their roles as future fathers and mothers. To this end, the programs urge young children to question their gender and to balk at the "pressures" and "expectations" placed upon them to fulfill their "sex roles".[116] They tell stories and show films about people who find supreme happiness in reversing their sex roles and extol famous people in history who have been homosexuals.[117]

The instruction stresses the normality of homosexuality and the abnormality of those who disapprove of it, dubbing them as having "homophobia".[118] The sex educators teach children the techniques of homosexual intercourse and how to "come out" if they suspect that they are homosexual.[119] They emphasize that even in heterosexual marriage, roles are changing[120]—women choose careers, and men become homemakers—and some people delay, or entirely forego, childbearing.[121]

With true zeal the new teaching proceeds with its messianic task of remaking the human material. By a steady, relentless process of interrogating, informing, and repeating, using all the techniques of group pressure known to modern psychology, the modern sex educators pursue their goal. Obviously, the few

[113] Ibid., p. 101.

[114] Calderone, "Sex Education and . . . ", op. cit., pp. 54–60; William H. Genné, "The Churches and Sexuality", SIECUS Newsletter, vol. 2, no. 3, Fall 1966.

[115] McCoy and Wibbelsman, op. cit., p. 152.

[116] California State Department of Education, op. cit., pp. 73, 75.

[117] J. Katz, Gay American History—Lesbians and Gay Men in the U.S.A. (New York: Avon Books, 1976), recommended in Sol Gordon, Sex Education and the Library: A Basic Bibliography for the General Public with Special Resources for the Librarian, ERIC Clearinghouse on Information Resources, Syracuse University, December 1979, prepared under NIE–HEW Contract #NIE-400-77-0015; see also California State Department of Education, Teacher Resource Kit, op. cit., Goal 3, Concept 3.

[118] Calderone and Johnson, op.cit., pp. 113–119; Johnson, op. cit., pp. 63–64; The Boston Women's Health Book Collective, Our Bodies, Ourselves: A Book By and For Women, 2nd ed. (New York: Simon & Schuster, 1976), recommended by California State Department of Education, op. cit., p. 104.

[119] The Boston Women's Health Book Collective, op. cit., chap. 5; Ruth Bell, et al., op. cit., pp. 117–122; McCoy and Wibbelsman, op. cit., pp. 150–153.

[120] Calderone and Johnson, op. cit., pp. 134–135.

[121] Ibid., p. 12.

minutes it would take to explain sexual reproduction alone are out of the question. For its ends, the program must be "mandated",[122] must extend from "kindergarten throughout a person's entire educational career".[123]

In reviewing their government-funded experiences both at home and abroad, the promoters of sex education admit that young people will not voluntarily come to birth control clinics for information or services.[124] Promotion is necessary, and sex education in the classroom is an obvious method of "outreach". Another common technique is "peer education" and "peer counseling", in which young people are engaged and trained to recruit their peers for sex education and birth control.[125] They will also offer youth a "range of activities", including sex education and birth control, through "multi-service centers", which are padded with other services such as vocational training, recreation, arts and crafts instruction, and entertainment. The model for this approach, which is now being duplicated in foreign countries, is The Door in New York City.[126] In the opinion of the proponents of "adolescent fertility management", such multi-service centers offer a "discrete [sic] and confidential alternative" to ordinary birth control clinics, which teenagers avoid.[127]

Sex education promoters in the United States and abroad lure young people through enticing entertainments and amusements, such as "condom blowing competitions", "youth contests on family planning themes (poster making, slogan writing, essay competition) . . . skits, plays, musical productions", as well as "letter columns in community newspapers, mobile shows, television and radio programming".[128] "Teens Only" newspaper columns provided by Planned Parenthood in the United States have explained "French" kissing,[129] "what happens if you forget to take your birth control pills for three or four days",[130] and "why . . . parents think sex is dirty".[131] The International Clearinghouse on Adolescent Fertility has reported on the "positive impact on the adolescent population of a current disco hit about condom usage".[132]

---

[122] Joseph S. Darden, Jr., "Mandated Family Life Education: A Rose Is a Rose Is a Rose Is a Rose", *The Journal of School Health,* vol. 51, no. 4, April 1981, pp. 292–294.

[123] Hacker, op. cit., p. 210.

[124] International Clearinghouse on Adolescent Fertility, Center for Population Options, *An Analysis of the Nature and Level of Adolescent Fertility Programming in Developing Countries* (Washington, D.C.: revised October 1983).

[125] Ibid., p. 5; The Center for Population Options, *Peer Education Programs* (Washington, D.C., 1983).

[126] International Clearinghouse on Adolescent Fertility, op. cit., p. 6.

[127] Ibid., p. 8.

[128] Ibid., p. 7.

[129] *Times Standard,* Eureka, California, March 26, 1978.

[130] *Times Standard,* Eureka, California, May 14, 1978.

[131] *Times Standard,* Eureka, California, February 26, 1978.

[132] International Clearinghouse on Adolescent Fertility, op. cit., p. 9.

The same agency has also reported that in some countries where "legal constraints" prevent birth controllers from openly distributing contraceptives to minors, they skirt the law by advertising their activities as "educational efforts only".[133] And in some places in the United States, sex educators distribute contraceptives in the schools.[134] It is hardly surprising that parents in the United States have objected to the programs, in some cases bringing lawsuits against them, and that citizens of foreign countries have complained that the sex educators are corrupting their youth.[135]

In promoting their program, the sex educators have shown they are masters of the system familiar to development planners. The initial public grants to sex education were used to create a demand for still more. Then, too, the new instruction required teachers, and teachers needed special training in special classes in colleges and universities. This in turn created a demand for textbooks, films, and other instructional materials, in addition to the books, pamphlets, and films prepared for children.

The sex educators have also mastered the art of "coalition-building", establishing friendly relations and cooperative projects with a slew of groups—the PTA, the Girl Scouts, Campfire, the YWCA, 4-H Clubs, the American Medical Association, the National Education Association, numerous church groups, and others. Their professional government-paid staff members provide information, publish bulletins, and offer workshops on how to build support, get government grants, and neutralize any opposition.[136] The strategy is always to make it appear that local parents are "demanding family life education" in the schools for their children. In its pamphlet *Creating a Climate of Support for Sex Education,* Planned Parenthood of Alameda-San Francisco summarizes the strategy: "Pack the board room with your supporters . . . avoid a public encounter . . . with the opposition." Special programs for parents, using teachers of their same ethnic background, can also help to create a "climate of support".[137] The result of this careful, publicly funded planning and

[133] Ibid., p. 6.

[134] Edward A. Brann et al., "Strategies for the Prevention of Pregnancy in Adolescents", reprinted by the U.S. Department of Health, Education, and Welfare, Public Health Service, from *Advances in Planned Parenthood,* vol. 14, no. 2, 1979; Ted Koppel, ABC *Nightline,* November 4, 1982, on the Johns Hopkins University program of distributing contraceptives in a Baltimore school.

[135] Statement by Comite Nacional Pro-Vida, A.C., Mexico, no date (probably 1984).

[136] See the *Network Report,* published twice a year at the offices of Planned Parenthood–Santa Cruz County, using funds supplied by the State of California Office of Family Planning. In 1981 the latter agency was offering to pay school districts to introduce or augment their sex instruction through a promotional program operated by ETR Associates of Santa Cruz under the auspices of San Diego State University Foundation. Also see *Preventing Adolescent Pregnancy: The Role of the Youth Serving Agency,* report of a conference co-sponsored by the Center for Population Options and the Center for Population and Family Health, March 1982.

[137] The Center for Population Options, *Sexuality Education Strategy and Resource Guide: Programs for Parents,* (Washington, D. C., 1983).

formation of alliances is, as in any war, to win control before the opposition can organize a defense.

The groups advocating sex education have maintained steady pressure on elementary and high school teachers, as well as the leaders of secular and religious youth groups, to take "sexuality" training, offering college credits for their courses. State law requires students at the California State Universities and Colleges to finish a course in "human integration" before graduation, and a course in sex will fulfill the requirement.[138] A 1976 law in California stimulated demand by requiring all persons applying for licenses as clinical social workers, marriage counselors, and trainees in related fields, to take training in "human sexuality".[139] Throughout the nation, new job classifications have come into being to staff the government-funded sex industry. In addition to the high-level "sexologists", who publish each other's articles in their proliferating sex journals, speak at each other's conferences, and recommend each other for honorary advanced degrees,[140] there were by 1980 many thousands of "health educators" who worked in the schools and abortion clinics and campaigned for sympathetic candidates for public office. This created members for new professional organizations and lobbying groups, such as the American Association of Sex Educators, Counselors and Therapists (AASECT).

Once in operation, the new sex programs called for "evaluation", which provided the occasion for still more millions in public grants. The evaluators in turn found that a principal effect of the programs is to "produce attitudinal change" and "to increase the students' tolerance of the sexual practices of others".[141] Such changes in "knowledge and attitudes" should, they thought, "facilitate a more positive and fulfilling sexuality".[142] A Falls Church evaluation found that after sex education more students regarded sex before marriage as "easy".[143] Two studies published by the Guttmacher Institute in 1986 found that youngsters who had received sex education had an elevated probability of engaging in premarital sex activity at an early age.[144] None of the evaluations has found that sex

---

[138] California Administrative Code, Title V, Sec. 40405.2(e); Office of the Chancellor, The California State University and Colleges, Executive Order 338, November 1, 1980.

[139] 22 California Business and Professions Code (25).

[140] See *Childhood and Sexuality: Proceedings of the International Symposium,* Études Vivantes 6700, Chemin Côte de Liesse, Saint-Laurent (Quebec), 1979.

[141] Douglas Kirby et al., "An Analysis of U.S. Sex Education Programs and Evaluation Methods", for the U.S. Department of Health, Education, and Welfare, Report No. CDC-2021-79-DK–FR, July 1979, p. 7.

[142] Ibid., p. 18.

[143] Susan Gustavus Philliber and Mary Lee Tatum, "The Impact of Sex Education on Students, Parents, and Faculty: A Report from Falls Church", November 1979, p. 11.

[144] William Marsiglio and Frank L. Mott, "The Impact of Sex Education on Sexual Activity . . . ", and Deborah Anne Dawson, "The Effects of Sex Education on Adolescent Behavior", *Family Planning Perspectives,* vol. 18, no. 4, July/August 1986.

education reduces adolescent pregnancy, though several report that where the school program includes ready access to abortion, teenagers have fewer babies.[145] Almost all studies, of course, have discovered a great need for more government funds for further research.

Since the accounting is extremely loose, it is not clear how much of the hundreds of millions of dollars annually spent by the U.S. government on domestic family planning is routed to sex education. The House Select Committee on Population reported in 1978 that "instead of being ear-marked for family life and sex education, funds are usually included among those for multi-service programs in health, welfare, social services, education, and maternal and infant care". The committee went on to state that federal sex education grants are provided by the Health Service Administration's Bureau of Community Health Services, the National Institute of Education, and the Bureau of Health Education within the Centers for Disease Control. Another ganglia of agencies that "may be devoting unspecified funds to sex education" include the National Institute of Mental Health, the Office of Child Development, the Bureau of Education for the Handicapped (sex education for the handicapped is now a thriving, federally supported business), and the Bureau of Indian Health Services.[146] Since this report, the federal Office of Adolescent Pregnancy has joined the list.

Additional sums are contributed by the states and private foundations. And drug companies, all too eager to sell their contraceptives and abortion supplies, have added muscle to the movement by advertising in its journals and making direct contributions.[147]

The operations of the new sex education have been justified by quantities of "research" into the most intimate aspects of human sexual behavior. The most famous center of such research is the Kinsey Institute for Research on Sex, Gender, Reproduction, Inc., at Indiana University. The founder of the institute, Alfred Kinsey, became famous for his minutely detailed descriptions of the sexual behavior of men, women, and children. Kinsey and his co-authors, including Wardell Pomeroy (author of sex books for children), portrayed hundreds of reactions of young children, some of them less than a year old, undergoing a variety of sexual stimulation. Kinsey reported that many of these children, subjected to "prolonged and varied and repeated stimulation" for as long as twenty-four hours in some instances, struggled, wept, and went into convulsions. The experiments continued until Kinsey and his co-authors had amassed enough material to publish four

---

[145] Brann et al., op. cit.

[146] Select Committee on Population, *Report,* "Fertility and Contraception in the United States", U.S. House of Representatives, 95th Congress, 2nd Session (Washington: U.S. Government Printing Office, 1978), pp. 76–77.

[147] Calderone, "Sex Education and . . . ", op. cit., p. 56.

statistical tables describing the detailed sexual responses of young children to stimulation—by adults, by older boys, and by themselves.[148] (Scholars subsequently objecting to the manner of the research[149] were met by a resounding silence.)

The family planning/sex education industry now boasts thousands of employees dependent, one way or another, on government funding. For economic as well as ideological reasons, the industry is outraged by suggestions it should be weaned from public support. In the words of veteran sex grants recipient Peter Scales, those who oppose the new school sex education are "A Powerful Threat to a Democratic Society"—they seek to impose "censorship in the public schools", and threaten "our First Amendment freedoms, the freedom of speech and the freedom of and from religion". He sees great danger in the attempts of some groups to "remove . . . state and federal regulation over private schools" and is shocked that his critics have been permitted to buy television time to bring their case before the public.[150] Scales' motives, of course, are not merely economic. His rhetoric is aimed at enemies, enemies of the state, for objecting to having their schools used as instruments to impose the dogma of population control.

[148] Alfred C. Kinsey, Wardell B. Pomeroy, and Clyde E. Martin, *Sexual Behavior in the Human Male* (Philadelphia: W. B. Saunders Company, 1948), pp. 161, 176–181, Tables 31 to 34.

[149] Dr. Judith A. Reisman, The American University, Washington, D.C., formerly of the Department of Sociology, Haifa University, publication forthcoming; reported in *Washington Times,* June 23, 1983, p. 3c.

[150] Peter Scales, "The New Opposition to Sex Education: A Powerful Threat to a Democratic Society", *The Journal of School Health,* vol. 51, no. 4, April 1981, pp. 300–303.

CHAPTER SIX

ADOLESCENT PREGNANCY: GOVERNMENT FAMILY PLANNING ON THE HOME FRONT

In 1978 the birth rate among U.S. teenagers was at its lowest level in almost forty years. Nevertheless, well-advertised concern over the so-called "teenage pregnancy epidemic" had increased throughout the preceding decade, culminating in special federal legislation to combat the problem.

In the "Health Services and Centers Amendments of 1978" (Public Law 95-626, Titles VI, VII, VIII), the Congress found that "pregnancy and childbirth among adolescents . . . often results in severe adverse health, social, and economic consequences" and that therefore "federal policy . . . should encourage the development of . . . health, educational, and social services . . . in order to prevent unwanted early and repeat pregnancies . . . " The act authorized $190 million to be spent over a three-year period on pregnancy testing, maternity counseling, "referral services", "family planning", "educational services in sexuality", and related services to pregnant and nonpregnant "adolescents".

For these services, the act provided a national network of "public or nonprofit private" agencies "in easily accessible locations" to be supported by federal grants. The sums authorized constituted a net addition to the several hundred millions of dollars already authorized for the support of existing family planning services available to all age groups, including adolescents.

The act embodied the fruition of years of labor by such groups as Planned Parenthood, Zero Population Growth, the Population Council, and the Population Reference Bureau, as well as the Department of Health, Education, and Welfare, to gain official recognition of the unique "epidemic". A torrent of pamphlets, articles, and press releases had poured from these organizations in the preceding years in a replay of the publicity expended on the "population explosion" a decade earlier. In the spring of 1978 the newly created Select Committee on Population held hearings and issued reports on "World Population: Myths and Realities", "Population and Development Assistance", "Legal and Illegal Immigration to the United States", and "Fertility and Contraception in America", giving three days of attention to "Adolescent and Pre-Adolescent Pregnancy". The committee's report found adolescent pregnancy so "alarming" that it called for strenuous federal action.

Adolescent pregnancy had received offical scrutiny as early as 1969, when President Nixon's Commission on Population Growth and the American Future sponsored several *Research Reports* on the topic.[1] The reports discussed statistical trends, "medical aspects", "illegitimacy", "unwanted" pregnancies, and "genetic implications", but failed to discover any special problems for teenage parenthood beyond low income. In fact, where no income differences existed, teenage mothers proved to have a lower proportion of low-birth-weight infants than mothers over twenty.[2] One of the most interesting features in the reports was the discovery that public birth control programs do not reduce illegitimacy.[3]

But the *Research Reports* had a more pressing object than merely reducing illegitimacy or the number of low-birth-weight infants. As they themselves were quick to point out, the *size of the population could be significantly reduced by eliminating all teenage births.*[4] *Accordingly, the commission "deplore*[d] the various consequences of teenage pregnancy" and recommended free "birth control information and services" and public sex education for teenagers,[5] and proposed the elimination of all restrictions on voluntary sterilization[6] and that "abortions ... be performed on request" at public expense.[7]

The idea of reducing the size of the population by blocking teenage births reappeared in 1974 in a major study written by Dorothy Nortman and published by the Population Council.[8] The introduction states that the concept had come from Bernard Berelson, then president of the Population Council, who devoted his Annual Report of 1971 to the topic "18–35 in place of 15–45?"; and in her final paragraphs Nortman discusses Berelson's seminal idea—the "Demographic Implications of Eliminating Births at Ages of Reproductive Inefficiency". She asks, "Suppose, then, that women were to reproduce only during the fifteen-year period from age 20 through age 34", rather than during the normal thirty-year period (15–44) of female fertility. Using estimates from various countries of the number of births by age of mother, she calculates that shortening the childbearing period by fifteen years would reduce the annual world population growth rate from its 1970 level of 20 per thousand population to about 13 per thousand. "The impact of this", she says, "can be seen in the fact that, at a growth rate of 20 per

---

[1] Commission on Population Growth and the American Future, *Research Reports,* vol. 1 (Washington: U.S. Government Printing Office, 1972).

[2] Jane A. Menken, "Teenage Childbearing: Its Medical Aspects and Implications for the United States Population", Commission on Population Growth and the American Future, op. cit., p. 349.

[3] Commission on Population Growth and the American Future, op. cit., pp. 419–421.

[4] Ibid., p. 350.

[5] *Population and the American Future: The Report of the Commission on Population Growth and the American Future* (New York: New American Library, 1972), pp. 189–190.

[6] Ibid., p. 171.

[7] Ibid., p. 178.

[8] Dorothy Nortman, "Parental Age as a Factor in Pregnancy Outcome and Child Development", *Reports on Population/Family Planning* (New York: The Population Council), no. 16, August 1974.

thousand per year, the population doubles in 35 years compared with 53 years at a rate of 13 per thousand per year."[9] She concludes by saying that "the means by which to restrict fertility to ages 20–34 are beyond the scope of this paper" but that a successful program of this type "would ... bring relief to a world coping with growth rates that retard economic development and threaten nature's ecological balance".[10]

Two years after the publication of the Nortman study, the Alan Guttmacher Institute, which is the "Research and Development Division" of the Planned Parenthood Federation of America, launched its media campaign against the "teenage pregnancy epidemic". The barrage began with the publication of the Institute's pamphlet *11 Million Teenagers: What Can Be Done about the Epidemic of Adolescent Pregnancies in the United States.*[11] The pamphlet, which sensationalized the epidemic, was spread nationwide and was quoted by leaders in Congress, by the media, by parent-teachers organizations, churches, youth organizations, and other creators of public opinion. Its message is reproduced *in toto* in the Hearings of the House Select Committee on Population.[12] Many of its claims and colorful headlines were quoted not only in the final Report of the Select Committee but in countless letters-to-the-editor and reports to community groups throughout the country—"U.S. Teenage Childbearing Rates Are Among the World's Highest", "11 Million Teenagers Are Sexually Active", "One Million Teenagers Become Pregnant Each Year", and more of the same stripe.

By the following year, the Guttmacher Institute was ready to publish its plan for action, *Planned Births, the Future of the Family and the Quality of American Life: Towards a Comprehensive National Policy and Program.* Sponsors of the plan included not only Planned Parenthood itself but also Zero Population Growth, the Population Section of the American Public Health Association, and other "family planning" organizations. It demanded "a high priority national program of services, education, and research related to fertility, and *a shift in public policy to one which supports the regulation of fertility as a universal service,* with government prepared to intervene to assist those who are disadvantaged

---

[9] Ibid., p. 49.

[10] Ibid.

[11] Alan Guttmacher Institute, *11 Million Teenagers: What Can Be Done about the Epidemic of Adolescent Pregnancies in the United States* (New York: Planned Parenthood Federation of America, Inc., 1976).

[12] *Hearings* before the Select Committee on Population, "Fertility and Contraception in America: Adolescent and Pre-Adolescent Pregnancy", 95th Congress, 2nd Session, vol. II (Washington: U.S. Government Printing Office, 1978), pp. 553–613.

for any reason in obtaining the services they need and want . . . " (emphasis added).[13]

The plan broke new ground, calling for a more intrusive public approach to "fertility regulation"[14]; and it did not contain this "universal service" to voluntary recipients. The plan expressed particular concerns regarding pregnancy among "women younger than age 20", based on its own assertion that these pregnancies are largely "unintended".[15] To "reduce . . . the number of unintended pregnancies and births among teenagers",[16] it called for "new initiatives" — the creation of a "national network for early detection of pregnancy", "school-based education programs", "community information and outreach programs", and programs to "encourage hospitals to provide abortion services".[17] In order to launch this assault on "unintended fertility",[18] it demanded "immediate attention from the Administration and Congressional leadership"[19] and federal spending in 1979 of $410 million on domestic "family planning", to be increased to $783 million by 1981.[20]

"Immediate attention" was, indeed, forthcoming from a compliant administration and Congress. The president of the Guttmacher Institute was a featured witness before the Select Committee on Population,[21] but other witnesses also called for a national network of "pregnancy detection centers"[22] to prevent not only first births, but "recidivism"[23] (i.e., additional births) among women under twenty.

The demographic leanings of the Select Committee are suggested in its questions, "Is the right of parents to determine the number of children they will have an absolute one? Is it unethical to restrict population size through legislative action? What is compulsion?"[24] Several witnesses had reached beyond concerns about demographic size to eugenic purity in their statements on adolescent pregnancy. Mr. Sargent Shriver, for example, spoke of "this Committee's interest in improv-

[13] *Planned Births, the Future of the Family and the Quality of American Life* (Planned Parenthood et al., June 1977), p. 2.

[14] Ibid., pp. 10–17.

[15] Ibid., p. 8.

[16] Ibid., p. 3.

[17] Ibid., Table 1, pp. 18–19.

[18] Ibid., p. 8.

[19] Ibid., p. 30.

[20] Ibid., pp. 26–28.

[21] *Hearings,* op. cit., pp. 170–177.

[22] Ibid., p. 169.

[23] Ibid., p. 163.

[24] Select Committee on Population, Report, "World Population: Myths and Realities", U.S. House of Representatives, 95th Congress, 2nd Session (Washington: U.S. Government Printing Office, 1978), p. 7.

ing the quality of life and enhancing the biological product of this society, rather than just controlling or limiting births".[25]

Granted, in its Letter of Transmittal to the Speaker of the House, the committee professed that its report on fertility and contraception merely "reviews the methods, means, and services available to help American men and women achieve their family size goals".[26] But the report proceeded to list a series of measures in support of the committee's belief that the government had the responsibility to influence those "family size goals" in major ways—by distributing "public service messages concerning . . . family planning and its medical and socioeconomic advantages",[27] by "measures . . . to increase the acceptability of . . . contraceptives",[28] by "further research on motivation",[29] by "further effort . . . to investigate more acceptable . . . fertility regulation for adolescent males and females . . . and for women over 35",[30] by devoting more resources to the "urgent need for contraceptive services among rural women",[31] by supporting "outreach activities to attract males to these [contraceptive] services",[32] and by evaluating "sterilization regulations to protect individuals from undergoing this procedure without careful consideration, with the goal of ensuring that these regulations do not hinder voluntary and informed access to this procedure",[33] and more.

In short, the committee felt it was the obligation of the government to intervene in and regulate the fertility of the individual. The committee obviously intended that the weight of U.S. policy should land against childbearing. It was a startling reversal of the traditional deference to personal choice.

Given the unabated outcry regarding adolescent pregnancy that has dominated public utterance for more than a decade, the statistics come as a surprise. There is, first, the very large decline (prior to the uproar) in fertility among this age group, as shown in Chart 6-1. The decline of 47 percent in teenage fertility during the 1957–1985 period was the same as the decline among women of all ages. When pressed, the public family-planning advocates will occasionally admit the facts, only to insist "the decline has been restricted to older adolescents".[34] But the data

---

[25] *Hearings,* op. cit., p. 178.

[26] Select Committee on Population, *Report,* "Fertility and Contraception in the United States", U.S. House of Representatives, 95th Congress, 2nd Session (Washington: U.S. Government Printing Office, 1978), p. iii.

[27] Ibid., p. 11.

[28] Ibid., p. 17.

[29] Ibid.

[30] Ibid., pp. 16–17.

[31] Ibid., p. 11.

[32] Ibid.

[33] Ibid.

[34] Alan Guttmacher Institute, *11 Million Teenagers,* op. cit., p. 12.

tell a different story, as Table 6-1 indicates. Though smaller than for women over 18, there was a definite decline among girls aged 15 to 17 during the period for which data are available. The table also shows that births to teenagers are heavily concentrated among women over 18. Less than four out of a hundred girls aged 15 to 17 (and about one out of a thousand girls under age 15) give birth in a typical year. The very low birth rate for the youngest group varies on a year-to-year basis by as much as 20 percent, mostly random changes in a small number, having little statistical significance. It is arguable that the very low rates and small numbers represent some irreducible minimum of adolescent indiscretion that should not be expected to follow the trends for adults.

Not only birth rates but numbers of births to women under 20 have been falling—there was a decline of almost 180,000 births between 1970 and 1985.

While trends in births out-of-wedlock have compounded the general alarm, the statistics are somewhat ambiguous. Twelve states, including California, New York, and Ohio, have not required legitimacy status to be reported on birth certificates. The data, therefore, are estimates only, and the apparent trends may be affected by underregistration in earlier years.[35] As Table 6-2 shows, although the estimated proportion of illegitimate births has increased markedly, the *rate* per 1,000 unmarried women in the 15–19 year age-group has not. Three out of a hundred unmarried women in the 15–19 year age-group give birth out-of-wedlock each year. The reason that the proportion has risen so much more than the *rate* is that birth rates among married teenagers have fallen steeply.

It appears, then, that although young mothers are having fewer babies, they are having a larger proportion outside of marriage. There are other signs that marriage is falling even more precipitately than childbearing among the young. Rising proportions of both sexes have never married. For example, in 1960, 76 percent of all eighteen-year-old females had never been married; by 1985, the proportion had risen to 91 percent.[36]

Another symptom of the dread epidemic of teenage pregnancy has been its supposed prevalence in the United States compared with other countries. The allegation appears in the Guttmacher Institute–Planned Parenthood booklet *11 Million Teenagers*, repeated as fact, and even submitted in testimony to Congress. The statement is based on a graph[37] comparing births to women under 20 in several countries, most of which had higher rates than the United States. There is,

[35] See U.S. Department of Health, Education, and Welfare, Public Health Service, National Center for Health Statistics, *Vital Statistics of the United States,* 1973, vol. 1, Natality, Technical Appendix; also Phillips Cutright, "Illegitimacy in the United States: 1920–1968", Commission on Population Growth and the American Future, *Research Reports,* vol. 1 (Washington: U.S. Government Printing Office, 1972), pp. 429–433.

[36] U.S. Bureau of the Census, *Statistical Abstract of the United States: 1985* (Washington: U.S. Government Printing Office, 1985), p. 39.

[37] Alan Guttmacher Institute, *11 Million Teenagers,* op. cit., p. 7; also *Hearings,* op. cit., p. 556.

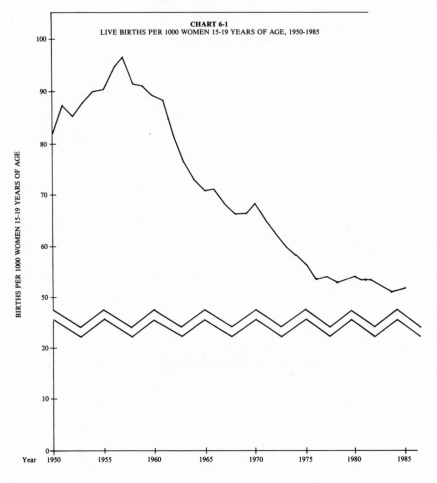

CHART 6-1
LIVE BIRTHS PER 1000 WOMEN 15-19 YEARS OF AGE, 1950-1985

Source: National Center for Health Statistics, Vital Statistics of
the United States, annual, and Monthly Vital Statistics.

Table 6-1
Birth Rates, by Age of Mother, and Numbers of Births
to Women Aged 15–19, 1966, 1970, and 1985

Year	(1) Births per 1000 Women 15–19	(2) Number of Births to Women 15–19	(3) Births per 1000 Women 18–19	(4) Births per 1000 Girls 15–17	(5) Births per 1000 Girls Under 15
1966	70.6	621,426	121.2	35.8	0.9
1970	68.3	644,708	114.7	38.8	1.2
1985	51.3	467,485	80.8	31.1	1.2
Percent Change, 1966–85	−27.3%	−24.8%	−33.3%	−13.1%	+33.3%
Percent Change, 1970–85	−24.9%	−27.5%	−29.6%	−19.8%	0

SOURCES: Derived from U.S. Department of Health, Education, and Welfare, Public Health Service, National Center for Health Statistics, *Monthly Vital Statistics Report* for September 8, 1977, and March 29, 1978, and *Vital Statistics of the United States,* annual, and *Monthly Vital Statistics Report,* Advance Report of Final Natality Statistics, 1985 (PHS) 87-1120, vol. 36, no. 4, *Supplement,* July 17, 1987.

Table 6-2
Estimated Live Births Out-of-Wedlock per Thousand Unmarried Women 15–19,
and as a Proportion of All Births to Women 15–19, 1970 and 1985

Year	Estimated Live Births Out-of-Wedlock per Thousand Unmarried Women, 15–19	Estimated Live Births Out-of-Wedlock as a Percent of All Births to Women, 15–19
1970	22.4	29.5%
1985	31.6	58.0%

SOURCE: Derived from U.S. Department of Health, Education, and Welfare, Public Health Service, National Center for Health Statistics, *Monthly Vital Statistics Reports,* September 8, 1977, and Advance Report of Final Natality Statistics, 1985 (PHS) 87-1120, vol., 36, no. 4, Supplement, July 17, 1987. See text for discussion of the problem of estimating out-of-wedlock births.

however, a slight omission. The Planned Parenthood statisticians simply left out all but three of the more than thirty countries with rates higher than the United States! In fact, on a scale of all adolescent birth rates for which United Nations estimates are available, the United States stands in the lower one-third.[38] In response to well-earned criticism, the Guttmacher Institute added a few countries to its graph and reran it in its 1981 publication, *Teenage Pregnancy: The Problem*

[38] Based on data appearing in the United Nations *Demographic Yearbook,* issues for 1975 and 1981.

That Hasn't Gone Away. And once again, by making comparisons with countries carefully selected for their low fertility, the chart erroneously shows that the United States has one of the world's highest rates of teenage childbearing. In fact, the rate of childbearing among white American teenagers is at the midpoint on the scale for Europe. Taking into account that more than a fifth of all American teenagers are Hispanic or black or "other non-white", it is possible to estimate what our teenage fertility "should" be, based on the geographic and cultural origins of our people. And the actual rate is just what it "should" be by this criterion, or a bit lower.[39]

The whole Planned Parenthood performance concerning "high" adolescent fertility points up what William Ball has called the essential "standardlessness" of the population control effort.[40] The would-be controllers have never defined "high" other than to tell us that ours is "too high". Obviously, with "high" left dangling, it will be impossible ever to decide *a priori* when determined national action will have lowered childbearing levels to less than "too high". Without objective standards, we can only continue to rely, as we are being urged to do, on the solomonic judgment of the public planning advocates.

The proponents of government family planning have made their case for reduced teenage fertility to the public and to Congress on a number of grounds, ably assisted by their selective presentation of statistics. For instance, writing in the *New England Journal of Medicine*, in August 1980, the physicians Hollingsworth and Kreutner reported:

> Teenage pregnancy has become a common occurrence in American society. Although there has been a decline in the total national birth rate, the proportion of deliveries by adolescents (age 11 to 18 years old) increased from 17 per cent in 1966 to 19 per cent in 1975. Today, one in five births is to a woman 18 years of age or younger. The pattern of early pregnancy is shifting; births to older teenagers have decreased but births to mothers 15 to 17 years old have increased 22 percent, with the peak occurring at the age of 16.[41]

The reader is deluded into believing that teenage pregnancy and fertility have increased. Careful perusal reveals that this is not quite what the authors have said, but quite clearly what they want to impart. To create the appropriate alarm, they rather badly garble the information in the official source on which they rely,

---

[39] Based on midpoint teenage fertility in Europe and teenage fertility in Mexico and Latin America and among American blacks and other nonwhites, weighted in accordance with their estimated proportions in the U.S. teenage population. The resulting expected rate is 55 compared with the actual rate of 53 for 1982.

[40] William B. Ball, *Population Control* (Export, Pennsylvania: U.S. Coalition for Life, reprinted from Donald A. Grannella, ed., *Religion and the Public Order*, no. 4, Cornell University Press, 1968).

[41] Dorothy Reycroft Hollingsworth, M.D., and A. Karen Kessler Kreutner, M.D., "Teenage Pregnancy: Solutions Are Evolving", *The New England Journal of Medicine*, vol. 303, no. 9, August 28, 1980, pp. 516–518.

misquoting the age-categories for which the original data were given and even referring to a "peak" for sixteen-year-olds that appears nowhere in the original source.

The original source, a special government report titled *Teenage Childbearing: United States, 1966–75* by Stephanie J. Ventura of the Division of Vital Statistics, itself presents the case in the worst possible light within the limits of statistical accuracy. Rather than report teenage childbearing for all women under 20 or for those aged 15 to 19, as previous reports had done, this one reported separately on fertility among women aged 18–19, 15–17 and 10–14. While it noted the large decline in fertility among the older members, where most of the group's childbearing is concentrated, it made much of the fact that there was no corresponding decline among the younger girls. It omitted altogether the very large decline for the group as a whole, and then commented, "The phenomenon of unchanged teenage childbearing is puzzling . . . " —which of course contradicts its own statistical assertions.[42]

The Hollingsworth-Kreutner article follows the usual pattern of spreading dismay by stressing the increasing proportion of teenage births. But the increase is smaller than the alarmists indicate and has an explanation they fail to mention. As a proportion of all births, those to women 15 to 19 increased from 14 percent in 1960 to 19 percent in 1972–1975 and then declined to 12 percent in 1985. But, as mentioned, the decline in fertility for this group was as great as the average decline for all women. The explanation of the shifting proportions is that much greater-than-average declines were occurring during the 1960s and 1970s among older women and among those having three, four, or more children. The period saw the virtual disappearance of the larger family. The declining proportion of births of three and more children means, of course, that the proportion of first and second births, those born to younger women, must increase, even though the fertility of the younger group was declining. Charts 6-2 and 6-3 illustrate these changes.

It is possible, of course, that such errors and distortions as appear in the Hollingsworth-Kreutner article and others are due to carelessness or lack of familiarity with statistical analysis. But if so, the question occurs—why do all the errors exaggerate the problem? Surely random errors would be rather evenly distributed between minimizing and overstating the case. But the errors run consistently high in the case of adolescent pregnancy.

The Hollingsworth-Kreutner article also exemplifies the government family planners' tendency to use shifting definitions of adolescence to cement their case. The term is capable of elastic definition, depending on the purposes in hand.

---

[42] U.S. Department of Health, Education, and Welfare, National Center for Health Statistics, "Teenage Childbearing: United States, 1966–75", *Monthly Vital Statistics Report: Natality Statistics,* (HRA) 77-1120, vol. 26, no. 5, Supplement, September 8, 1977.

CHART 6-2
BIRTH RATES BY AGE OF MOTHER: UNITED STATES, 1950-1980

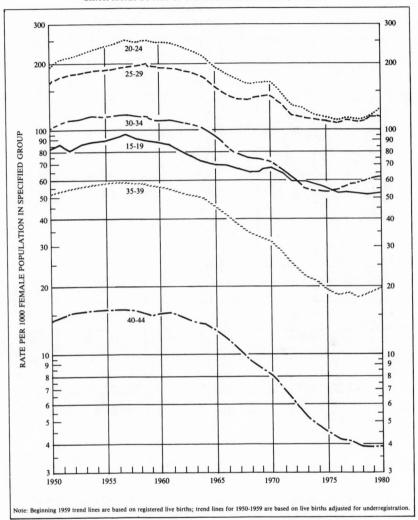

Note: Beginning 1959 trend lines are based on registered live births; trend lines for 1950-1959 are based on live births adjusted for underregistration.

Source: Reproduced from National Center for Health Statistics, Advance Report of
Final Natality Statistics, 1980, (PHS) 83-1120, Vol. 31, No. 8, Supplement, November 30, 1982.

CHART 6-3
BIRTH RATES BY LIVE BIRTH ORDER: UNITED STATES, 1950-1980

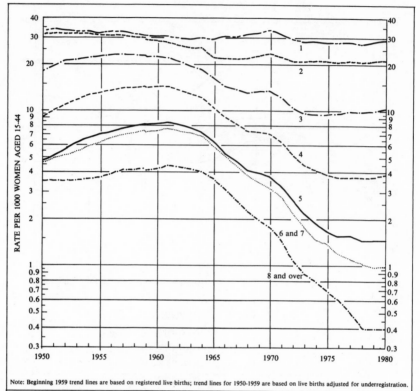

Note: Beginning 1959 trend lines are based on registered live births; trend lines for 1950-1959 are based on live births adjusted for underregistration.

Source: Reproduced from National Center for Health Statistics, Advance Report of
Final Natality Statistics, 1980, (PHS) 83-1120, Vol. 31, No. 8, Supplement, November 30, 1982.

Webster defines "adolescence" as the "time of life between puberty and maturity" and an "adolescent" as a "person in his teens". Legally, individuals in our society reach maturity at different ages for different purposes, and physically, they mature at widely differing ages.

Recent literature has broadened "adolescent pregnancy" to refer to that of women under 20. The term is relatively new, to fit the new concern. A generation or so ago, a young married woman aged 17, 18, or 19 starting her family was not regarded as a cause for public consternation. Four out of ten births to women under 20 occur in this older, married category but are now reported with dismay as part of a teenage epidemic. But in discussing the fancied problems, the focus is put on the younger members of the group, as when Hollingsworth and Kreutner report in detail on the pregnancy problems of girls aged 11 to 15 without mentioning that only 2 percent of all teenage births—10,000 per year—occur in this younger age-group.

By toying with definitions, antinatalists bend the truth to accommodate their ends—teenage pregnancy is portrayed as abounding and portending great physical, social, and emotional risks rather than being what it is, a natural, though declining, phenomenon among young women arriving at physical maturity.

Federal and state governments show the same tendency to shift definitions for different purposes. On the one hand, the courts have held that no girl is too young to obtain an abortion without her parents' permission or knowledge.[43] Nor is any child too young to be given sex information or to procure contraceptives, again without parental consent or knowledge.[44] Yet on the other hand, while the Health Services Centers and Amendments of 1978 did not include "adolescent" in its six paragraphs of "definitions" (although the stated purpose of the act was to provide them with a wide range of new "services"), the act did define an "adolescent parent" to mean a "parent under the age of 21". Thus federal law now holds that persons who are parents do not mature until they are 21, putting them in a unique category since it is years later than the date of legal maturity for other purposes.

It is probably unnecessary to point out that the term "adolescence" may, whenever convenient, be redefined to suit the policymakers' choice. Once again, the standardlessness of the government family-planning movement is appallingly apparent.

Promoters of the epidemic describe the ravages of teenage maternity in painful detail. The House Select Committee on Population, for example, in its indictment of young motherhood reiterated the standard statement that "pregnancy is the single most common cause of school drop-out among young girls".[45] Now

[43] *Planned Parenthood v. Danforth,* 428 U.S. 52, 1976; *Belotti v. Baird,* 47 LW 4969, July 2, 1979.

[44] Kathy McCoy and Charles Wibbelsman, M.D., *The Teenage Body Book* (New York: Simon & Schuster, 1978), p. 173.

[45] Select Committee on Population, Report, "Fertility and Contraception in the United States", op. cit., p. 63.

obviously, that type of conclusion depends on how the "causes of school drop-out" are listed and categorized. Pregnancy will loom as a more-or-less important cause to the degree that other causes are listed in more-or-less detail. In cold fact, the committee had received testimony that two-thirds of girls leave school for reasons other than pregnancy.[46] To give it credit, the committee did the best it could with what it had at hand.

In the same spirit, it is commonly alleged that teenagers have higher maternal mortality rates than older mothers. For example, the California Department of Education announced in the introduction to its new sex curriculum that "the mortality rates for mothers under twenty years of age are 30 percent higher than for those in the next higher age group (twenty to twenty-four)."[47]

But Table 6-3, which presents the most recent official statistics available in 1987, shows that these assertions were not true, for maternal mortality was not only lower among teenagers, it rose steeply as women aged.

Table 6-3
Maternal Mortality Rates,*
By Age, United States, 1979, 1983

Age Group	1979 Rate*	1983 Rate*
Total	9.6	8.0
Under 20 Years	6.2	5.4
20–24 Years	7.5	7.5
25–29 Years	7.6	6.6
30–34 Years	12.8	9.1
35–39 Years	33.3	20.0
40–44 Years	65.2	27.0
45 Years and Over	414.9**	—

SOURCE: National Center for Health Statistics, *Vital Statistics of the United States.*
*Maternal death rates per 100,000 live births in specified group.
**Rate computed by relating deaths to women 45 years and over to live births to women 45–49 years.

The California Department of Education had several other strings to its bow. "Toxemia deaths for teenage mothers are 50 percent higher," it charged.[48] Also not true. United States vital statistics for 1983 show that the teenage maternal toxemia death rate was one-third as high as the rate for all women.

In another twist of the truth, the department claimed that "children born to mothers aged fifteen to nineteen are 36 percent more likely to be premature (as measured by birth weight) than to [sic] children born to mothers over

---

[46] *Hearings,* op. cit., p. 34.
[47] California State Department of Education, *Education for Human Sexuality: A Resource Book and Instructional Guide to Sex Education for Kindergarten Through Grade Twelve, 1979,* p. 1.
[48] Ibid.

nineteen . . . "[49] But, as mentioned previously, birth-weight differences are affected by income differences, and where they do not exist, teenage mothers deliver fewer low-birth-weight infants than mothers over 20.[50] In 1985 the National Center for Health Statistics reported that 9 percent of all babies born to women aged 15–19 in the United States fell within its definition of low birth-weight in that they weighed less than 5½ pounds. This compares with 7 percent of the babies born to women aged 20–24, which is the same as the percentage for all women. Of the low-birth-weight babies born to teenagers, the great majority—more than 60 percent—weighed more than 4 pounds 7 ounces.[51]

Even more damaging to the thesis that teenagers bear a higher proportion of babies with low birth-weight and associated medical problems, a recent major study of 11,000 teenage mothers and 28,000 older mothers found that "teenage mothers tend to be of small stature and weight . . . The small size of their infants is in proportion to their smaller size and not to their early age at conception."[52]

Moreover, by age seven the children of teenage mothers were no smaller than those of older mothers.[53] In addition,

> undesirable pregnancy outcomes are not necessarily more common in teenage pregnancies or in the younger teenage pregnancies . . . some undesirable pregnancy outcomes are actually less frequent in the progeny of teenage mothers.[54]

Continuing its note of grave alarm, the California Department of Education reported that "adolescent mothers have a suicide rate many times higher than the general population."[55] No source is given, perhaps because national suicide statistics have no separate information for "adolescent mothers". Yet the assertion frequently appears in the teenage-pregnancy discussions, and about as frequently without reference to any source. An exception is a source offered by F. Ivan Nye in his study "School-Age Parenthood", written for the Cooperative Extension Service of Washington State University.[56] Nye emphasizes that "the number of teenage mothers who attempt suicide is seven times the rate for teenage girls without children" and refers to articles by Braen et al and Gabrielson et al as sources. Braen et al, writing in *The Journal of School Health* in 1975, claim that the rate of suicide attempts among pregnant students under age 18 was ten times

---

[49] Ibid.

[50] Menken, op. cit., p. 349.

[51] National Center for Health Statistics, *Monthly Vital Statistics Report, Advance Report, Final Natality Statistics, 1985,* (PHS) 87–1120, vol. 36, no. 4, Supplement, July 17, 1987.

[52] Stanley M. Garn and Audrey S. Petzold, "Characteristics of the Mother and Child in Teenage Pregnancy", *American Journal of Diseases of Children,* vol. 137, April 1983, pp. 365–368.

[53] Ibid.

[54] Ibid.

[55] California State Department of Education, op. cit., p. 1.

[56] Extension Bulletin 667, Family Research Institute, Washington State University, no date.

greater than the rate among the nonpregnant population,[57] and quote Gabrielson et al and Otto as sources.

Gabrielson et al in turn report on a study they made of 105 pregnant teenagers admitted to the Yale-New Haven Hospital during 1959 and 1960.[58] There were no suicides in the group, but fourteen of the young women "were known to have made subsequently one or more self-destructive *attempts or threats* serious enough to require care or to be reported to a physician at the hospital"[59] (emphasis added). The investigators made no effort to determine whether their tiny local study group resembled or differed from the national population of young expectant mothers. On the basis of such a small and probably unique local sample, no honest investigator would draw general conclusions. But adolescent-pregnancy experts are not bound by ordinary standards. They not only draw conclusions, they boldly leap to them and broadcast them as national suicide *rates.*

Much the same can be said about the cited study by Otto. The investigation was conducted in Sweden in 1955–1959. It did not compare the suicide rates of pregnant and nonpregnant women, but instead studied a group of women under 21 who had attempted suicide and found that less than 6 percent were pregnant[60]— about the same proportion as would be expected to be pregnant in the general Swedish population of this age.[61]

In full confidence that no one will ever check on its shoddy statistics, the California Department of Education adds to its indictment of young motherhood by claiming that "a 30 percent higher risk of infant mortality exists among children born to adolescent mothers than those born to mothers twenty to twenty-four".[62] Here again no regularly published national data exist. In her 1974 study of "Parental Age as a Factor in Pregnancy Outcome and Child Development" previously mentioned, Dorothy Nortman examined a number of studies conducted in several different cities, states, and countries during the 1950s and 1960s. Infant mortality by age of mother varied widely in the different study groups. Among the American Indian population of Arizona in 1967, infant mortality was less than half as high among the babies of teenagers as among those of women 20–34. Among white New Yorkers in 1966–1967, infant mortality was reported to be 56 percent higher among the babies of teenagers than among those of women 20–34. In Denmark, where health care has long been freely available to

[57] Bernard P. Braen and Janet Bell Forbush, "School Age Parenthood: A National Overview", *The Journal of School Health,* vol. 45, no. 5, May 1975, pp. 256–262.

[58] Ira W. Gabrielson et al., "Suicide Attempts in a Population Pregnant as Teenagers", *American Journal of Publich Health,* vol. 60, no. 12, December 1970, pp. 2289–2301.

[59] Ibid., p. 2289.

[60] U. Otto, "Suicidal Attempts Made by Pregnant Women under 21 Years", *Acta Paedopsychiatrica,* vol. 32, 1965, pp. 276–288.

[61] Based on Swedish births by age in 1958, appearing in *Demographic Yearbook of the United Nations,* 1960.

[62] California State Department of Education, op. cit., p. 1.

all age groups, infants born to teenage mothers had lower mortality rates than those born to older mothers. In Taiwan the rates were about the same for teenagers as for older mothers.[63]

Nortman reported that the median ratio between infant mortality among babies of mothers under 20 and those of mothers aged 20–34 was 128 percent.[64] This is probably the origin of the "30 percent higher risk" claimed by the California Department of Education. But it should be noted that this is only a median or a middle number, derived from several samples of different sizes; it is not a weighted average. It is based on studies of various sizes conducted at various times and places, all more than a decade ago. And it seems likely that the data largely reflect varying access to health care as a number of investigators have concluded, and as will be shown shortly.

Denouncers of teenage pregnancy are also fond of claiming that younger mothers are child abusers. In the words of the House Select Committee on Population, "there are indications that child abuse is more prevalent among young mothers than among older mothers",[65] but in 689 pages of testimony by twenty-four expert witnesses over a period of three days no corroborative evidence was submitted.

Contrary to claims by the alarmists, studies of the mental and social development of the children of teenage mothers have discovered no real differences between them and other children. A major study of 375,000 children in the United States found that the former showed somewhat less academic aptitude in high school than other children but that the disparity tended to disappear when children of similar family background—that is, matched in respect to living with both parents and so on—were compared. The study followed the same children up to age 30 by which time, although they had had less formal education, they were earning as much income as those born to older parents.[66] The author, summing up, found "much smaller consequences for the future lives of the children involved" than previous studies with their forebodings about the "enormous impact" of teenage childbearing.[67]

But the essence of the case against teenage childbearing, publicized in numerous articles and studies, is that it causes "soaring welfare costs". On the face of it the charge is patently untrue because Aid to Families with Dependent Children (AFDC), the public program principally affected by dependency among teenage mothers, is one of the few government programs whose costs are *not* soaring, but

[63] Nortman, op. cit., p. 33.

[64] Ibid.

[65] Select Committee on Population, *Report,* "Fertility and Contraception in the United States", op. cit., p. 65.

[66] Josefina J. Card, "Long-Term Consequences for Children of Teenage Parents", *Demography,* vol. 18, no. 2, May 1981, pp. 137–156.

[67] Ibid., p. 154.

instead have remained at roughly the same level since the mid-1970s. It is a relatively small public transfer program directly accounting for less than 2 percent of all public expenditures and for no more than a possible 4 percent when allowance is made for the addition of food stamps, health care, and housing assistance.

Only about 7 percent of the mothers on AFDC are teenagers,[68] and no one knows what proportion of women giving birth under the age of 20 become dependent on welfare. One study found that 70 percent of teenage mothers were living with their own parents at the time of birth.[69] And though it has been estimated that perhaps a third become dependent for a time,[70] recent data indicate that the proportion may be much lower, closer to a quarter or a fifth.[71] Another study found that almost two-thirds of unwed young mothers married within five years after giving birth, 60 percent of these within a year of delivery.[72] Not surprisingly, the sooner the young father found a job, the greater the likelihood of marriage[73] and, therefore, economic independence.

The findings probe the importance of economic factors in the escalation of illegitimate teenage births. A young unmarried couple without much income can avoid the inflating private medical costs of childbirth by qualifying for Medicaid or for their parents' health insurance. Once this hurdle has been passed, they have less incentive to remain unmarried, although rising levels of unemployment among young males probably encourage illegitimacy as well.

One study of low-income adolescent mothers found that five years after delivery only 15 percent were totally dependent on welfare and only half of these had received such assistance for more than twelve months.[74] A conspicuous charge—that "half of all welfare expenditures go to women who were teenagers when they first gave birth"[75]—stems from an Urban Institute estimate based on data for 1975.[76] What the estimate, if accurate, actually suggested was that the women receiving AFDC were roughly similar to the rest of the female population, because in 1975 about a third of all first births to American women (and about half

[68] Social Security Administration, *Aid to Families with Dependent Children, 1979 Recipient Characteristics Study,* part 1: Demographic & Program Statistics, pp. 2, 50.

[69] Wendy Baldwin, Testimony, Hearing before Select Committee on Children, Youth, and Families, U.S. House of Representatives, 98th Congress, 1st Session, June 20, 1983, p. 12.

[70] Kristin A. Moore, Testimony, *Hearings* before the Select Committee on Population, "Fertility and Contraception in America: Adolescent and Pre-Adolescent Pregnancy", op. cit., p. 295.

[71] Derived from the 1979 number of AFDC mothers under 20 (see note 68) divided by the number of women under 20 who had had a first birth, derived from birth data for 1974–1979.

[72] Frank F. Furstenberg, Jr., "The Social Consequences of Teenage Parenthood", in Catherine S. Chilman, *Adolescent Pregnancy and Childbearing: Findings from Research,* U.S. Department of Health and Human Services, NIH Publication no. 81–2077, December 1980, p. 278.

[73] Ibid., p. 280.

[74] Furstenberg, op. cit., p. 294.

[75] Tim Zentler, for Planned Parenthood of Humboldt County, quoted in *The Union,* June 14, 1983.

[76] Moore, op.cit., p. 293.

of all black first births) were occurring to women under 20.[77] Nor did the study find any direct connection between early childbearing and dependence on public aid, though it alluded to an "indirect role".[78]

It is the poor who need public assistance and for whom the programs were designed. Although in the past the poor began their childbearing at earlier ages and had somewhat larger families on the average than the higher-income groups, the difference is growing smaller. In 1982 wives 18 to 29 years of age in all income groups had averaged fewer than two children and expected to have no more than two at the most.[79] Fertility has been below replacement levels in the United States since 1972.[80]

Sensational descriptions of the astronomical public welfare costs caused by teenage pregnancy have swamped the nation. One of the most creative was a 1979 study by John C. Robbins, who estimated that the present discounted value of the twenty-year public costs associated with births to teenagers in 1979 amounted to $8.3 billion.[81] In order to arrive at this staggering total, Robbins used fancifully high estimates of the average amounts and duration of future public costs.

The facts speak otherwise. The typical AFDC family in 1982 consisted of a mother and one child who had received public aid for less than three years.[82] A ten-year study of welfare dependency conducted by the Institute for Social Research at the University of Michigan found that half of all recipients were on the welfare rolls for no more than two years, and only one in twelve was heavily dependent for more than seven years.[83]

Another common claim is that the children of teenage parents "repeat the cycle" of poverty and welfare dependence. This error is evidenced by what we have already seen—by the age of 30 the children of teenage parents are earning just as high incomes as those of older parents—and surely suggests that they have no higher probability of being dependent on public assistance than any other group. Strengthening this conclusion, research at the University of Michigan Survey Research Center found that persons whose parents have received public aid are not much more likely to become dependent than any other group.[84] The authors

[77] U. S. Bureau of the Census, *Current Population Reports,* Series P-20, no. 358, "Fertility of American Women: June 1979", Table 17, p. 62.

[78] Moore, op. cit., p. 289.

[79] U.S. Bureau of the Census, *Current Population Reports,* Series P-20, no. 387, "Fertility of American Women: June 1982", p. 22.

[80] U.S. Bureau of the Census, *Statistical Abstract of the United States: 1980,* p. 61.

[81] SRI International, *An Analysis of Government Expenditures Consequent on Teenage Childbirth* (Menlo Park: SRI International, April 1979).

[82] U.S. Bureau of the Census, *Statistical Abstract of the United States: 1985,* p. 382.

[83] Greg J. Duncan, *Years of Poverty, Years of Plenty* (Ann Arbor: The University of Michigan, Institute for Social Research, 1984) pp. 77, 90.

[84] Martha S. Hill et al., "Motivation and Economic Mobility of the Poor" (Ann Arbor: University of Michigan Survey Research Center, August 3, 1983).

proceeded to refute a number of other spurious claims regarding the bad effects of teenage pregnancy:

> Our results do not support the intergenerational arguments of the culture-of-poverty, underclass, and welfare-dependence theories. We observe a great deal of income mobility from one generation to the next, even among the poorest households. Links between parents' and children's economic circumstances do exist. However, long-term welfare dependency as a child does not cause long-term welfare dependency as an adult, at least among blacks. Parental attitudes and values had little effect on children's later economic outcomes and welfare dependence.[85]

The lamenters of the "costs of teenage pregnancy" prefer never to mention any benefits generated by the children born to young mothers, who, like other children, grow up to be productive members of society. Though it is impossible for any one human being to determine the true worth of any other, a smaller question is relatively easy to answer—whether the *public economic costs* of these children are greater or smaller than their *public economic benefits*. These children do grow up and do become income-producers and taxpayers. The average baby born in the United States in 1983 will spend about 47 years in the labor force, will earn more than two-thirds of a million dollars in his lifetime and will pay over a quarter of a million dollars in taxes.

The stark figures prove that these tax payments will vastly exceed the cost of public assistance, even for those very rare children (no more than two out of a hundred)[86] who spend their entire childhood on welfare. For the baby of a typical teenage welfare mother who spends less than three years on public assistance before becoming self-supporting, Table 6-4 shows that the present value in 1983 dollars of the expected future taxes paid by that child during his adult life is 3.6 times as great as the present value of the public assistance costs incurred on his behalf. In other words, the public assistance expenditures made on behalf of these dependent children are investments in human capital that promise high rates of return to the public over long periods of time.

Even if we use the inflated costs, high ratios, and duration of welfare dependence of the more flagrant studies, the conclusion holds true. For example, the $8 billion teenage pregnancy "costs" announced by Robbins still yield a benefit-to-cost ratio of 2.2 when compared with the present discounted value of the expected lifetime tax payments to be made by the children in question. In general, any public investment having a benefit-to-cost ratio greater than one is regarded as acceptable, since its benefits will pay for its costs. In this example, the ratio indicates that the public

---

[85] Martha S. Hill and Michael Ponza, "Poverty and Welfare Dependence Across Generations", *Economic Outlook USA* (Ann Arbor: The University of Michigan Survey Research Center), vol. 10, no. 3, Summer 1983, p. 64.

[86] Duncan, op cit., p. 75.

Table 6-4
Public Benefit-Cost Calculation for a Baby of a Teenage AFDC Mother, 1983

Expected Public Benefits		Expected Public Costs	
Expected average annual tax		Cost of delivery	$ 2,174**
payment during adulthood	$ 5,394	Annual public assistance costs,	
Total expected taxes to be paid		1983, for mother and child***	
during lifetime	$253,518	AFDC cash payment	$ 2,567
Present discounted value* in		Food stamps	971
1983 of total taxes	$56,031	Medical costs	906
		School lunch	200
		Housing assistance	834
		Total annual costs	$ 5,478
		Present discounted value* of	
		costs of delivery and annual	
		public assistance for 2½ years	$15,451

$$\frac{\text{Benefit}}{\text{Cost}} \text{Ratio} = \frac{\text{Present value of taxes to be paid}}{\text{Present value of public assistance costs}} = \frac{\$56,031}{\$15,451} = 3.6$$

*Discounted at 4 percent real rate.

**Estimated from actual Medicaid costs in Califronia, 1980, corrected by 1983 medical care price index.

***Estimated from actual payments and numbers of recipients reported in *Statistical Abstract of the U.S.: 1984*, and *Social Security Bulletin.*

benefits of teenage births will pay over twice their public costs, even when the costs are exaggerated. This benefit-to-cost ratio is significantly higher than those typical of public investments.

The same reasoning applies to the frequent allegations that abortion is the "economical solution" to teenage pregnancy. To overlook the potential benefits of the lives destroyed, and calculate only the costs "saved" by eliminating the living is, if logically pursued, a good reason to abolish all human life, and patently foolish. They even fail on their own grounds, in their attempts to put a monetary value on human life. For if we subtract from the typical child's future earnings[87] his cost-of-living over his lifetime,[88] and express future dollars at their present value, using a 4 percent real rate of discount, the net present value of the life of a new baby in 1983 amounts to about $70,000. This represents the value in dollars of 1983 purchasing power of the lifelong contribution the child will make to society's wealth. It is a broader measurement than just the taxes he will pay, because

[87] Assuming average real weekly earnings as in 1983. Since this forecast does not take into account probable future increases in average worker productivity, it is probably an *underestimate* of both future earnings and future taxes paid.

[88] Based on cost-of-living allowances for foster children in California and family budgets as estimated by the U.S. Bureau of Labor Statistics in *Statistical Abstract of the U.S.: 1982–83*, p. 465.

it includes all his productivity minus his own maintenance—the value of his taxes together with his personal additions to his family's and the nation's wealth. It is the net present value of the financial loss caused by an abortion. Multiplying this figure by the 450,000 annual abortions now performed on women under 20, the *net costs* of teenage abortion amount to $32 billion annually, and those of the 1.5 million abortions to all women reach a staggering $105 billion annually.

It might be posited that the lives destroyed by abortion could be replaced later under more propitious circumstances for both society and the families. Leaving aside the moral objection, it begs the question by assuming what has not been shown to be the case—that the circumstances of the children in question are "inferior" to those of other children. It further assumes that abortion has no effects on subsequent fertility, also untrue, since significant research testifies that abortion reduces subsequent fertility and affects it in various adverse ways, on which more later.

The publicists of the adolescent pregnancy epidemic splice their case for government intervention with a mixture of careful selection, arrangement, and presentation of assumptions and data. A good part of their case has rested on obstetrical behavior according to age, long familiar to experts in the field. Older obstetrics books have routinely noted, for example, that maternal mortality rises with the age of the mother,[89] as does the risk of Down's syndrome in the baby,[90] though the risks are still surprisingly low at any age, despite the recent fuss. The maternal mortality rate for women aged 35–39 was 2 per 10,000 live births in 1983, though it was several times as high as for those in their twenties and younger.[91]Similarly, the risk of a Down's syndrome baby was reported to be 1 in 100 for mothers of age 40, compared with less than 1 in 1,000 for women up to age 30.[92]It is also well-known that the incidence of breast cancer is lowest among women who have had a first child while under the age of 20.[93]

Far from showing greatly elevated risks for younger mothers, the data showed the converse. As Nortman noted, " . . . by age 18 or 19, the human female may be at or close to her prime physical condition for reproduction."[94] She nevertheless speculated—she never, of course, proved—that risks were higher for women under 18. Other investigators differ. The physicians Semmens and Lamers studied a large number of teenage pregnancies and found that "complications are rare",

[89] Louis M. Hellman et al., *Williams Obstetrics,* 14th ed. (New York: Appleton-Century-Crofts, 1971), p. 5.

[90] Ibid., p. 1064.

[91] National Center for Health Statistics, *Vital Statistics of the United States,* 1983, vol. II–Mortality, Part A.

[92] Hellman et al., op. cit., p. 1073.

[93] W. P. D. Logan, "Cancer of the Female Breast—International Mortality Trends", *World Health Statistics Report* 28: 232–251, World Health Organization, 1975.

[94] Nortman, op. cit., p. 4.

and that the incidence of prenatal death of the baby was only a fraction as high as in the general population.[95] The Rochester Adolescent Maternity Project studied predominantly black, inner-city teenagers averaging 16 at delivery—that is, a group, according to the new teaching, that would be expected to have a high rate of multiple problems. But they found no greater obstetric or neonatal risks among them than among women in their twenties.[96] A Johns Hopkins study, as reported in *Ob. Gyn. News,* found that "with optimal care, the outcome of an adolescent pregnancy can be as successful as the outcome of a nonadolescent pregnancy".[97]

Several investigators believe economic difficulties and limited access to health care have been primarily responsible for past maternal problems. As Hollingsworth noted, "The single most important factor determining a favorable or unfavorable pregnancy outcome is the economic level of the patient and her family."[98]

Undeterred, the spokesmen for the epidemic have not only continued their efforts but have apparently, in a number of cases, been carried away by their own managed news. Dr. Jane Hodgson, in a discussion of adolescent pregnancy at a conference of the National Abortion Federation in Washington, D.C., in 1980, actually called for compulsory abortion for young pregnant teenagers.[99]

The eugenic concerns of the antinatalists are never far beneath the surface. Sargent Shriver's call for "improving the quality of life and enhancing the biological product of this society" is a case in point.[100] Once again, the standardlessness of the population control movement leaps into view. What is "enhancement"? How can the "quality of life" be "improved"? Shriver's emphasis on "enhancing the biological product" is revealing and typical of the movement. Men of other ages believed that moral or spiritual excellence was the desired good, but the evangelical zeal of the government family planning leaders has been fired by the quest for physical perfection, however vaguely defined. All things being equal, no one wants more one-armed children to be born, but the quest for physical perfection carries its own perils, not the least of which are the problems of definition and permissible action. Planned Parenthood emphasizes the crucial importance of

[95] James P. Semmens, M.D., and William M. Lamers, Jr., M.D., *Teen-Age Pregnancy* (Springfield: Charles C. Thomas, 1968), pp. 93, 86.

[96] Elizabeth R. McAnarney, M.D., et al., "Obstetric, Neonatal and Psychosocial Outcome of Pregnant Adolescents", prepublication manuscript presented in part at the American Public Health Association meetings, Miami, Florida, October 21, 1976.

[97] "Pregnant Teens Needn't Bear Low Birth-Weight Infants", *Ob. Gyn. News,* vol. 14, no. 24, December 15, 1979.

[98] A. Karen Kessler Kreutner, M.D., and Dorothy Reycroft Hollingsworth, M.D., eds., *Adolescent Obstetrics and Gynecology* (Chicago: Yearbook Medical Publishers, Inc., 1978), p. 121.

[99] *MCCL News,* June 1980.

[100] Statement of Hon. Sargent Shriver, Chairman, International Advisory Board, Joseph and Rose Kennedy Institute for the Study of Human Reproduction and Bioethics, Georgetown University, in *Hearings* before the Select Committee on Population, "Fertility and Contraception in America", op. cit., p. 178.

"genetic screening", "amniocentesis and prenatal diagnosis", and, of course, abortion in its "Program for Improving Fertility Regulation".[101] The object of these activities, they say, is to "reduce incidence of retardation and of disability among infants".[102] But the organization fails to define either "retardation" or "disability", although it demands huge public funds to search out and destroy the targeted infants.

The opposing moral view, holds that these infants cannot be destroyed, being members of the human race with the full rights accorded to all persons. But the eugenic views of such groups as Planned Parenthood insist that human beings meet some standards of quality, *pass a test,* before they can claim their human rights. The traditional view expressed in our country by Jefferson in the Declaration of Independence is that human beings are *endowed* with rights by virtue of their humanity alone, not by reason of the captious standards of others. These rights are the unalienable gift of a divine Creator who holds all men to be of equal and inestimable value. That is, the value of a human being is intrinsic, not conditional; his entitlement to human rights does not depend on the eugenic norms of any man.

Once, however, the doctrine that we should "improve our biological product" by regulating fertility and destroying human beings with "disabilities" is adopted, enormous problems, even of a practical nature, emerge. What is the test? Who makes it up? Who decides what constitutes a passing grade? When customary ethics are attacked and destroyed, someone must and will impose a new orthodoxy. If in the name of "progress" or "freedom" traditional values are abandoned, new values will fill the void and, as history attests, they are usually more harshly enforced.

The eugenic energies of the family planners are, unfortunately, not consumed by their quest for physical perfection. The literature on adolescent pregnancy bristles with concern over the fertility of the "lower" classes[103] and the "low socio-economic" groups.[104] The slick magazines and booklets abound with photographs of dark-skinned young women, obviously poor, and just as obviously pregnant.

Frederick S. Jaffe and Joy G. Dryfoos of the Guttmacher Institute put it this way: "With the overall decline in fertility in the United States, concern has shifted from numbers of births to insuring that those children being born have fewer physical, social, and economic handicaps."[105] Jaffe and Dryfoos offer no definition of these "handicaps", but are content to refer vaguely to the "adverse health,

---

[101] *Planned Births, the Future of the Family and the Quality of American Life,* op. cit., Table 1.
[102] Ibid.
[103] Furstenberg, Jr., op. cit., pp. 269, 275.
[104] Alan Guttmacher Institute, *Teenage Pregnancy: The Problem That Hasn't Gone Away,* op. cit., p. 30.
[105] Frederick S. Jaffe and Joy G. Dryfoos, "Fertility Control Services for Adolescents: Access and Utilization", in Chilman, op. cit., p. 129.

economic, social, and emotional outcomes" of adolescent pregnancy.[106] They are ambiguous as to whether a "handicap" is an undefined something more likely to increase by being born to a mother under 20, or whether being born to a mother under 20 is by definition a handicap. The authors also comment on the "low-income attitudes and practices toward fertility control and ... black attitudes toward abortion"[107] that have perennially disconcerted the government family planners. Obscurity again overcomes the authors: do they believe these conditions increase the likelihood of handicap? Are they themselves the handicap? These are hardly quibbles—they go to the very heart of what can be tolerated as our country's public policy.

It makes a profound difference whether the official position holds that the young, the poor, and the black are prone to be disadvantaged; or that youth, and blackness, are themselves the disadvantage—are, in themselves, an inferiority. A policy of helping young women with the difficulties of motherhood is utterly distinct from a policy to stamp out the children of young women. A policy to help overcome the handicaps associated with being poor or black is a far cry from a policy to exterminate births among the poor and the black.

Jaffe and Dryfoos, in common with government family planners generally, claim that the object of their programs is to prevent "unintended" pregnancies by providing suitable "access" to fertility control. Here again the troubling problem of definitions arises. What is an "unintended" pregnancy? Throughout the population discussions, the words "unwanted", "unplanned", "unintended", "born out-of-wedlock", and even "conceived out-of-wedlock", have for years been used interchangeably, without definition, and in the face of repeated protests.[108] An unintended pregnancy rarely results in an unwanted child, nor does a pregnancy conceived out-of-wedlock. The fact that at present an estimated 96 percent of unwed mothers under the age of 20 keep their children, despite the demand for adoptable babies, surely suggests that few babies are unwanted.

There has, moreover, been a dismal failure to find the dread effects stemming from these "unwanted" or "unintended" pregnancies, as admitted by Pohlman[109] and noted by Ford. [110] The norm is otherwise—most births always have resulted from unintended pregnancies.[111]

---

[106] Ibid.

[107] Ibid., p. 148.

[108] Juan Ryan, Statement, Hearing before the Subcommittee on Public Health and Welfare of the Committee on Interstate and Foreign Commerce, "Family Planning Services", U.S. House of Representatives, 91st Congress 2nd Session, Serial No. 91–70 (Washington: U.S. Government Printing Office, 1970), pp. 448–453.

[109] E. H. Pohlman, *Psychology of Birth Planning* (Cambridge: Schenkman Publishing, 1969), p. 332.

[110] James Ford, M.D., Testimony before United States Senate Committee on Labor and Human Resources, March 31, 1981.

[111] Ford, op. cit., Part II, p. 5.

The question of "access" to fertility control is also equivocal. As already pointed out, the present literature and the practice of government family planning does away with any pretense that making the means of birth control available is, if it ever was, adequate. "Motivation" is the new operative word, and it denotes further largesse by the government. The new sex programs, on top of telling young people where they can get their preventive appliances and services, pursue the young pregnant to "find them where they are" with "intensive, one-on-one" counseling. These programs have served their purpose—fertility has succumbed to high levels of abortion.[112] William Ball made plain more than a decade ago that the public programs of family planning contained no guarantees against coercion,[113] and as actions since attest, it was not idle oversight but the result of design.

Can Government "Solve" Teenage Pregnancy?

The common thread running through almost all of the recent adolescent-pregnancy debates has been the bland assumption that government has the responsibility somehow to solve or alleviate what a coterie has chosen to consider a malignancy. Even when the disputable nature of the statistics is recognized, there are those who insist that the problem of "children . . . having children" (whatever that means) is such that "it would be irresponsible to ignore teenage pregnancy" and, therefore, that government action is justifiable.[114] One essential question is not only unanswered but unasked—whether, even if you grant that adolescent pregnancy is a problem, government can improve matters.

The record is far from reassuring. During the period between the late 1960s and the early 1980s, the government-subsidized family-planning/sex-education effort expanded at an unprecedented rate. The Guttmacher Institute, whose figures on federal spending are often more accurate than those of the government (perhaps because it receives so much of it), reports that expenditures swelled from $13.5 million in 1968 to $279 million in one decade, a nineteen-fold increase. And by 1981, state and federal outlays had bloated to $377.5 million.[115] Again citing the Guttmacher Institute, the enrollment of teenagers in family-planning clinics grew by seven times between 1970 and 1979.[116] Frederick Jaffe, president of the Institute, estimated in 1978 that of 11 million nonvirgin teenagers in the United

[112] Edward A. Brann et al., "Strategies for the Prevention of Pregnancy in Adolescents", reprinted by the U.S. Department of Health, Education, and Welfare, Public Health Service, from *Advances in Planned Parenthood,* vol. 14, no. 2, 1979.

[113] Ball, op. cit.

[114] Gilbert Y. Steiner, *The Futility of Family Policy* (Washington: The Brookings Institution, 1981), pp. 71–88.

[115] Alan Guttmacher Institute, *Informing Social Change* (New York: The Alan Guttmacher Institute, 1980), p. 7; *Family Planning Perspectives,* vol. 14, no. 4, July/August 1982, p. 200.

[116] *Family Planning Perspectives,* vol. 13, no. 3, May/June 1981, p. 108.

States only 2 million, or less than one-fifth, lacked "access" to family planning services.[117] Since contraceptives were by this time available in drug stores, markets, and public restrooms, and given the enormous expansion in the school sex education programs, it is hard to believe that any teenager could possibly lack "access".

And what was the result of this unprecedented expansion of public birth-control services to teenagers? As mentioned, and whether for good or bad, fertility among women under 20 had been declining since 1957. But unambiguous signs revealed that all was not well. Surveys divulged sharp increases in sexual activity among unwed young people. Zelnik and Kantner reported:

> The proportion of U.S. teenage women residing in metropolitan areas who have had premarital sexual experience rose from 30 percent in 1971 to 43 percent in 1976 and to 50 percent in 1979 ... The proportion of all teenage women who have ever been premaritally pregnant rose from nine percent in 1971 to 13 percent in 1976 and to 16 percent in 1979 ... [118]

They reported more grim news—though the use of contraceptives, as well as abortion, was increasing, the premarital pregnancy rate was increasing even faster than the rising level of premarital sex activity, and there was even "a rise between 1976 and 1979 in the proportion of premarital pregnancies occurring among those who reported that they had always used a contraceptive method ... "[119] This, of course, was precisely the sort of thing that government promotion of family planning was supposed to correct.

Though the Zelnik-Kantner findings were based on questionnaires, the least reliable source of information, national vital statistics disclosed the same disturbing trends. Chart 6-4 shows the increase in teenage pregnancy and abortion rates along with the decline in birth rates during the 1970s. There was, moreover, as previously noted, a sharp increase in the proportion of out-of-wedlock births to teenage mothers. The rising trends in pregnancies and abortions were charted by the Guttmacher Institute in its booklet *Teenage Pregnancy: The Problem That Hasn't Gone Away*, which was prepared in time for the 1981 congressional hearings on federal funding for family planning and was supplied not only to members of Congress but to every school board in the nation and various other key people.[120] The headline over the Guttmacher chart proclaimed, quite misleadingly, that

---

[117] Frederick S. Jaffe, Testimony in *Hearings* before the Select Committee on Population, "Fertility and Contraception in America", op. cit., pp. 537–550.

[118] Melvin Zelnik and John F. Kantner, "Sexual Activity, Contraceptive Use and Pregnancy Among Metropolitan-Area Teenagers: 1971–1979", *Family Planning Perspectives*, vol. 12, no. 5, September/October 1980, p. 230.

[119] Ibid.

[120] Alan Guttmacher Institute, *Teenage Pregnancy: The Problem That Hasn't Gone Away*, op. cit., pp. 18–19.

"Better Use of Contraceptives Brings Teen Pregnancy Down".[121] Since teen pregnancy was rising tangibly, how could the authors claim the opposite, with a second chart in support? The strategy was to express total pregnancies, both marital and premarital, as a rate per the number of women estimated to be sexually active. Thus *by dividing the rising number of teen pregnancies by the rising numbers of teenage women estimated to be sexually active,* Planned Parenthood manufactured the appearance of a success!

At the same congressional hearings, Susan Roylance presented other and disturbing statistics. Her figures, some of which are reproduced in Table 6-5, showed that the adolescent-pregnancy rate in the United States, calculated as the sum of the birth rate and the abortion rate for this age group, had increased by 36 percent during the decade of the 1970s, moving upward closely behind the annual federal expenditures on family planning. The statistical correspondence between expenditures in given years and adolescent pregnancy two years later was very high, yielding a correlation coefficient of .882 for the cross-lag correlation.[122] Although Mrs. Roylance did not make this calculation, her chart and figures indicate that, in the late 1970s, every additional million dollars granted to the family planners by the federal government was followed in two years by another two thousand adolescent pregnancies.

Even more damaging to the programs was another Roylance demonstration: in fifteen states with similar social-demographic characteristics and rates of teenage pregnancy in 1970, those with the highest expenditures on family planning showed the largest increases in abortions and illegitimate births among teenagers between 1970 and 1979.[123]

At the same committee hearings, other testimony corroborated Roylance's findings. The adolescent pregnancy rate—that is, the rate of births plus the rate of abortions—had declined between 1957 and 1971, at which time the new federally funded sex programs began to expand in earnest, and at which time there began a step-by-step increase in adolescent pregnancy. Although fertility—that is, live births per thousand women of age 15 to 19—continued downward, the pregnancy rate—that is, births plus abortions per thousand women—began to increase.[124] The reason, of course, that the increasing pregnancies did not result in higher fertility was that the teenage abortion rate increased explosively after 1972, so that by the end of the decade 45 percent of all pregnancies among teenagers were being aborted. And as Charts 6-1 and 6-4 and Table 6-5 show, even these high levels of abortion barely counteracted the upward surge in teen pregnancies so that *after*

[121] Ibid., p. 19.

[122] Susan Roylance, Testimony before the United States Senate Committee on Labor and Human Resources, March 31, 1981.

[123] Ibid.

[124] Jacqueline R. Kasun, Testimony before the United States Senate Committee on Labor and Human Resources, March 31, 1981.

ADOLESCENT PREGNANCY

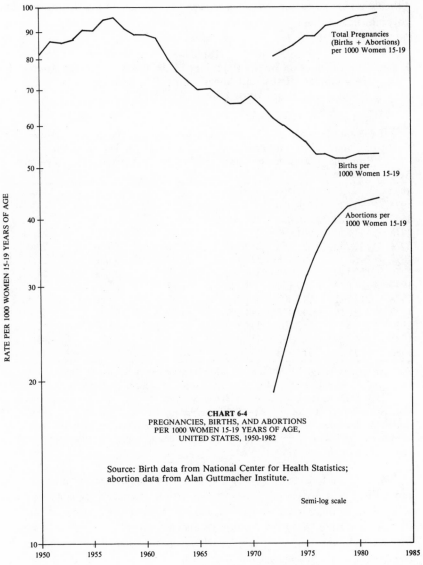

RATE PER 1000 WOMEN 15-19 YEARS OF AGE

Total Pregnancies
(Births + Abortions)
per 1000 Women 15-19

Births per
1000 Women 15-19

Abortions per
1000 Women 15-19

CHART 6-4
PREGNANCIES, BIRTHS, AND ABORTIONS
PER 1000 WOMEN 15-19 YEARS OF AGE,
UNITED STATES, 1950-1982

Source: Birth data from National Center for Health Statistics;
abortion data from Alan Guttmacher Institute.

Semi-log scale

1976 there were no further declines in teenage fertility, despite massive increases in government spending.

Table 6-5

Federal Expenditures on Family Planning; Births and Abortions to Women 15–19; Pregnancies, Births, and Abortions per Thousand Women 15–19, United States, 1970–1982

Year	Federal Expenditures on Family Planning ($ millions)	Births to Women 15–19	Abortions to Women 15–19	Pregnancies per Thousand Women 15–19	Births per Thousand Women 15–19	Abortions per Thousand Women 15–19
1970	—	644,708	—	68.32	68.32	—
1971	80,000	628,000	—	64.66	64.66	—
1972	99,420	616,280	191,000	81.22	62.01	19.22
1973	137,280	604,096	231,890	82.61	59.69	22.91
1974	142,780	595,466	279,700	85.36	58.08	27.28
1975	148,220	582,238	325,780	87.77	56.28	31.49
1976	157,140	558,744	362,680	88.26	53.52	34.74
1977	184,620	559,154	397,720	91.87	53.69	38.19
1978	217,771	543,407	418,790	92.82	52.42	40.40
1979	233,031	549,472	444,600	94.7	52.3	42.4
1980	298,572	552,161	444,800	95.7	53.0	42.7
1981	324,977	527,392	433,000	96.0	52.7	43.3
1982	326,000	513,758	430,000	97.2	52.9	44.3

SOURCE: Figures for 1970–1978 from Susan Roylance testimony before U.S. Senate Committee on Labor and Human Resources, March 31, 1981, based on data from National Center for Health Statistics, U.S. Department of Health and Human Services, U.S. Bureau of the Census, and the Alan Guttmacher Institute; figures for 1979–1982 from National Center for Health Statistics and the Alan Guttmacher Institute. The figures for family-planning expenditures are estimates of certain categories of spending only. While they appear to be internally consistent, they are substantially smaller than other estimates of the same kinds of spending.

Not only did teenage pregnancy increase when the government intervened to control it, but it was subsequently discovered that teenage pregnancy *decreased* when visits to the government-funded family-planning clinics declined. In 1980 the state of Utah passed a law requiring parental consent for contraceptives given to minors. In the following year there was a decline in clinic attendance by teenagers, and the pregnancy rate—which had been increasing among girls of 15–17—declined for the age-group, as did abortion and birth rates.[125]

These facts are indisputable. For some, they clearly demonstrate the failure of the public programs and the justification for their termination. For those holding this view, the fact that the burgeoning pregnancy rates are joined inexorably to

[125] Press release by United Families of America, March 8, 1983, quoting figures from Utah Department of Health.

expanding premarital sex activity, which has led to ballooning abortion rates, constitutes the final nails in the coffin for the public programs. The problems the promoters are facing are those they have created, which in turn are defying their stratagems to correct them.

It is here that the debate is joined, but it unveils a shift in perspective. For in the public family planners' claim that the programs have not failed *because adolescent fertility has declined,* lies the true impulse of the movement. Only now does a Guttmacher author, who admits that pregnancy has increased, call reduction in fertility "an especially stringent criterion".[126] Numerous recent statements and publications by spokesmen for the public family-planning lobby have finally admitted that, in their view, the primary object is not to prevent or alleviate pregnancy, but to reduce fertility. The president of Planned Parenthood, for example, testified at the 1981 Senate hearings that the public family-planning program had succeeded because it had prevented "1.4 million unwanted births" in a six-year period.[127]

A major statistical study written by Jacqueline Darroch Forrest and published by the Guttmacher Institute in 1980 credited the U.S. family-planning programs with reducing adolescent fertility. How far proponents are willing to go appears in an earlier article by Jacqueline Forrest and John Ross, in which they describe the effects of such strategies as giving or withholding food and jobs as incentives for abiding by the officially prescribed quota of children.[128]

In the same vein, the previously mentioned article by Hollingsworth and Kreutner spoke favorably of the public programs that provide "intensive, one-to-one, 'find-them-where-they-are'" counseling for young pregnant women as an effective solution to fertility. They described such a program in St. Paul, Minnesota, and one in San Bernardino, California, where the health department gave "one-to-one counseling sessions for adolescents who came to the department for pregnancy tests". The "easy access to abortion" combined with "active worker involvement" —read, the aggressive promotion of abortion—did the job.[129] A local outfit applied for a grant to send social workers out in their cars to corral young pregnant women for intensive "counseling"[130]—again, abortion.

An article by Brann et al in 1979 described the methods used in various "model" programs, such as one in St. Paul, where a federally funded family

[126] Jacqueline Darroch Forrest, *Exploration of the Effects of Organized Family Planning Programs in the United States on Adolescent Fertility,* Final Report, Alan Guttmacher Institute, October 1980, p. 26.

[127] Faye Wattleton, Testimony before the Appropriations Subcommittee on Labor, Health, and Human Services and Education, U.S. Senate, March 16, 1981, p. 2.

[128] Jacqueline Darroch Forrest and John A. Ross, "Fertility Effects of Family Planning Programs: A Methodol`gcal Review", *Social Biology,* vol. 25, Summer 1978, pp. 145–163.

[129] Hollingsworth and Kreutner, "Teenage Pregnancy: Solutions Are Evolving", op. cit.

[130] Humboldt–Del Norte Health Department, Grant Application for "Adolescent Parenting Project", no. 13.975, March 11, 1980, pp. 2, 16, 18, 58.

planning and abortion referral clinic has since 1973 operated within the Mechanic Arts Junior-Senior High School and two other high schools. The article reports that "students who miss appointments are called to the clinic", and that "members of the staff . . . reach most students in the classrooms during the year." It has achieved a remarkable reduction in births.[131]

The Brann article also approves of the San Bernardino program, where "four full-time social workers . . . conduct one-to-one, in-school follow-up counseling sessions with adolescent women who come to the health department for a pregnancy test." The methods are termed "activist"—i.e., "within one week of their health department visit, students are contacted at their school by what appears to classmates to be a routine call to visit the nurse or guidance personnel". Almost none of the girls so "contacted" has refused to "participate", most especially since the social workers make an average of "three to four visits per student".[132] In Hackensack, New Jersey, Planned Parenthood and other family planners boasted a 74 percent rate of abortions on pregnant teenagers. This remarkable federally funded Operation Cleansweep was executed, according to the Brann article, by means of an extremely energetic "outreach" program that coordinated the pressures of the schools, the health department, and several family planning and abortion clinics.[133]

The methods of the controllers are obviously "activist". The pregnant teenager, faced with repeated summons from the school authorities and counseling sessions with public health department officials, is at the least intimidated, if not coerced. Even young married women have been subjected to intense pressure to choose abortion.[134] But since the methods are deemed "successful", their dubious ethics are swept aside.

This claim of "success" deserves examination on its own grounds—that is, the assumption that government has the right to reduce adolescent fertility.

But first, if the assumption is granted, have the programs really reduced fertility? We know that fertility had been falling steeply for some time before the programs began, and that it continued to drop *until 1976 but has not fallen since.* The increase in teen pregnancy that began when the new sex programs were introduced finally swamped even the explosive increase in teen abortions, so that teen fertility has remained at approximately the same level since 1976. This, together with the fact that premarital sex activity has increased so sharply among teenage women and that they are increasingly reporting contraceptive "failure", suggests that their fertility might be lower, or at least no higher, if there were no programs at all.

The states that spend the least on family planning also have the lowest rates of

[131] Brann, et al., op. cit.
[132] Ibid.
[133] Ibid., p. 75.
[134] Personal interviews with the author.

teenage abortion and out-of-wedlock births.[135] A comparison between the United States in the early 1970s and two subareas where family planning was enthusiastically promoted—California and Humboldt County—is enlightening. Between 1970 and 1976 teenage fertility declined in the nation and in the two subareas to the same level of 50–55 births per thousand women aged 15–19. But in California, the pregnancy rate among this group rose twenty times as much as the national rate, and in Humboldt County, forty times as much. In both areas the excess pregnancies were aborted, at rates almost twice as high as for the nation, with the result that fertility in 1976 was the same in all three areas.

The data suggest that what the government programs have chiefly done is to influence the means by which a reduction in fertility, which would have occurred in any case, was accomplished. The government programs have encouraged abortion. And, in doing so, they may have encouraged behavior that might not otherwise occur. For example, when the states of Ohio and Georgia stopped paying for abortions in 1977, not only abortions but births and pregnancies declined among Medicaid-eligible women.[136]

The advocates of government family planning insist that, from their early years, children should receive explicit, comprehensive sex education, and that by puberty, they should have complete birth control and abortion information, including the information that their parents can be kept from knowing about their use of the services.[137] The sex educators know—they admit it in writing—that such explicit instruction is arousing.[138] They must also know—though they do not admit—that the natural outcome is an increase in sex activity, which they duly report so as to propose that they neutralize it by contraception, sterilization, and abortion.

There is no proof, then, nor even any strong indication, that the recent government infusions of money cause a decline in adolescent fertility. The decline may more reasonably have occurred due to the same social and economic factors that account for later marriage. The chief effects of the government programs have probably been to encourage abortions to terminate the pregnancies incited by the programs themselves.

Second, even if you can still assume that the programs have been effective, are the costs acceptable? Do the programs stimulate sex activity and, in consequence, increase the cost of reducing fertility? That would, of course, be to the economic

---

[135] Jacqueline R. Kasun, *Teenage Pregnancy: What Comparisons among States and Countries Show* (Stafford, Virginia: American Life League, 1986).

[136] Jacqueline R. Kasun, "Cutoff of Abortion Funds Doesn't Deliver Welfare Babies", *Wall Street Journal,* December 30, 1986.

[137] Alan Guttmacher Institute, *Teenage Pregnancy: The Problem that Hasn't Gone Away,* op. cit., pp. 64–68.

[138] Robert Crooks and Karla Baur, *Our Sexuality* (Menlo Park: The Benjamin/Cummings Publishing Company, Inc., 1980), pp. 204–206.

advantage of the family planners, for they can create constantly growing markets for their contraceptive and abortion and "counseling" services. An "actively-involved" abortion counselor must seem impressive to a young girl. And, how measure the cost of such matters as giving youngsters ready access to contraceptives and abortions without their parents' knowledge?

The increasingly frank and heavy reliance on abortion as a "solution" must surely raise questions. In 1973, the first year of legalized abortion-on-demand in the United States, less than 28 percent of adolescent pregnancies were aborted. By 1980 the ratio had risen to 45 percent. And the rates rise steeply where public urgings are intense. In California, for example, almost 60 percent of teenage pregnancies are aborted.[139]

Though the adolescent pregnancy controllers have reported exhaustively on the spurious dangers of youthful motherhood, they have been remarkably sanguine regarding the effects of abortion. They do not, in fact, hesitate to proclaim frequently that abortion is safer than motherhood,[140] even though there is a large body of statistical data and medical literature charging abortion with some serious and lasting physical and psychological effects, perhaps especially on younger women. These begin with the injuries or even deaths during the abortion itself. A leading California abortionist was ingenuously open about the risks when he appeared at a state legislative hearing to testify on a proposed change in the state payment for abortions. Dr. Kenneth Wright, operator of several large-scale abortion facilities, enumerated the hazards of "perforation of the uterus, laceration of the cervix, the injury to the bowel, injury to the bladder, the hemorrhage, the infection . . . those things you're all aware of". He continued,

> The other thing you may not be aware of is the cervix has to be handled with delicacy and care because while a woman may be receiving a therapeutic abortion at the time and be well, her subsequent child-bearing capabilities may be impaired by microlacerations . . . If that cervix is injured, there may be problems encountered in future childbearing. She may have repeated spontaneous abortions due to incompetent cervical os.[141]

He went on to describe the procedure performed on young girls: " . . . the cervix is infantile in many cases. It's very snug. It is not meant physiologically for dilation." He stated that abortions after the sixteenth week of gestation of the baby are especially difficult:

[139] Alan Guttmacher Institute, *Teenage Pregnancy: The Problem That Hasn't Gone Away,* op. cit., Factbook, p. 31.

[140] See, for example, Willard Cates' speech to adolescent pregnancy conference sponsored by Johns Hopkins University School of Medicine, reported in *Family Practice News,* vol. 10, no. 2; also Christopher Tietze and Marjorie Cooper Murstein, *Induced Abortion: 1975 Factbook* (New York: Population Council, 1975), p. 61. ·

[141] Dr. Kenneth Wright, Testimony, Official Transcript of Public Hearing on Regulations, California State Department of Health Services, March 25, 1980, pp. 31–35.

Some of it is distasteful, but the facts are that the parts are now large and they are hard ... There are large grasping instruments which must be used to remove parts ... Again, we don't even know yet whether we are causing in these women a situation which might exist for them to have repeated spontaneous miscarriages.[142]

He noted that the saline solution procedure, which is used in late abortions, is "hazardous and potentially lethal". Dr. Wright's testimony, based on what he referred to as his professional experience with "literally hundreds of thousands of women", is, as we shall see, at variance with the latest findings emerging from the government-funded research of the family-planning statistical experts. But more of that later.

At the same hearing Alison Lohnberg also appeared, identifying herself as the administrator of an abortion clinic. She too mentioned the "risk of puncture of the uterus, bowel injury, and possible hemorrhage", especially during abortions performed in the second trimester. She added that among women having abortions, "guilt, depression, anger, and fear are all common reactions ... which, without counseling, stands (sic) a good chance of never being resolved. A woman could conceivably be scarred for the rest of her life ... "[143] Along with Dr. Wright, Mrs. Lohnberg seems to have been too busy with a large clinical practice to keep up with the absolutions granted by the most recent findings of the federally funded statisticians.

Lending credence to Wright's and Lohnberg's testimony, Christopher Tietze of the Population Council estimated that in the early 1970s in the United States over 12 percent of all abortion patients had complications. The rates varied from less than 10 percent of women having abortions in the first trimester to more than a third of those who aborted later in pregnancy. About 6.5 percent of the women having complications had major difficulties—cardiac arrest, convulsions, endotoxic shock, hemorrhage, injury to the bladder, ureter or intestines, pulmonary embolism, thrombophlebitis, death.[144]

The long-run effects of abortion have been extensively documented. Women who have had abortions have been found to have an elevated probability of delivering subsequent babies prematurely.[145] In various study groups, the propor-

---

[142] Ibid.

[143] Alison Lohnberg, Testimony, Official Transcript of Public Hearing on Regulations, op. cit., pp. 110–115.

[144] Christopher Tietze, *Induced Abortion: 1979*, 3rd ed. (New York: The Population Council, 1979), pp. 79–81.

[145] Leslie Iffy, M.D., et al., "Perinatal Statistics: The Effect Internationally of Liberalized Abortion", in Thomas W. Hilgers, M.D., et al., *New Perspectives on Human Abortion* (Frederick, Maryland: University Publications of America, 1981), pp. 92–127; S. Harlap and A. M. Davies, "Late Sequelae of Induced Abortion: Complications and Outcome of Pregnancy and Labor", *American Journal of Epidemiology*, vol. 102, no. 3, September 1975, pp. 217–224; T. W. Hilgers, M.D., *Abortion and Social Justice* (Thaxton: Sunlife, 1972).

tion of babies delivered prematurely varied between 40 percent higher to almost three times as high among mothers who had previously had induced abortions as compared with those who had not.[146] There is no dodging the facts, and the very real damage they do to the shibboleth that massive abortions performed on teenagers will improve the "biological product". Premature birth (usually measured by low birth-weight) is known to be significantly associated with mental retardation and other health problems,[147] and is, in fact, one of the most common arguments against adolescent motherhood.[148] The higher occurrence of premature babies to women who have undergone abortions should, for material reasons alone, undermine the position that abortion is a practical treatment for adolescent pregnancy.

Not surprisingly, the statistics involved, although reported in numerous studies, have been disputed. Chung and Steinhoff reported that they found no tendency in women who had aborted to deliver subsequent babies prematurely.[149] Daling and Emanuel, reporting on the results of their federally funded research at the University of Washington, contended that there were no higher levels of prematurity among babies born to women who had had abortions than among babies of other women. In fact, their research led them to "suggest the possibility" that, for women under 20, "abortion has a less deleterious effect than the natural completion of the first pregnancy".[150] These unique findings have not been corroborated by other scholars.

By way of repudiation, and in a larger study, using the method of multiple regression to control for demographic and health factors that might influence the outcome, Harlap and Davies found low birth-weight to be significantly associated with previous induced abortion.[151]

Similarly, one of the largest investigations into the effects of induced abortion, a six-year follow-up study of 20,000 New York women who underwent abortion in 1970–1971, showed that these women subsequently delivered a notably higher

[146] Iffy, op. cit.; John A. Richardson and Geoffrey Dixon, "Effects of Legal Termination on Subsequent Pregnancy", British Medical Journal, 1976, 1, pp. 1303–1304; Hungarian Central Statistical Office, "The Effect of the Number of Abortions on Premature Births and Perinatal Mortality in Hungary", Budapest, 1972; Marriage and Family Newsletter, vol. 4, nos. 2,3,4, February, March, April, 1973.

[147] Alan Guttmacher Institute, Teenage Pregnancy: The Problem That Hasn't Gone Away, op. cit., p. 29.

[148] Ibid.

[149] Chin Sik Chung and Patricia G. Steinhoff, et al., "The Effects of Induced Abortion on Subsequent Reproductive Function and Pregnancy Outcome: Hawaii" (Honolulu: The East West Population Institute, Paper no. 86, June 1983).

[150] Janet R. Daling and Irvin Emanuel, "Induced Abortion and Subsequent Outcome of Pregnancy in a Series of American Women", The New England Journal of Medicine, vol. 297, no. 23, December 8, 1977, pp. 1241–1245.

[151] Harlap and Davies, op. cit.

percentage of premature infants—61 percent higher—than a matched control group of women whose first babies were born live.[152] The study went on to discover other baneful consequences of abortion. The women who had abortions had rates of complications during subsequent pregnancies several times as high as those who did not.[153] There was a 53 percent greater incidence of fetal death within the group who had had abortions.[154] There was a 25 percent higher incidence of neonatal mortality among their babies and a 26 percent higher incidence of congenital malformations, although the authors did not view the latter results as statistically significant.[155]

The large study of Harlap and Davies also found that prior abortions were associated not only with significantly elevated prematurity rates, but with abnormally high neonatal deaths and malformations in children born subsequently. Other studies have similarly noted problems associated with a history of abortion.[156]

On the other hand, a number of articles, including one by the U.S. Department of Health, Education, and Welfare, have attributed the declining trends over time in prematurity, fetal deaths, and infant mortality to rising rates of abortion.[157] But a more recent statistical study rejects the hypothesis, and suggests the contrary— that the rising incidence of abortion has such adverse effects on subsequent pregnancies that it may increase fetal and infant mortality rates in the future.[158]

Nevertheless, the adolescent-pregnancy controllers doggedly insist that abortion is better for women than childbirth. One Planned Parenthood physician actually said that "since abortion is so much safer than childbirth, from a strict medical standpoint, every pregnancy should be aborted."[159]

True to the new orthodoxy, school sex programs stress that abortion is "a

---

[152] Vito M. Logrillo, et al., *Effect of Induced Abortion on Subsequent Reproductive Function, Final Report,* New York State Department of Health, Office of Biostatistics, April 18, 1980, Contract no. N01-HD-6-2802, National Institute of Child Health and Human Development, Table 43. The data cited are for white women. Separate computations for nonwhites were not statistically significant because of the small number of observations.

[153] Ibid., Table 49.

[154] Ibid., Table 58.

[155] Ibid., Table 52 and Table 61.

[156] See, for example, Ann Aschengrau Levin et al., "Association of Induced Abortion with Subsequent Pregnancy Loss", *Journal of the American Medical Association,* vol. 243, no. 24, June 27, 1980, pp. 2495–2499; also Richardson and Dixon, op. cit.

[157] For a review of this literature, see Karl E. Bauman and Ann E. Anderson, "Legal Abortions and Trends in Fetal and Infant Mortality Rates in the United States", *American Journal of Obstetrics and Gynecology,* vol. 136, no. 2, January 15, 1980, pp. 194–202.

[158] Ibid.

[159] Dr. Lise Fortier, address before Association of Planned Parenthood Physicians, 1980, reported in *Ob Gyn News,* December 1, 1980.

relatively safe, uncomplicated procedure"[160] whereas childbirth entails the "risk of death", or of bearing a child who is mentally retarded, afflicted with cerebral palsy, epilepsy, or an assortment of other dire maladies.[161]

One of the most indefatigable supporters of the doctrine is Willard Cates, Jr., former chief of the abortion surveillance branch at the U.S. Center for Disease Control. Dr. Cates has reported that mortality among teenagers giving birth is five times as high as among those having abortions.[162] This was countered by a careful statistical study of comparative mortality among women who have abortions at various stages of pregnancy and women who deliver babies, in which Thomas Hilgers and Dennis O'Hare concluded that natural pregnancy is safer than abortion in every stage of pregnancy.[163]

But despite the profuse evidence against abortion, the same claims that it is beneficial will continue to pour out from the same quarters as long as the federal government is willing to subsidize the myth.

On one point, there is virtually complete agreement—women who have had induced abortions bear fewer children after the fact than other women. The Guttmacher Institute reported in 1981 that only 10 percent of teenagers whose first pregnancies ended in abortion were pregnant again within a year, as compared with 17.5 percent of those whose first pregnancies resulted in a live birth.[164] The institute attributed this "at least in part" to the easy availability of contraceptives to those who had aborted.[165] But for years, investigators in many countries have reported on the comparative infertility of women who have had abortions.[166]

In line with this is the discovery that, as compared with women as a whole, several times as high a proportion of women being treated for infertility have had induced abortions.[167] The large New York study previously mentioned found that women who had aborted had 37 percent fewer pregnancies and less than half as many live births in the six following years than women who had not.[168] Further suggesting the consequences of rising abortion rates among teenagers, the National Survey of Family Growth conducted by the National Center for Health

---

[160] Planned Parenthood–Santa Cruz County, *Family Life Education: Teacher's Guide*, 1979, developed under contract with the U.S. Department of Health, Education, and Welfare, Grant #09-H-00260-08-0 FT-H70, p. 163.

[161] Ibid., p. 167.

[162] Reported in *Family Practice News*, vol. 10, no. 2.

[163] Thomas W. Hilgers, M.D., and Dennis O'Hare, "Abortion Related Maternal Mortality: An In-Depth Analysis", in Hilgers, et al., *New Perspectives on Human Abortion*, op. cit., pp. 69–91.

[164] The Alan Guttmacher Institute, *Teenage Pregnancy: The Problem That Hasn't Gone Away*, op. cit., p. 21.

[165] Ibid.

[166] Tietze and Murstein, *Induced Abortion: 1975 Factbook*, op.cit., p. 50.

[167] D. Trichopoulos, et al., "Induced Abortion and Secondary Infertility", *British Journal of Obstetrics and Gynecology*, vol. 83, August 1976, pp. 645–650.

[168] Logrillo et al., op. cit., p. 10.

Statistics found that the rate of infertility among American wives aged 20–24 almost tripled between 1965 and 1982 and that infertility rose most markedly among young black wives.[169] For the proponents of overpopulation, the benefits are real: abortion is a two-pronged weapon—it not only reduces fertility directly but it promises an adverse impact on subsequent fertility. Little wonder that Planned Parenthood and its companion, the Guttmacher Institute, demand that government give free access to abortions-on-demand.[170] In keeping with this rigid antinatalism, the Guttmacher Institute estimated that "at least" 579,000 women aged 15–19 "needed" abortions in 1978,[171] 160,000 more than those who had actually aborted. It would have added up to a majority of abortions for the total pregnancies of women under 20.

Though contraception and free abortion are most openly favored by government family planners, sterilization is a popular alternative. Currently more than 1 million men and women are sterilized annually in the United States, almost 30 percent more than during the early 1970s.[172] The federal government finances about 100,000 sterilizations through Medicaid each year,[173] the new sex education programs begin to laud their advantages in elementary school,[174] and free public vasectomy services are heavily advertised and promoted in communities with high concentrations of young people.[175]

State laws permit the sterilization of teenagers, and provide for compulsory sterilization in some cases.[176] In California, for example, young people can legally consent to their own sterilizations as early as age 18.[177] Federal regulations restrict federal funding for sterilization to patients who are at least 21 years old who have given informed consent, but violators, if they are detected, have only to return the federal funds. A consumer advocacy group reported in 1979 that seven out of ten

---

[169] William F. Pratt et al., "Understanding U.S. Fertility: Findings from the National Survey of Family Growth, Cycle III", *Population Bulletin*, vol. 39, no. 5, December 1984, pp. 27–28, published by the Population Reference Bureau. The survey defines infertility as the inability to conceive after a year of intercourse without contraception.

[170] Alan Guttmacher Institute, *Teenage Pregnancy: The Problem That Hasn't Gone Away*, op. cit., pp. 64–71.

[171] Ibid., p. 57.

[172] *Family Planning Perspectives*, vol. 12, no. 2, March/April 1980, p. 113.

[173] *Family Planning Perspectives*, vol. 11, no. 6, November/December 1979, pp. 366–367.

[174] *Arcata School District Family Life/Sex Education Curriculum Guide* (Arcata, California, June 1976).

[175] "How Men Can Help with Birth Control", informational brochure distributed by Everyman's Center to students at Humboldt State University; "Humboldt Open Door Clinic Presents Everyman's Center", distributed to students at Humboldt State University; "Vasectomies", in *Humboldt Life and Times*, November 12, 1980, distributed free to all residents of Arcata, home of Humboldt State University.

[176] Christian S. White IV, *Situation Report: Sterilization in the United States* (Stafford, Virginia: The American Life Lobby, 1981).

[177] California Civil Code 25.1, 34.5.

hospitals surveyed were violating the federal guidelines—sterilizing persons under 21 and without their informed consent—and even wresting "consent" from women in labor and under false pretenses.[178]

An audit of federally funded sterilizations performed in nine states in 1979–1980 discovered numerous cases where the federal law was being broken, and the nine states were asked to return nearly $1 million to the federal treasury.[179]

To return to the question of whether government can do anything about adolescent pregnancy, the answer is clearly yes. Though the government-subsidized adolescent pregnancy programs have shown no ability to prevent pregnancy—in fact, the more funding, the more pregnancies—they can abort pregnancy. The data show that the aggressive promotion of abortion through "intensive, one-on-one, find-them-where-they-are" pregnancy counseling is highly effective in the short run, with fewer subsequent children in the offing. But this solution is repugnant to a large number of people, to tax-paying citizens. And there is evidence that the whole gamut of government programs—sex education, free contraception, abortion—does not achieve anything that could not be attained without them.

No less a friend of population limitation than the sociologist Kingsley Davis has offered the opinion that "the problem of teenage pregnancy will not be solved by further promotion of contraception and abortion for children",[180] an opinion backed by empirical evidence. The facts also unearth that the costs are very high, not only in terms of money, but in terms of the health and welfare of our young people.

Filtered through the maze of statistics, a clear picture emerges. The publicly funded programs to combat adolescent pregnancy began with the desire of the population-control groups to reduce fertility among younger women. Substantial reductions in total fertility could result if the 15 percent or so of all births to women under 20 were eliminated. Accordingly, they launched their campaign to convert the public image of pregnancy among women under 20 from a natural phenomenon into an epidemic. With the aid of millions of federal dollars, a politicized research establishment operating within the hallowed halls of some leading universities, and the population organizations themselves, the campaign amassed and publicized spurious evidence condemning "teenage pregnancy" as a scourge. Though much of the evidence evaporates under dispassionate examination, the campaign grinds on, calling for special legislative initiatives and massive injections of public funding to combat the dread effects of the synthetic plague. In

---

[178] *Family Planning Perspectives,* vol. 11, no. 6, November/December 1979, pp. 366–367.

[179] U.S. Department of Health and Human Services, *State Assessment Guide: Abortion, Sterilization, and Family Planning,* 1979 and 1980.

[180] Kingsley Davis, "A Theory of Teenage Pregnancy in the United States", in Chilman, op. cit., p. 335.

near panic, Congress has established a publicly funded national sex industry, which presumes to educate the young, to form their values, and to deal with the fruits of their sexual lives. Their purposes are not only to restrict population growth, but, as they frankly acknowledge, to delve into eugenics.

Focusing on the young is essential to the aims of the movement. In order to foster a public belief in the need for the government to limit population and a tolerance for whatever methods this entails, the efficient way is to begin with children in the formative stage of life, whose attitudes and reproductive lives can be molded, and who can transmit the new orthodoxy to coming, though shrinking, generations. Critics of the policy object that the new sex programs are busily attempting to correct self-created problems. But there is a more fundamental reservation: should the government of a free society devote itself to manipulating the hearts and minds and bodies of its people in a direction dictated by special interest groups? Adolescent-pregnancy controllers have no standards of value, or of method, other than to reduce fertility, and to that end they do not hesitate to distort the facts or to use means that intimidate and flirt with coercion. Whether a campaign so authoritarian as to impose the ideology of a select group on the general population should be stamped with a government's approval and promoted with all its resources and power is the vital question.

CHAPTER SEVEN

THE MOVEMENT, ITS HISTORY, AND ITS LEADERS

When in 1900 the firm of Krupps sponsored a prize-essay competition on Social Darwinism, scholars joined in an outpouring of thought on the scientific discoveries of the nineteenth century and their implications for organizing society. Basing their ideas on the theories of Darwin, Spencer, Sumner, Galton, Pearson, and others, they postulated that progress was the central theme of history.

This view holds that man and society are continually evolving toward a better future by a natural process that, however, requires optimal conditions to operate beneficially. The problem with the modern state, the thinkers agreed, is that it clings to outmoded ideas that give precedence to the innate rights of the individual over his usefulness to society. Unless society is to be hopelessly burdened, even crippled, by caring for the poor, it must shed the socially inept, reimpose the equivalent of the process of natural selection, and ensure that its "biological product" is improved, not debased, by its social legislation.[1]

The nineteenth century had witnessed a revolution in social and scientific thought, with inevitable reverberations in the concept of population. Thomas Robert Malthus (1766–1834) first broached the subject with his notion that the size of the population must press against the limits of the food supply because of the breeding habits of the "lower classes of society". But Malthus stopped well short of the notion that government should adopt an antinatalist policy: "leave every man to his own free choice and responsible only to God for the evil which he does in either way; this is all I contend for; I would on no account do more . . . "[2] He believed that by denying the poor all charity, public or private, they would experience fully both the costs and benefits of their reproductive decisions and conform their marriages and childbearing with their earning abilities.[3] Before the end of his life, Malthus modified his opinions, but what has endured is the influence of his earlier work, especially his fear of excessive population growth.

Charles Darwin (1809–1882) acknowledged that he had been inspired by

---

[1] Helmut Krausnick, "Social Darwinism", in Helmut Krausnick et al., *Anatomy of the SS State* (New York: Walker and Co., 1968), pp. 10–19.

[2] Thomas Robert Malthus, *An Essay on the Principle of Population*, in Leonard Dalton Abbott, ed., *Masterworks of Economics*, 3 vols., (New York: McGraw-Hill Book Company, 1973), vol. 1, p. 228.

[3] Ibid.

Malthus[4] in his own study of the "struggle for existence" and the process by which "favorable variations . . . tend to be preserved and unfavorable ones to be destroyed".[5] But he did not apply his biological theories to the social and political life of man, and appeared not to understand those who did. He wrote to one of the German Social Darwinists that it had not occurred to him that his biological theories were applicable to social matters.[6] Others nevertheless proceeded to find in Darwin's theories what they were disposed to find, often with apparently contradictory results. Not only did supporters of unregulated business competition admire him but so did Marx, who proposed to dedicate the English translation of his *Das Kapital* to Darwin. (Darwin refused the honor.) Himmelfarb suggested that what these diverse admirers had in common was an affinity for the idea of struggle, unmitigated by the strictures of traditional ethics and religion, leading to human progress.[7] This apparent justification for throwing off time-honored religious and ethical restraints has appealed to many — not only aspiring business magnates, but revolutionary socialists, scientists yearning for more freedom to experiment, and assorted social planners as well.

It fell to Herbert Spencer (1820–1903) to coin the phrase "survival of the fittest"[8] and, in his *Social Statics*, to describe the process of competition by which optimal development occurs in social systems. The benefits derived from the competitive process, i.e., weeding out the unfit, led him to oppose any government interference that might frustrate the process.[9] Spencer and his ideas greatly inspired the business magnates of his time, such as John D. Rockefeller, Sr.[10]

William Graham Sumner (1840–1910), author of *Folkways* and other works,[11] had ideas similar to Spencer's regarding the benefits of competition. Both men illustrate the radical departure of Social Darwinism from Adam Smith's concept of competition. Smith held that *competition is good because it leads men to serve one another,* no matter their intent; whereas Spencer and Sumner considered competition good because it eliminates the "unfit", and with full intent. The Social Darwinist theory was embraced by the emerging private business monopolies that wanted to avoid government regulation, though not government subsidies. The vision of Smith was less benign toward big business, most especially toward the

[4] Abbott, op. cit., p. 185.

[5] Ibid.

[6] Gertrude Himmelfarb, *Darwin and the Darwinian Revolution* (New York: Doubleday Anchor Books, 1959), p. 390.

[7] Ibid., chap. 19.

[8] Herbert Spencer, *The Man Versus the State,* in *The Works of Herbert Spencer* (Osnabruck: Otto Zeller, 1966), vol. XI.

[9] Herbert Spencer, *Social Statics,* in *The Works,* op. cit.

[10] Allan Chase, *The Legacy of Malthus: The Social Costs of the New Scientific Racism* (New York: Alfred A. Knopf, 1977), p. 8.

[11] William Graham Sumner, *Folkways: A Study of the Sociological Importance of Usages, Manners, Customs, Mores, and Morals* (Boston: Ginn and Company, 1906).

marriage of big government and big business, perceiving that large combinations of public and private power posed a threat to the social interest.

Crucial to the Social Darwinists' theory was their view of individual human beings—not as creatures of innate worth and dignity, regardless of their earthly condition, but as factors on a scale of social value. Without hesitation or embarrassment, the Social Darwinists determined the scale itself and undertook to measure other men by it. Not surprisingly, those who shared the social and economic attributes of the movement's leaders rated highest.

The idea of natural selection encouraged the study of heredity and the statistical laws of probability that governed it. The statistician Sir Francis Galton (1822–1911) was the founder of the study of eugenics, or "good birth". As Chase recounts in his monumental history of scientific racism, Galton hoped by his research to give the "more suitable races or strains of blood a better chance of prevailing speedily over the less suitable".[12] He believed that blacks were genetically inferior,[13] that Jews were "parasitical",[14] and that poverty was transmitted in the genes.[15]

Karl Pearson (1857–1936), another statistician and a disciple of Galton, discussed "the sterilization of those sections of the community of small civic worth . . ."[16]

The notion that progress is achieved by the eugenic process of weeding out the unfit quickly took hold, and in 1907, as Chase recounts, Indiana passed the world's first compulsory sterilization law, aimed at "confirmed criminals, idiots, rapists, and imbeciles". Thirty states and Puerto Rico followed suit, drawing heavily from a Model Eugenical Law written by Harry Laughlin,[17] and have been charged with having inspired the Nazi compulsory sterilization laws.[18]

In 1912 the First International Congress of Eugenics was held at the University of London. Its vice-presidents included Winston Churchill, Charles Eliot (president emeritus of Harvard), David Starr Jordan (president of Stanford University), and other notables. Its goal: the "prevention of the propagation of the unfit".[19]

Subsequent congresses were held in 1921 and 1932, again attracting many of the luminaries of the time. The third congress, in 1932, featured a call for the

[12] Francis Galton, *Inquiries into Human Faculty* (London: Macmillan, 1883), pp. 24–25, quoted in Chase, op. cit., p. 13.

[13] Francis Galton, *Hereditary Genius: An Inquiry into Its Laws and Consequences* (New York: Horizon Press, 1952), pp. 326–328.

[14] Karl Pearson, *Life, Letters and Labours of Francis Galton*, 4 vols. (Cambridge, England: Cambridge University Press, 1914–40), vol. II, p. 209, quoted in Chase, op. cit., p. 14.

[15] Chase, op. cit., pp. 100–104.

[16] Pearson, op. cit., vol. III, pp. 218–220, quoted in Chase, op. cit., p. 15.

[17] Chase, op.cit., pp. 15–16.

[18] Elasah Drogin, "Margaret Sanger: Founder of Modern Society", reprinted from *International Review of Natural Family Planning*, vol. 3, no. 2, Summer 1979.

[19] Chase, op. cit., p. 19.

sterilization of 14 million Americans with low intelligence-test scores.[20]

One of the most energetic and enthusiastic eugenicists of the time was Margaret Sanger (1883–1966), founder of Planned Parenthood. Reputedly called by H. G. Wells "the greatest woman in the world",[21] Sanger imbibed deeply of the prevailing views on the importance of "a good birth". Early in her career of spreading birth control information and services to the poor, Sanger concluded that their greatest handicap was their biological inheritance, as Drogin documents in her careful biography.

In 1919 Sanger wrote in her magazine, *Birth Control Review*, "More children from the fit, less from the unfit—that is the chief issue of birth control."[22] In 1922 she zeroed in on the target—free maternity care for the poor, forces "the healthier and more normal sections of the world to shoulder ... the unthinking and indiscriminate fecundity of others; which brings with it ... a dead weight of human waste ... "[23] Planned Parenthood's present prejudice against helping adolescent mothers and its preference for abortions and contraceptives is dutiful to the traditions.[24]

In later statements Mrs. Sanger clarified her point with rigor. In 1932 her *Birth Control Review* carried her injunction for "a stern and rigid policy of sterilization and segregation" of those persons "already tainted" by their heredity. Such people, she contended, should be offered pensions in return for their consent to be sterilized, but if they refused, they should be segregated from the general population so that their "tainted" inheritance would not infect future generations. The afflicted would be relegated, for life, to designated "farm lands and homesteads" where "they would be taught to work under competent instructors",[25] and she sentenced "fifteen or twenty million of our population"[26] to this exile.

In 1933 her *Birth Control Review* delved deeply into eugenic sterilization. In a featured article, "Eugenic Sterilization: An Urgent Need", Professor Dr. Ernst Rudin, curator of the Kaiser Wilhelm Institute for Anthropology, Human Genetics, and Eugenics, demanded rousing action to "prevent the multiplication of bad stocks" and "increase the birth-rate of the sound average population".[27]

Sanger herself devised the cost-benefit justification for selective birth control that has been promulgated by Planned Parenthood. She urged her disciples to "ask

---

[20] Chase, op. cit., p. 20.

[21] Miriam Allen de Ford, "The Woman Rebel", *Humanist,* Special Issue, Spring 1965, p. 96.

[22] *Birth Control Review,* May 1919, quoted in Chase, op. cit., p. 55.

[23] Margaret Sanger, *Pivot of Civilization* (New York: Brentano's, 1922), p. 177, quoted in Drogin, op. cit.

[24] See Frederick S. Jaffe, Testimony in *Hearings* before the Select Committee on Population, "Fertility and Contraception in America: Adolescent and Pre-Adolescent Pregnancy", 95th Congress, 2nd Session, vol. II (Washington: U.S. Government Printing Office, 1978), pp. 538–550.

[25] *Birth Control Review,* vol. 16, no. 4, April 1932, p. 107, quoted in Drogin, op. cit.

[26] Ibid.

[27] *Birth Control Review,* vol. 17, no. 4, April 1933, p. 102, quoted in Drogin, op. cit.

the government to . . . take the burden of the insane and feebleminded from your back. Sterilization for these is the solution."[28] And she decried the democratic process, in which "a moron's vote [is] as good as the vote of a genius"[29] and "funds that should be used to raise the standard of our civilization are diverted to maintenance of those who never should have been born".[30]

Sanger corresponded with Clarence Gamble, another early leader of the population-control movement and founder of the influential Pathfinder Fund, and told him of her plan to persuade American blacks to practice birth control. Her strategy was to use black ministers "with engaging personalities" to spearhead the movement and thus neutralize black opposition.[31]

Sanger was an intimate friend of Havelock Ellis, the great sexologist, who is credited with converting her from her original emphasis on quantity, in her birth-control pursuits, to eugenics.[32] Sanger was one of the most influential people of her time, and counted among her friends and associates many of the richest and most powerful of the age. In 1916 she organized her first birth control clinic under the auspices of her National Birth Control League, and in 1921, founded the American Birth Control League, which in 1939 became the Birth Control Federation, the parent of today's Planned Parenthood.[33]

During World War II and for some years after, the birth control-eugenics furor subsided in the Allied Countries in response to the pall the Nazi experiments in scientific racism cast on eugenic dabblings—the attempts to improve the biological product. But voices were not entirely stilled. In 1945, for example, eugenicist Guy Irving Burch, founder of the Population Reference Bureau, published a book, *Population Roads to Peace or War,* which he offered as a guide to the peace negotiations. The book counseled compulsory sterilization of "all persons who are inadequate, either biologically or socially", and asked the peace negotiators to "recommend" such laws for "all nations", but to "insist" on them in the conquered countries.[34] Unless such laws were passed, Burch warned, endless disasters would ensue and the new peace would be "as transitory as were the results of the Versailles Treaty".[35]

Burch and his compatriots worked throughout the fifties, regrouping, renaming

[28] *Birth Control Review,* October 1926, quoted in Drogin, op. cit.

[29] *Birth Control Review,* April 1925, quoted in Drogin, op. cit.

[30] Sanger, *Pivot of Civilization,* op. cit., p. 279, quoted in Drogin, op.cit.

[31] Linda Gordon, *Woman's Body, Woman's Right: A Social History of Birth Control* (New York: Grossman Publishing Co., 1976), pp. 332–333, quoted in Drogin, op. cit.

[32] Chase, op. cit., p. 294.

[33] Alan F. Guttmacher, "The Planned Parenthood Federation of America, Inc., General Program", in Mary Steichen Calderone, ed., *Manual of Family Planning and Contraceptive Practice.* 2nd ed. (Baltimore: The Williams & Wilkins Co., 1970), pp. 91–96; and *Encyclopaedia Britannica,* 1953 ed.

[34] Guy Irving Burch and Elmer Pendell, *Population Roads to Peace or War* (Washington: Population Reference Bureau, 1945), p. 103.

[35] Ibid., p. 130.

their organizations, forming new ones, and, above all, burrowing into the councils of power. In the early 1960s the movement reemerged as a Campaign to Check the Population Explosion and, sounding the alarm regarding the "population bomb", it captured the imagination of the mass media.

Playing up fear of the bomb, according to historians of the movement, was largely the work of one man. Elizabeth Moore and Lawrence Lader recount that Hugh Moore of the Dixie Cup fortune was persuaded of the threat of overpopulation by a 1948 book by William Vogt, a former official of Planned Parenthood. From then on, Moore devoted much of his fortune and energies to publicizing the "bomb" and enlisting support. In 1954 he sent his pamphlet *The Population Bomb* to one thousand leaders in business and the professions,[36] and subsequently to another million-and-a-half, and gave Paul Ehrlich permission to use the title for his 1968 book.

As chairman of the Population Reference Bureau, Moore labored to commit the federal government to population control abroad. His friendship with like-minded General William Draper, Jr., bore fruit in 1958 when President Eisenhower appointed Draper chairman of a committee to investigate the impact of foreign aid on economic growth in foreign countries. Draper made sure that Moore's population materials, published by the Population Reference Bureau and the Hugh Moore Fund, deluged the committee, which responded by issuing the 1959 Draper Report, the "first official government report to take a stand on birth control".[37]

In 1960 Moore began the World Population Emergency Campaign, which raised enormous sums of money and merged with the International Planned Parenthood Federation in 1961 to form Planned Parenthood–World Population.[38]

In 1961 the Hugh Moore Fund began its full-page advertising campaign in the *New York Times,* the *Washington Post,* the *Wall Street Journal,* and *Time* magazine. Droves of influential people signed the advertisements—Thurman Arnold, Frank Abrams, Joseph Wood Krutch, Reinhold Niebuhr, Mark Van Doren, Jonas Salk, Draper and Moore themselves, and many others.[39] Moore served as president of the Association for Voluntary Sterilization and he founded the Population Crisis Committee, enlisting the rich, the powerful, and the ambitious to lobby in Washington. He was tireless. He created the Campaign to Check the Population Explosion to involve people in public relations and advertising and, in 1970, brought the full force of his capabilities to bear on "Earth Day", distributing some 300,000 flyers on his population bomb to the demonstrators, and a free tape of Paul Ehrlich and environmentalist David Brower to radio stations. College newspa-

---

[36] Elizabeth Moore, "How American Big Business Sold Us the Population Bomb", *The Uncertified Human,* August 1978, pp. 3–6.

[37] Moore, op. cit.

[38] Ibid.

[39] For reproductions of some of these advertisements, see Chase, op. cit., pp. 384–385.

pers ran his free cartoons, and his newspaper ads proclaimed that pollution was primarily caused by too many people.[40]

But by the time in 1970 that Hugh Moore captured the fancy of young nature lovers on Earth Day with his slogan that "people pollute", he and his band had already conquered the U.S. government. Back in the mid-1960s, in response to heavy pressure, Congress voted to provide birth control services both at home and abroad. In his 1966 message on health and education, President Johnson stated that "it is essential that all families have access to information and services that will allow freedom to choose the number and spacing of their children within the dictates of individual conscience".[41]

In the preceding year, as part of the War on Poverty, the Office of Economic Opportunity had begun to make family-planning grants to community action agencies.[42] In 1967 Congress amended the Social Security Act to provide funds for family planning in maternal and child health programs; Title V, Title XIX and Title XX of the act became major vehicles for federal funding of family planning. That same year Congress amended the Foreign Assistance Act to finance family planning and population programs in countries receiving U.S. foreign aid; Title X of the act was the vehicle in this case.

The steamroller bore on. In 1968 President Johnson appointed a Committee on Population and Family Planning, and, as expected, it recommended further doses of domestic and foreign expenditures on birth control and a major public program of biomedical and behavioral research to undergird the federal designs for birth control.[43]

Richard Nixon was the first president to send a message directly to Congress calling for even greater funding of the population programs,[44] and in 1970 he struck new ground by appointing the now-famous Commission on Population Growth and the American Future, under the chairmanship of John D. Rockefeller III, founder of the Population Council and a dedicated member of the antinatalist movement. The commission, whose membership and staff were substantially of the same die, threw its weight behind a host of population deterrents—free abortion-on-demand, sex education, easier voluntary sterilization, and public solicitation of teenagers to adopt contraceptives.[45] In his letter transmitting the commission's Report to Congress, Rockefeller ordained that since further popula-

[40] Moore, op. cit.

[41] Quoted in Population Reference Bureau, *World Population Growth and Response: 1965–1975—A Decade of Global Action* (Washington: The Population Reference Bureau, April 1976), p. 184.

[42] Ibid.

[43] Ibid., p. 185.

[44] Ibid.

[45] *Population and the American Future: The Report of the Commission on Population Growth and the American Future* (New York: New American Library, 1972), pp. 137, 171, 178, 189–190.

tion growth would not advance such essential national interests as "the vitality of business", it had better stop.[46]

President Nixon received the report with what the Guttmacher Institute described as "reserve". The President in fact restated his opposition to abortion and to the provision of contraceptives to minors, and ignored its other recommendations.[47]

But in the same year, 1970, without waiting for the commission's Report, an impatient Congress passed the Family Planning Services and Population Research Act, amending Title X of the Public Health Services Act and authorizing $382 million for a three-year program. It has become the vehicle for the largest continuing federal funding of birth control.

Through its battery of legislation, Congress provided for the world's largest program of publicly financed birth control, both at home and abroad, and undertook 90 percent of the worldwide research on population and family planning.[48]

The muscle for the legislation, together with the supporting speeches, was based on materials supplied to the President and the Congress by Planned Parenthood and its research arm, the Alan Guttmacher Institute.[49] Though the domestic program was slated to be administered by an Office of Population Affairs in the Department of Health, Education, and Welfare, with a corresponding office for the foreign programs in the Department of State, these programs have grown so large and so complex, and are scattered through so many parts of the federal bureaucracy, that no agency seems to know what is going on or how much money is involved. For example, the Population Reference Bureau, which has a great stake in the size of its massive funding, estimated that in fiscal 1975 the Department of Health, Education, and Welfare provided $201 million for organized family-planning programs. But the department itself reported only $148 million to the Senate Committee on Labor and Human Resources.[50] Recent but by no means all-inclusive estimates by the General Accounting Office show that Department of Health and Human Services obligations for selected categories of family-planning and population research activities amounted to more than $600 million in fiscal 1984.[51]

[46] John D. Rockefeller III, Letter to the President and Congress, transmitting the Final Report of the Commission on Population Growth and the American Future, dated March 27, 1972.

[47] Alan Guttmacher Institute, *Informing Social Change* (New York: The Alan Guttmacher Institute, 1980), p. 19.

[48] Population Reference Bureau, *World Population Growth and Response,* op. cit., p. 187.

[49] Alan Guttmacher Institute, op. cit., p. 17.

[50] Population Reference Bureau figure from *World Population Growth and Response,* op. cit., p. 187; U.S. Department of Health and Human Services figures compiled for the Senate Committee on Labor and Human Resources and appearing in Susan Roylance, Testimony before the Committee, March 31, 1981.

[51] U.S. Department of Health and Human Services, *Report on Population and Family Planning Activity: A Report to the House Committee on Appropriations,* January 1985, and personal letter from Jo Ann Gasper to Jacqueline R. Kasun, dated May 21, 1985.

Whatever the size of the expenditures, the program reaches into a morass of public agencies and surpasses the combined efforts of all other countries.[52] Even then, since so many other government expenditures carry conditions—submission one way or the other to family planning—the force of the movement outweighs the money involved. Federal law, for example, requires that all persons who receive federally funded public assistance, "including minors who can be considered to be sexually active", must be offered family planning services.[53] Personal statements by aid recipients indicate that many believe they must practice birth control in order to receive public aid, even though federal law states that acceptance shall be "voluntary ... and ... not ... a prerequisite to eligibility for ... any other service".[54]

In addition to this battery of legislation, federal law requires health maintenance organizations to provide family planning services, and state laws are pitted with family planning projects, varying from sex education in the schools to sterilization, abortion, and "genetic screening".

The Population Reference Bureau reports that by 1974 the purposes of federally assisted family planning as originally stated by President Johnson had been substantially achieved. By that year, 95 percent of all counties in the United States had publicly funded family-planning services; the remaining 5 percent of counties were sparsely settled and had few low-income women.[55]

But Congress, again reacting to persistent antinatalist pressures, continued its expansion and funding, especially during the Carter administration.

In 1977, in the Career Education Incentive Act, Congress presented to the new sex educators and birth controllers the wish dearest to their hearts—funds for "the elimination of bias and stereotyping ... on account of race, sex, age, economic status, or handicap".[56] It authorized grants to enable states to integrate career education into the regular education programs offered in elementary and secondary schools, employing "such staff as are necessary" to eliminate the said "stereotyping".[57] Such grants, of course, are crucial to a public school system that lost some 3 million pupils due to birth declines, compounded by the stampede to private schooling during the 1970s. The "anti-stereotyping" grants guarantee that all school materials will be screened so as to buttress the ideological leanings of the government birth controllers and sex educators—depicting women in hard hats or judicial robes, and men in kitchen aprons holding babies.

In 1978, Congress moved further into the public control of reproduction. Free access to birth control was now not enough, the government had actually to

[52] Population Reference Bureau, *World Population Growth and Response,* op. cit., p. 226.
[53] 42 U.S. Code, sec. 602(a).
[54] Ibid.
[55] Population Reference Bureau, *World Population Growth and Response,* op. cit., p. 188.
[56] PL 95–207, 20 U.S. Code, sec. 2602.
[57] 20 U.S. Code, sec. 2605.

"prevent unwanted early and repeat pregnancies ... " In the Adolescent Pregnancy Act of 1978,[58] in words inspired by the Guttmacher Institute, Congress found that "pregnancy and childbirth among adolescents ... often results in severe adverse health, social, and economic consequences" and that federal policy must gear up to prevent such pregnancies. Well beyond mere "family planning clinics", the act dictated the use "to the maximum extent feasible" of "health care centers ... children and youth centers, maternal and infant health centers, regional rural health facilities, school and other educational programs, nutrition programs, recreation programs ... "—in short, the mobilization of the entire educational, health, welfare, and recreation structure of the nation to prevent adolescent pregnancy.

Still not satisfied, in the same year Congress passed the Population Education Act,[59] authorizing federal funds for the development and provision of population education in elementary and secondary schools. Population education was to be injected into "a broad array of subject fields such as geography, history, science, biology, social studies, and home economics". Further grants were authorized for curriculum development, teacher training, and a national "clearinghouse" of population education in the National Institute of Education.[60] It gave additional thrust to the push by organizations such as the Population Reference Bureau to implant their overpopulation ideology in the schools. The Bureau was now in the happy position of receiving grants to produce materials that schools would be paid to use.

The foreign population-control programs operated by the United States are even more frankly antinatalist than their domestic counterparts. Under the terms of Sections 102 and 104(d) of the International Development and Food Assistance Act of 1978, the entire foreign aid program must be geared to encourage smaller families in all countries receiving U.S. aid. U.S. appropriations explicitly designated for foreign population assistance amounted to $185 million in fiscal 1980, $290 million in 1985, and $230 million in 1987. Implicitly, of course, the full amount spent on foreign aid—$12 billion in 1985—is tainted by the antinatalist ideology.

In tandem with their success in the United States during the 1960s and 1970s, the American antipopulation activists made strides in the United Nations and the World Bank. The United Nations Fund for Population Activities, the United Nations Children's Fund (UNICEF), the Food and Agriculture Organization, and the World Health Organization combined forces to reduce world fertility, focusing on the less-developed nations.[61] The World Bank, under the direction of Robert S. McNamara, became fervently committed to the cause of governmental

[58] PL 95-626, 42 U.S. Code, sec. 300a-21 to 300a-41.
[59] PL 89-10, 20 U.S. Code, sec. 3061 to 3062.
[60] Ibid.
[61] Population Reference Bureau, *World Population Growth and Response,* op. cit., pp. 197–202.

population control. Altogether the agencies spent hundreds of millions of dollars, mainly supplied by the U.S. government, to shrink the population.

In 1973 the United Nations announced its plans for "World Population Year 1974". The multimillion dollar gala media event was galvanized by countless country conferences. A flood of news releases and World Population Year *Bulletins* heralded the special events paving the road to the great occasion—films and pamphlets, an "Encounter for Journalists",[62] and splashy posters proclaiming "a small family is a happy family".[63] An Ad Hoc Advisory Group on Youth was convened to discuss population,[64] and an essay contest for young people[65] and a drawing contest for children were organized.[66] There were special exhibits on "Spaceship Earth",[67] and a specially written article entitled "Stop at Two!"[68] And, in a dreary appendage, a No Pregnancy Year Campaign was launched in the Republic of Korea.[69]

The stars of the American population movement gave their best to the production of the conference and to the promotion of world acceptance of its Draft Plan, prepared well in advance. Publications, conferences, and more were produced by, among others, Planned Parenthood, the Population Council, the Population Reference Bureau—even the Girl Scouts.[70] The dean of the American activists, John D. Rockefeller III, addressed the assembled delegates to stress that "population planning" should be incorporated into all plans for economic development. "Population planning" to quote him, "must be a fundamental and integral part of any modern development program, recognized as such by national leadership and supported fully."[71]

Rockefeller's star status was acknowledged by the World Population Year *Bulletin*, which gave front-page headlines to his speech:

> "If anyone else had said it, it would have been a fairly ordinary speech. But he is a bellwether of population opinion . . . " "He" is John D. Rockefeller 3rd, and the speaker was one of his audience at the Population Tribune in Bucharest . . . [72]

---

[62] United Nations Centre for Economic and Social Information, OPI/CESI NOTE POP/32/Rev. 1, 22 July 1974.

[63] United Nations Population Task Force, CESI–WPY-11, 73-14555.

[64] *WPY Bulletin*, no. 5, September 1973.

[65] *WPY Bulletin*, no. 11, March–April 1974.

[66] *WPY Bulletin*, no. 13, June 1974.

[67] *WPY Bulletin*, no. 7, November 1973.

[68] Alastair Matheson, "Stop at Two! Mauritius Takes Family Planning Action" (UN Children's Fund, World Population Year 1974).

[69] *WPY Bulletin*, no. 13, June 1974.

[70] *WPY Bulletin*, no. 6, October 1973.

[71] The Population Council, *Studies in Family Planning*, vol. 5, no. 12, December 1974, "A Report on Bucharest", p. 369.

[72] *WPY Bulletin*, no. 16, September–October 1974.

Though the conference, after an often acrimonious debate, deleted all mention of world "targets" from the antinatalist Draft Plan, the "World Population Plan of Action", which was finally adopted, had something for everyone. It left population policy to the discretion of national governments, who might wish to "affect fertility"[73] while, simultaneously, governments were to "respect . . . the right of persons to determine . . . the number and spacing of their children".[74] The plan made no effort to resolve the paradoxical recommendations.

One of the most interesting outcomes of the conference was the light shed on the profound difference between the U.S. delegation's enthusiasm for government control of fertility and the resentment it engendered in the other countries.[75] The Rockefeller-created Population Council blamed it on a failure in advance planning: "The organizers . . . did not anticipate the political problems . . . They consulted scientific and technical experts in preparation of the Draft Plan, but failed to . . . identify possible sources of political controversy."[76]

The Bucharest Conference, however, was by no means a setback for the antinatalists, for it had put its population ideology internationally on center stage. And it resulted in a World Plan of Action, dedicated to the "improvement of the quality of life", which translated into impressing upon countries various methods for reducing population growth — putting more women to work, adjusting the legal age of marriage, and offering "incentive and disincentive schemes".[77]

Again in 1984, at the International Conference on Population in Mexico City, there were marked differences between the positions of the United States and the other delegations. This time, however, there were no slip-ups in advance planning. After two decades of heavy public funding and intergovernmental arm-twisting, especially on the part of the U.S. Agency for International Development, the world population network was superbly organized, with rank upon rank of government agencies, United Nations organizations, publicly supported private agencies, and private foundations active in the cause of worldwide population control. The advance preparations began two-and-a-half years before the conference. There were preparatory meetings, international conferences, expert reports, consultations with International Planned Parenthood and other "NGOs" (nongovernmental organizations), publications, posters, and a specially produced film. The conference itself attracted more than 1,000 official delegates from 136 countries, 367 representatives of nongovernmental organizations, and, reflecting their great importance in spreading the population message, 800 media representatives. The

[73] *World Population Plan of Action,* (c)(1)(c)(31), reproduced in Population Council, op. cit.
[74] Ibid., (c)(1)(c)(29)(a).
[75] The Population Council, op.cit.
[76] Ibid., p. 379.
[77] *World Population Plan of Action,* op. cit., (c)(1)(c).

event cost more than $2 million, not including the cost of the preparatory proceedings.[78]

Some weeks before the conference, however, there were rumblings that the U.S. delegation might not represent the same antinatalist views as in the past. Senator Jeremiah Denton inserted in the *Congressional Record* of June 18 the so-called White House Draft Statement, together with two rival proposed statements—one prepared by the U.S. Agency for International Development, the other by the State Department—and a critique of the White House statement by the Alan Guttmacher Institute, the "research" arm of Planned Parenthood. Though pledging continued support for population programs abroad, the White House draft contained statements that were sure to raise the hackles of the population network: "population growth", it said, "is . . . a neutral phenomenon . . . not necessarily good or ill . . . More people do not necessarily mean less growth." And it stated that there had been an "over-reaction by some" to the fact of population growth. Adding insult to injury, it claimed that "government control of economies" had "impaired" or even "crippled" economic growth, and blamed "government price fixing" and "confiscatory taxes" for destroying the incentives for production and growth—"agriculture was devastated" and job creation in industry was "hampered" by these wrong-headed policies. Moreover, "too many governments pursued population control measures . . . rather than sound economic policies that create the rise in living standards historically associated with declines in fertility . . . " As if this were not enough, it denounced abortion and said that U.S. funds would not be used for it or for involuntary sterilization or for "population activities involving coercion".

The response was immediate and furious. Former senators and long-time population activists Robert Taft, Jr. and Joseph Tydings issued a formal statement saying that the White House draft represented "a 180-degree reversal . . . of U.S. population policy developed over a 20-year period" and was "a potential foreign policy embarrassment of serious proportions". They were especially irate over the antiabortion statements. The *New York Times* denounced the administration's "ignorant new policy on population control",[79] and was echoed by the *Los Angeles Times,* which called it an "irresponsible crusade".[80] The Population Crisis Committee forecast that it would "cripple U.S. assistance efforts"[81]; the House Subcommittee on Census and Population held hearings; delegations representing the conflicting points of view descended upon the White House; and Evans and Novak reported that Richard Benedick, the State Department's coordinator of population affairs, was packing the delegation with antinatalists.[82]

---

[78] Rafael M. Salas, "Report on the International Conference on Population", Speech Series No. 117, UN Fund for Population Activities, October 30, 1984.

[79] "Free Market as Contraceptive", *New York Times,* June 21, 1984, p. A22.

[80] "An Irresponsible Crusade", *Los Angeles Times,* July 17, 1984.

[81] "End Urged to Aiding Population Control", *Washington Post,* June 14, 1984.

[82] "The Population Policy Battle", *Washington Post,* June 13, 1984.

In the end, however, the White House statement, with only slight modifications, went to Mexico City. Former Senator James Buckley, known to be in sympathy with the sentiments of the statement, headed the U.S. delegation, which was composed predominantly of persons with views similar to Buckley's.[83] The indignation increased: Mr. Benedick, not selected as a delegate, asked for and was granted reassignment;[84] six angry antinatalist congressmen decided to attend the conference to contradict the official U.S. message;[85] A. W. Clausen, current president of the World Bank, delivered a passionate warning that population growth could "plunge countries into chaos";[86] Robert McNamara, former head of the World Bank, predicted that the United States would be "laughed out of the conference";[87] Werner Fornos of the Population Institute called it "rhetoric which conflicts with U.S. law and which Congress will not carry out";[88] the *Washington Post* speculated that International Planned Parenthood could lose up to $12 million in U.S. support as a result of the ban on abortion funding,[89] and conference delegates from the Soviet Union,[90] the United Kingdom,[91] Australia,[92] and China[93] criticized the U.S. statement.

The rage on the part of the population planners and agencies receiving U.S. money for population control did not subside even when Mr. Buckley assured them that U.S. support for foreign population programs would continue and increase.[94] Sharon Camp of the Population Crisis Committee called the U.S. position "voo-doo demographics".[95]

But, be it noted, delegates to the conference did not laugh at the United States. In fact, they voted to urge governments "to take appropriate steps to help women avoid abortion".[96] They even went so far as to recommend that countries

---

[83] The Population Reference Bureau, *Population Today,* October 1984, p. 2.

[84] Ibid.

[85] "Politics Crowds in on Population Talks", *Christian Science Monitor,* August 13, 1984.

[86] Associated Press, (Eureka) *Times Standard,* August 11, 1984.

[87] "U.S. Population Control Stance Called Laughable", *Rocky Mountain News,* August 6, 1984.

[88] David K. Willis, "People vs. Resources", *Christian Science Monitor,* August 8, 1984.

[89] "U.S. Flips Policy on Population", *Washington Post,* August 5, 1984.

[90] "U.S. Policy on Population Causes Outcry at Mexico Conference", (London) *Times,* August 10, 1984.

[91] Ibid.

[92] "U.S. Abortion Fund Cuts Attacked", (Manchester) *Guardian,* August 8, 1984.

[93] "Delegates to U.N. Population Talks Defend Family-Planning Programs", *International Herald Tribune* (France), August 11, 1984.

[94] "Population Conference Hears New U.S. Policy Banning Abortion Funds", *Washington Times,* August 10, 1984.

[95] "U.S. Stands Firm on Population Control", (Manchester) *Guardian,* August 10, 1984.

[96] International Conference on Population, "Recommendations for the Further Implementation of the World Population Plan of Action", Recommendation 18(e), in *Report of the International Conference on Population, 1984* (New York: United Nations, 1984).

"encourage ... wherever appropriate, entrepreneurial initiatives",[97] albeit at the end of a long list of development strategies that government planners might employ. The United States, however, did not succeed in getting the conference to acknowledge that government-planning mistakes rather than "overpopulation" might be at the root of some problems. As James Buckley later wrote, "To have succeeded would have required that a significant number of delegations acknowledge the responsibility of their own governments for much of the misery experienced by their people."[98] Once again, the importance of overpopulation as an alibi for government-planning mistakes leaps into view.

The conference also affirmed "the basic human right of all couples and individuals to decide freely and responsibly the number and spacing of their children".[99] Conference delegates spelled this out by saying that "couples and individuals in the exercise of this right should take into account the needs of their living and future children and their responsibilities towards the community",[100] that "governments should ... make universally available ... all medically approved and appropriate methods of family planning",[101] that "governments should provide more money for family planning,[102] that governments might use "incentives and disincentives" to achieve population goals but these must not be "coercive" or "discriminatory",[103] and that governments should ensure that all adolescents receive sex education.[104]

Thus, as before, there was something for everyone in the final recommendations. In addition, the Population Institute's *Popline* reported with satisfaction that Rafael Salas, head of the UN Fund for Population Activities, had called for stabilization of global population at fertility levels no higher than 2.1 children per woman "within the shortest period possible before the end of the century".[105] The conference did not go this far officially, although the assumption underlying most of its recommendations, as had been true of the 1974 statement, was clear: population growth is bad.

Besides the U.S. delegation with its iconoclastic statement, there were at the conference a few other dissenters from the dominant antinatalist ideology. Well-known economic demographer Julian Simon attended unofficially, but when some groups tried to distribute his articles showing that population growth does

[97] Ibid., Recommendation 3.
[98] James L. Buckley, "All Alone at the U.N.", *National Review*, vol. 36, no. 24, December 14, 1984, pp. 25–28.
[99] International Conference on Population, op. cit., Section 3 (25).
[100] Ibid., Recommendation 30.
[101] Ibid., Recommendation 25.
[102] Ibid., Recommendations 27 and 82.
[103] Ibid., Recommendation 31.
[104] Ibid., Recommendation 29.
[105] The Population Institute, *Popline*, vol. 6, no. 8, August 1984, p. 1.

not reduce resources, the directors of the conference forbade it.[106] Some nations—including Kuwait, Costa Rica, Bolivia, Bhutan, Chile, Iran, the Central African Republic, the League of Arab Nations, and others—saw population growth as good and necessary for economic development.[107] And thousands of women demonstrated against abortion outside the conference halls.[108]

The impression left by Mexico City was that of a powerful world movement, better financed than ever and commanding the attention of rulers and people, facing and absorbing minor challenges to its supremacy. So long as its revenues continued, especially those from its principal donor, the United States, it had no need to worry.

Since World War II the number of organizations devoted to limiting the population has burgeoned. United States government transfusions of money for birth-control services and research pump the lifeblood of the worldwide network. Unquenched, the proliferating "private, non profit" population agencies prod and plead, immerse Congress, the media, and the public in statistics at politically strategic moments. The most active of these private groups are briefly discussed in alphabetical order:

The Alan Guttmacher Institute (AGI), 111 Fifth Avenue, New York, New York 10003.

The institute came into existence as an arm of Planned Parenthood in 1968 when it received Office of Economic Opportunity funds to search all 3,072 counties in the United States for their "poor, fecund, sexually active women not seeking pregnancy who needed subsidized family planning services".[109] Repeated in 1969 and 1971, the county studies, according to the institute, became "the principal program-planning and priority-setting guide for federal, state, and local public and private agencies".[110] The institute publishes the widely disseminated *Family Planning Perspectives* to publicize the agency's research, promote its views on politics, and serve as a trade journal for drug companies advertising birth-control technology.

The Guttmacher Institute's biweekly *Planned Parenthood-World Population Washington Memo* "keeps its finger on the political pulse in Washington", reporting to its nationwide constituency on "who takes what position on which issues" and "how individual congressmen act on each question" in the birth-control population

---

[106] Sara Brown, "From the United Nations Population Conference", *Scottish Catholic Observer*, August 31, 1984.

[107] Ibid.; *Report of the International Conference on Population*, op. cit., p. 54, paragraph 56.

[108] "Population Conference Divided", (London) *Times*, August 13, 1984.

[109] Alan Guttmacher Institute, *Informing Social Change*, op. cit., p. 13.

[110] Ibid.

area.[111] Its bimonthly *Family Planning/Population Reporter* does the same for both state and federal legislation and all court decisions affecting "fertility control, women's rights and reproductive freedom . . . "[112]

The institute takes credit for being a "major source of the material incorporated into President Nixon's 1969 message to Congress on population" and "a source of inspiration" for the landmark Family Planning Services and Population Research Act of 1970 that followed. By its own account, "key legislators" funneled AGI material into the 1970 legislation and expert witnesses relied on AGI sources for their testimony on the proposed law, which was passed overwhelmingly by Congress.[113] The institute masterminded the six major planning documents—submitted to Congress in the form of "reports" by the Secretary of the Department of Health, Education, and Welfare—on which congressional family planning appropriations over the past decade have been based. They form what the institute likes to call a "national blueprint for the orderly expansion of services . . . "[114] The institute also prepared the much-quoted "cost-benefit" studies that purport to show the great tax savings achieved by the federal family-planning grants and that have been so effective in increasing the flow of congressional appropriations.[115] The AGI publications employ questionable statistical methods and reasoning that would justify the elimination of almost all births in most countries.

The institute prepared "need and service studies" for each of the fifty states as guides for their public birth-control plans, as well as instruction manuals for establishing family-planning services.

AGI has worked tirelessly for legalized, publicly financed abortion-on-demand.[116] It has "proved", to its disciples at least, that abortion is safe, and enlisted the president of the Rockefeller Foundation to demand its routine provision in public hospitals.[117] Its presses methodically grind out figures, county by county, on the "need" for more and more abortions in the United States,[118] as for instance an additional half-million to the one-and-a-half million actually performed each year.[119]

The institute created the two booklets, *11 Million Teenagers: What Can Be Done about the Epidemic of Adolescent Pregnancies in the United States* (1976) and *Teenage Pregnancy: The Problem That Hasn't Gone Away* (1981), which fueled and oiled the federal drive to stamp out adolescent pregnancy. And AGI materials

[111] Ibid., p. 22.
[112] Ibid.
[113] Ibid., p. 15.
[114] Ibid., p. 17.
[115] Ibid., p. 19.
[116] Ibid., pp. 23–29.
[117] Ibid., p. 23.
[118] Ibid.
[119] Ibid., p. 25.

served as major sources for the House Select Committee on Population, which reproduced *11 Million Teenagers* in its entirety in its committee hearings.[120]

As both "expert" and advocate, the institute has relentlessly promoted compulsory sex education in the public schools, complete with free contraceptives and abortions for minors without parental consent.[121] The institute, along with working tirelessly to set up a "citizens' coalition" of "parents, religious leaders, health and social service professionals and the young" to press for its objectives,[122] has never ceased to demand that the public and private sectors pump funds into reproductive "research", estimating, for instance, that $290 million should have been allocated in 1978, as compared to the $111 million actually spent.[123] (By the mid-1980s, federal population research expenditures amounted to almost $200 million a year.)[124]

The Guttmacher Institute has masterminded the public manipulation of reproduction in the United States. Its sights are currently set on expanding the use of sterilization, amniocentesis, and genetic screening, and on extending its foreign operations.[125] In 1981, alarmed by the strength of the opposition to the encroachments of government, the institute mounted a strenuous campaign to "mobilize opposition" to the pro-lifers. With forty allied organizations, it distributed legislative alerts to thousands in key positions, held countless conferences, and testified to Congress. The institute once again insisted that public population programs were "cost effective" and managed to save Title X of the Public Health Services Act from being combined with other health block grants, despite the Reagan administration's request.[126] A tax-exempt organization, the institute had an income of $3 million a year in the early 1980s, mostly derived from the Ford, Mellon, Rockefeller and Hewlett foundations, government-supported Planned Parenthood, and government contracts. Its officers, Jeannie Rosoff and Richard Lincoln, were paid $100,000 a year.[127]

Among AGI's directors in the 1980s were such notables as Dr. Beverlee M. Myers, director of the California State Department of Health Services, and Robin Chandler Duke, one of the most socially prominent women in America, who has served as president and fundraiser for the National Abortion Rights Action

[120] *Hearings* before the Select Committee on Population, "Fertility and Contraception in America", op. cit., pp. 553–613.
[121] Alan Guttmacher Institute, *Informing Social Change,* op. cit., pp. 23, 33.
[122] Ibid., p. 33.
[123] Ibid., p. 35.
[124] U.S. Department of Health and Human Services, NIH, PHS, *Inventory and Analysis of Federal Population Research,* Annual.
[125] Alan Guttmacher Institute, *Informing Social Change,* op. cit., pp. 41–43.
[126] Alan Guttmacher Institute, *Annual Report 1981.*
[127] Ibid.; Alan Guttmacher Institute, *Annual Report 1982;* New York Department of State, Annual Report–Charitable Organization, Alan Guttmacher Institute, Year Ended December 31, 1983.

League, national co-chairman of the Population Crisis Committee, consultant on population for the Carter administration to the United Nations, and member of the board of Planned Parenthood.[128]

American Association for the Advancement of Science (AAAS), 1776 Massachusetts Avenue, N.W., Washington, D.C. 20036.

This professional association has published several of its own studies on population, and works closely with the National Academy of Sciences. It publishes the magazine *Science* that frequently features articles on "excessive population growth" and the solutions thereof—birth licenses, taxes levied on families whose children outnumber the legal limit, compulsory sterilization, and fertility control agents in water supplies.[129] In preparation for World Population Year 1974, the AAAS received a $1.2 million federal contract "to provide policymakers with information on consequences of rapid population growth" and to help administrators "identify and modify cultural factors associated with expansion and improvement of family planning delivery systems". The product, *Culture and Population Change*, concluded, falsely, that "population is outrunning the immediately available resources,"[130] and that, to rectify this, an "assumption which needs to be discarded is that population regulation is a new thing".[131] It reported on the past usage of abortion, infanticide, and contraception,[132] and advised that governments "reward villages or other groups for reduced fertility",[133] a proposal that was in short order enthusiastically adopted by the U.S. Agency for International Development.

American Home Economics Association (AHEA), 2010 Massachusetts Avenue, N.W., Washington, D.C. 20036.

The association began to receive federal grants for its family planning activities in 1971 and has been active ever since. It conducts workshops and conferences of women throughout the world to sharpen their awareness of overpopulation and their rights and their "roles" as women. Integration of birth control instruction into home economics education at all school levels also preoccupies the association, which cooperates with other population groups in this endeavor.

AHEA has been in the forefront of those seeking to redefine the family to

---

[128] Gail Sheehy, "Hers", *New York Times,* January 3, 1980.

[129] Bernard Berelson, "Beyond Family Planning", *Science.* vol. 163, pp. 533–543, February 7, 1969; see also Priscilla Reining and Irene Tinker, eds., *Population: Dynamics, Ethics, and Policy* (Washington: American Association for the Advancement of Science, 1975).

[130] Irene Tinker et al., *Culture and Population Change: A Document from the Office of International Science, AAAS, prepared under the direction of its Advisory Committee on Cultural Factors in Population Programs* (Washington, 1974), p. 6.

[131] Ibid., p. 8.

[132] Ibid., section IV.

[133] Ibid., p. 9.

include the new "optional" forms not necessarily based on heterosexual marriage, blood or adoption.[134]

The American Humanist Association, 7 Harwood Drive, Amherst, New York 14226.

The American Humanist Association promotes the view that "excessive population growth must be checked by international concord."[135] Highly influential, the association counts among the signatories to its three "manifestos" well-known authors (such as Isaac Asimov), professors (such as B. F. Skinner), and religious and political leaders (such as Sidney H. Scheur, chairman of the National Committee for an Effective Congress). It is dedicated to the dogma that "belief in the existence of a supernatural . . . is either meaningless or irrelevant to the question of survival and fulfillment of the human race."[136] It pleads for *"cooperative planning concerning the use of rapidly depleting resources"* (emphasis in the original), "deplore[s] the division of humankind on nationalistic grounds",[137] and advocates "situational" ethics, abortion, suicide, euthanasia, and all forms of sexual behavior between consenting adults.[138]

It works to thrust sex education on the entire spectrum of society — the public schools, colleges and universities, the mass media, churches and service clubs, and the institutions training teachers, lawyers, theologians, journalists, and law enforcement officers.[139] Its views are disseminated through *The Humanist,* a magazine frequently found in university libraries, which is filled with antinatalist manifestos calling for "commitment" to governmental population control, with ringing calls that the United States "overcome" the Roman Catholic Church for opposition to their beliefs.[140] The magazine serves as a forum for vehement antinatalist propaganda of subsidized population research agencies.[141]

---

[134] The Population Reference Bureau, *World Population Growth and Response,* op. cit., pp. 231–233; Onalee McGraw, *The Family, Feminism and the Therapeutic State* (Washington: The Heritage Foundation, 1980), p. 5. The definition of family that is rejected by the American Home Economics Association is the one used by the U.S. Bureau of the Census — "a group of two or more persons related by blood, marriage, or adoption and residing together in a household". (See *Statistical Abstract of the United States: 1980,* p. 3.)

[135] *Humanist Manifesto II,* 1973, published in *The Humanist,* September/October 1973.

[136] Ibid.

[137] Ibid.

[138] Ibid.

[139] Lester A. Kirkendall, "Sex Education: A Reappraisal", *The Humanist,* Special Issue, Spring 1965, pp. 77–83.

[140] See *The Humanist,* various issues, especially Steven Mumford, "Population Growth and Global Security: Toward an American Strategic Commitment," *The Humanist,* vol. 41, no. 1, January/February 1981, pp. 6–25.

[141] Mumford, op. cit.

The American Public Health Association (APHA), 1015 15th Street, N.W., Washington, D.C. 20005.

Founded in 1872, the association was one of the first organizations outside the strictly population-oriented field to espouse antinatalism. In 1959 it came out officially for "public health organizations at all levels of government [to] give increased attention to the impact of population change on health". The statement said that "scientific research" on the determinants of fertility should be "greatly expanded", that "all population groups" should have "full freedom" of access to "methods for the regulation of family size", and that "public and private programs concerned with population growth and family size should be integral parts of the health program . . . "[142] In pursuance of all this, it created a Maternal and Child Health Section Committee on Population Control, later renamed the Committee on Family and Population Planning. In 1967 the Ford Foundation financed a family planning staff for APHA.[143] APHA has conducted studies and conferences in cooperation with the Carolina Population Center, Planned Parenthood, the Family Service Association of America, and others to train nurses and physicians in family planning.

The association has campaigned tirelessly for free abortion and sex education. Its "Population Section" joined with Planned Parenthood and Zero Population Growth to issue the 1977 booklet *Planned Births, the Future of the Family and the Quality of American Life,* yet another rallying cry for public "fertility regulation". APHA publishes the *American Journal of Public Health, The Nation's Health,* and *Salubritas.* In 1982 $4 million in government grants and contracts provided most of its $7 million income, only one-seventh stemming from membership dues. Joy Dryfoos, a frequent contributor to the Guttmacher/Planned Parenthood literature on family planning, has served as chairperson of its Population Section. The U.S. Agency for International Development hires the American Public Health Association to audit the activities of Family Planning International Assistance, the international arm of Planned Parenthood. Not surprisingly, APHA invariably discovers that Planned Parenthood programs are deserving of government funding.[144]

The Association for Voluntary Surgical Contraception (formerly *Association for Voluntary Sterilization),* 122 East 42nd Street, New York, New York 10168.

Incorporated in 1943 to promote worldwide male and female sterilization, the association received U.S. Agency for International Development funds in 1972 to

---

[142] Donald Harting and Leslie Corsa, "American Public Health Association", in Calderone, ed., *Manual of Family Planning and Contraceptive Practice,* op. cit., pp. 87–88.

[143] Ibid., p. 88.

[144] The Population Crisis Committee, "Private Organizations in the Population Field", *Population,* no. 10, September 1979, p. 1; U.S. Agency for International Development, Activity Data Sheet, FY 84; Form 990, Return of Organization Exempt from Income Tax, American Public Health Association, 1982.

organize its International Project. It spent $15 million, 91 percent of which came directly from the U.S. government, in 1985–86 to promote sterilization and to train health workers for the purpose in some sixty countries. Between 1972 and 1983 the association received $69 million from the Agency for International Development.[145]

In its *1983 Annual Report* AVS described its usefulness to the population-control aims of the U.S. Agency for International Development:

> In many places voluntary sterilization is still controversial, and established family planning organizations are reluctant to risk their hard-won gains by advancing sterilization. AVS and the groups it collaborates with have nothing to lose and are able to take the heat.[146]

Carolina Population Center, The University of North Carolina at Chapel Hill, University Square 300A, Chapel Hill, North Carolina 27514.

During the seminal decade, 1965–1975, when the federal government was nourishing the population infrastructure in the private sector, the U.S. Agency for International Development paid almost $100 million to universities for population projects.[147] The Carolina Population Center at Chapel Hill received an estimated $11 million, with the remainder parceled out to some thirty-four other universities, such as Johns Hopkins, George Washington, the University of California, the University of Michigan, and Columbia University.[148]

In addition to AID, research grants flowed from other federal agencies—most notably the Department of Health and Human Services—and by 1985, had expanded to an annual level of $198 million.[149] The flood of money engenders a cozy relationship between the federal populationists and the intellectual community, whose scholars embrace the list of "Research Problem Areas" published by the federal Interagency Committee on Population Research. Those who defy the prescribed wisdom—the threat of world population—are denied support,[150] allowing the prevailing views to reign unchallenged.

The Carolina Population Center has spearheaded the research on the "needs" of the poor to limit their families. It has probed their "beliefs and attitudes",[151] the

---

[145] The Population Crisis Committee, op. cit., p. 2; Association for Voluntary Sterilization, Inc., *1983 Annual Report:* Agency for International Development, Activity Data Sheet, FY 84.

[146] Association for Voluntary Sterilization, *1983 Annual Report,* p. 11.

[147] The Population Reference Bureau, *World Population Growth and Response,* op. cit., p. 228.

[148] *Pro Life Reporter* vol. 5, no. 14, Summer 1977, pp. 11–12.

[149] U.S. Department of Health and Human Services, NIH, PHS, *Inventory and Analysis of Federal Population Research,* Fiscal Year 1985.

[150] Julian L. Simon, *The Economics of Population Growth* (Princeton: Princeton University Press, 1977), p. xxvi.

[151] Robert R. Blake et al., *Beliefs and Attitudes About Contraception Among the Poor,* Monograph 5, Carolina Population Center.

"socioeconomic consequences of planned fertility reduction",[152] and the "implementation of family planning policy by public welfare".[153] Along with backing the "management of teenage pregnancy" (free abortion),[154] it has sponsored Edward Pohlman's research on paying people to be sterilized[155] and his book, *How to Kill Population*.[156] On top of federal funding, the Carolina Population Center has enjoyed the support of the Ford Foundation and other private organizations.[157]

Centre for Development and Population Activities, 1717 Massachusetts Avenue, N.W., Washington, D.C. 20036.

The U.S. Agency for International Development uses this organization to train operators of family planning programs in developing countries. Its annual budget in the early 1980s amounted to $1 to $2 million, largely from U.S. government sources. In common with many sister organizations, the agency also receives money from other U.S. government-supported population agencies, such as the Association for Voluntary Surgical Contraception, the Pathfinder Fund, International Planned Parenthood, and the UN Fund for Population Activities.[158]

Center for Population and Family Health, Columbia University, 60 Haven Avenue, New York, New York 10032.

This is yet another of the numerous great federally supported university centers for research, teaching, and practice in population and sexuality. With a grant from the Ford Foundation, the center was originally established in 1966 as the International Institute for the Study of Human Reproduction. Reorganized in 1975, it now carries on international research, provides, through the Columbia-Presbyterian Medical Center, "sexual health care" for women in the New York City area, conducts research on adolescent sexuality, and offers master's and doctoral degrees in Population and Family Health. Under the directorship of Allan Rosenfield, M.D., a well-known population activist, the center's goal is to "contribute to solutions" for the "alarming and unprecedented rate" of population growth in "a

[152] A. S. David and R. S. S. Sarma, *Potential Socioeconomic Consequences of Planned Fertility Reduction: North Carolina — Case Study*, Monograph 10, Carolina Population Center.

[153] Patricia B. Gustaveson, *Implementation of Family Planning Policy by Public Welfare*, Monograph 8, Carolina Population Center.

[154] James E. Allen with Deborah Bender, *Managing Teenage Pregnancy: Access to Abortion, Contraception, and Sex Education* (New York: Praeger, 1980).

[155] Edward Pohlman, *Incentives and Compensations in Birth Planning*, Monograph 11, Carolina Population Center, 1971.

[156] Edward Pohlman, *How to Kill Population* (Philadelphia: The Westminster Press, 1971).

[157] U.S. Department of Health and Human Services, PHS, NIH, *Inventory of Private Agency Population Research, 1978*.

[158] The Population Crisis Committee, op. cit., p. 2; Centre for Development and Population Activities, *Annual Reports* for 1980, 1982, 1983, 1986.

world whose limited resources are being threatened [and] where the majority of people go to bed hungry . . . "[159] The center specializes in innovative "outreach" programs that pay teenagers to search for young people in "parks, pools and recreational centers" for "peer counseling" in birth control.[160]

The center's 1986–1987 budget amounted to $8 million, much of it derived from U.S. government sources—including the Agency for International Development, as well as the Department of Health and Human Services, and the National Institutes of Health. It received contributions also from agencies funded by the U.S. government—the UN Fund for Population Activities, the World Bank, and the Pathfinder Fund—as well as the Mellon, Ford, Kaiser, Noyes, and Scherman Foundations and the Population Crisis Committee. Between 1976 and 1982 the center shared with several other population agencies $26 million provided by AID "to initiate and test the cost-effectiveness of family planning and basic health delivery systems".[161]

The Center for Population Options (CPO), 1012 14th Street, N.W., Washington, D.C. 20005.

Established to promote sex education and full access to all types of birth control for teenagers, the center conducts conferences and training sessions for leaders of "youth-serving agencies", such as the Salvation Army, Camp Fire, Girl Scouts, Big Brothers/Big Sisters, the Children's Defense Fund, Y.W.C.A., and the churches, to demonstrate the benefits of including sex education and birth-control counseling in their programs.[162] The center instructs key leaders in "facing the opposition", both national and local, to such sex information and services,[163] and its bibliographies of recommended sex books, pamphlets, and films list the standard Planned Parenthood materials discussed in Chapter 5.

The center takes credit for successfully "mobilizing" the Girls Clubs of America, the United Church of Christ, and other youth-serving agencies to oppose the requirement that federally financed agencies notify the parents of teenagers to whom they supply contraceptives.[164] In 1984 the center was "mobilizing over 40 . . . health, youth, religious, and women's organizations" to force television and radio stations to accept "tasteful, accurate contraceptive ads" to "increase adoles-

---

[159] Center for Population and Family Health, *1977–78 Annual Report.*

[160] Center for Population and Family Health, "Reaching Out to a Teenager in Washington Heights", reprint from the *Journal* of the College of Physicians and Surgeons, undated.

[161] U.S. Agency for International Development, Activity Data Sheet, FY 1984; Center for Population and Family Health, *Annual Report,* 1986–87.

[162] The Center for Population Options, *Annual Report 1983–1984; Preventing Adolescent Pregnancy: The Role of the Youth Serving Agency,* Report of a Conference Co-sponsored by the Center for Population Options and the Center for Population and Family Health, College of Physicians and Surgeons, Columbia University, March 2, 1982.

[163] *Preventing Adolescent Pregnancy,* op. cit., p. 3.

[164] CPO, *Annual Report,* op. cit., p. 8.

cent awareness of the need for practicing contraception".[165] It also sponsors a "research program" that has discovered that "school-based comprehensive health clinics" (i.e., birth control clinics in schools) reduce births (by increasing abortions, as Chapter 6 showed), and plans to help more schools to establish such clinics.[166] The center publishes information about current government funding and other public action on adolescent pregnancy. It receives support from the Ford, Rockefeller, and Stewart Mott Foundations, works closely with other population agencies, and includes among its officers many of the same people who are active in the other agencies—Joy Dryfoos, Karen Mulhauser, Stewart Mott, and others.[167]

Church World Service, 475 Riverside Drive, New York, New York 10115.

Supported by the U.S. government and members of the National Council of Churches, Church World Service has been active in the population field since 1965. The organization distributes contraceptives and sustains family-planning clinics in developing countries, stressing "multidisciplinary" programs—family planning interjected into services such as maternal and child health programs.[168] The organization has worked closely with Family Planning International Assistance, the international division of Planned Parenthood, to use religious hospitals in a successful stratagem to overcome local "opposition to family planning".[169] Such church-based programs, backed with U.S. government funds, have had persuasive effects in India, Brazil, the Philippines, Indonesia, Egypt, and other countries.[170] Church World Service was part of the forceful U.S. drive (described in Chapter 4) to curtail fertility in Thailand. The agency received $8 million in grants and commodies from the U.S. government in 1986, or about 17% of its total income.[171]

Family Health International (formerly "International Fertility Research Program"), Research Triangle Park, North Carolina 27709.

Another of the great North Carolina grouping of population organizations, it has published a vast quantity of research based on its clinical experience in forty-seven countries. One of its principal officials is Malcolm Potts, well known in population circles for his authorship of numerous works justifying abortion as essential to world population control. In Potts' own words, "There *is* a sense in which both the unwanted pregnancy and gonorrhea can be regarded, like the common cold, as 'sexually transmitted diseases'."[172] He is engrossed with the

---

[165] Ibid., p. 9.
[166] Ibid., pp. 10–11.
[167] *Preventing Adolescent Pregnancy,* op. cit.; CPO, *Annual Report,* op. cit.
[168] The Population Crisis Committee, op. cit., p. 2.
[169] The Population Reference Bureau, *World Population Growth and Response,* op. cit., p. 238.
[170] Ibid.
[171] *Annual Report Church World Service,* 1983, 1986.
[172] Malcolm Potts et al, *Abortion* (Cambridge: Cambridge University Press, 1977), p. 530.

"erosive effects of population growth"[173] and envisions "the hypothetical situation where a global abortion service is designed to bring the world population to zero growth rate".[174] Potts' work has been lavishly funded by the U.S. government, with $42 million donated by the U.S. Agency for International Development to his International Fertility Research Program between 1971 and 1983. Though AID provides the bulk of the agency's income, donations also come from foundations and pharmaceutical companies, including Norwich Eaton, G. D. Searle, Ortho, and Pfizer.[175] Studies done by Potts' agency have recently concluded that it is safe for "fieldworkers with only a few days of training" and "with minimal medical supervision" to dispense birth-control pills and other contraceptives, as is often done in population-control programs in less-developed countries.[176]

Family Planning International Assistance (FPIA), 810 Seventh Avenue, New York, New York 10019.

Established in 1971, this division of the Planned Parenthood Federation of America, though housed alongside its parent organization and also supported by the U.S. government, receives separate federal grants. It provides the usual birth-control products and assistance to family planning programs in developing countries, but with an emphasis on "outreach" to women's and youth groups and a commitment to the system that "motivates" people to use birth control. By subgranting its U.S. funds to local agencies in foreign countries, FPIA avoids disclosing some of the activities it finances. Its outlays of some $18 million per year are virtually entirely gifted by the U.S. Agency for International Development. On the occasions when FPIA has been audited, AID has arranged that it be conducted by enthusiastic boosters—AID itself and the American Public Health Association. Between 1971 and the end of fiscal 1983, FPIA received $132 million from the U.S. Agency for International Development.[177]

The Ford Foundation, 320 East 43rd Street, New York, New York 10017.

Many of the great American foundations played pivotal roles in labeling "overpopulation" as a peculiarly twentieth-century malady that must be stamped out by governments. The roster includes the Ford Foundation, the Rockefeller Foundation, the Airlie Foundation, the Kellogg Foundation, the General Ser-

[173] Ibid., p. 547.

[174] Ibid., p. 530.

[175] The Population Crisis Committee, op. cit., p. 3; U.S. Agency for International Development, Activity Data Sheet, FY 1984; Family Health International, *Annual Report 1983.*

[176] Family Health International, *Annual Report 1983,* p. 9.

[177] U.S. Agency for International Development, Activity Data Sheet FY 1984; FPIA, *Annual Report,* November 1982; Select Committee on Population, *Report,* "Population and Development Assistance", U.S. House of Representatives, 95th Congress, 2nd Session (Washington: U.S. Government Printing Office, 1978), p. 24.

vice Foundation, the Andrew Mellon Foundation, the Sunnen Foundation, the Tinker Foundation, and more.[178] Though less bountiful than the U.S. government, the private foundations have struck new paths and adopted activities that lacked public support. The Ford Foundation can claim star status in the population field. Active since 1952, it hired seven overseas population advisors in the late 1970s. Sharing honors frequently with its Rockefeller counterpart, the Ford Foundation name appears prominently among the sponsoring organizations in the population-control literature. In 1981 it made population grants of over $10 million, including $1 million to the Alan Guttmacher Institute and close to $7 million to the Population Council ($67 million since 1954).[179] The Ford and other foundations provided most of the 1982 income of Catholics for a Free Choice, a group agitating for Catholic approval of abortion.[180] Other foundations have contributed heavily to the Religious Coalition for Abortion Rights, which lobbies for unrestricted abortion at public expense.[181]

International Federation for Family Health, Research Triangle Park, North Carolina 27709.

This organization illustrates the complex, interlocking nature of the international population-control establishment. It is supported by the U.S. Agency for International Development, the United Nations Fund for Population Activities, and the National Council of Churches, and represents a coalition of sixteen foreign-based population organizations, together with the Family Health International, described above, which serves as "Consultant Office".[182] Like so many other U.S.-funded population agencies, it presses for "innovative approaches to the delivery of family health services",[183] a code phrase translated as insinuating "outreach" and "motivation" into U.S. foreign population programs, to overcome popular resistance and, many critics charge, to evade U.S. restrictions on the funding of abortion.

International Projects Assistance Services (IPAS), P.O. Box 100, Carrboro, North Carolina 27510.

The promoting arm of the abortion and sterilization activities of the North Carolina population complex, it sponsors clinics in developing countries and

---

[178] The Population Reference Bureau, *World Population Growth and Response,* op. cit., pp. 231–263.

[179] The Ford Foundation, *Annual Report 1980* and *Annual Report 1981;* Population Crisis Committee, op. cit., p. 3.

[180] Mary Meehan, "Funding the Abortion Pros", *National Catholic Register,* Special Report, Part 2, 1984.

[181] Ibid.

[182] The Population Crisis Committee, op. cit., p. 3; International Federation for Family Health, *Semiannual Report,* January 1, 1981–June 30, 1981.

[183] The Population Crisis Committee, op. cit., p. 3.

trains local health workers in these procedures.[184] In 1984 IPAS reported that since the Reagan administration was making it difficult to provide abortion with U.S. foreign aid, a compensatory private effort was "essential". It reported a 60 percent increase in its income over the preceding year, said that it had helped 5 million women to obtain abortions in 120 countries during the preceding ten years, and spoke of "nine distinguished private foundations" that contribute to IPAS. Gifts to IPAS are tax deductible.[185]

Johns Hopkins Program for International Education in Gynecology and Obstetrics, 624 North Broadway, Baltimore, Maryland 21205.

Yet another of the prestigious university population programs, it trains physicians and health workers to promote and provide birth control throughout the world. During the 1973–1983 period it received $52 million from the U.S. Agency for International Development.[186]

National Abortion Rights Action League (NARAL), 1424 K Street, N.W., Washington, D.C. 20005.

NARAL, with the single purpose of keeping abortion legal, has both an Educational Foundation and a Political Action Committee (NARAL–PAC) which publishes candidates' positions on abortion. Its many publications include the *Abortion Law Reporter,* which is disseminated in conjunction with the Antioch Law School. Its president in 1980 was Robin Chandler Duke and its executive director, Karen Mulhauser. Other well-known persons, including Mary Crisp, Lee Grant, Sarah Weddington, Carey Peck, and Episcopal Bishop Paul Moore, were members of its board or its advisory council.[187] In 1981 its income amounted to $3.4 million.[188]

National Academy of Sciences, 2101 Constitution Avenue, N.W., Washington, D.C. 20418.

The National Academy of Sciences has been disseminating publications about the mythical population crisis since 1965. It has published books and pamphlets on population growth, nutrition, legalized abortion, and other topics relevant to population policy. In 1969 its book *Resources and Man,* written by its Committee on Resources and Man, recommended that "efforts to limit population increase in the nation and the world be intensified by whatever means are practicable,

---

[184] The Population Crisis Committee, op. cit., p. 4.

[185] International Projects Assistance Service *Annual Report 1984.*

[186] U.S. Agency for International Development, Activity Data Sheet, FY 1984.

[187] The Population Crisis Committee, op. cit., p. 4; *NARAL 1980 Progress Report; The NARAL Foundation 1981 Mid-Year Report.*

[188] New York State Department of State, Annual Report–Charitable Organization, National Abortion Rights Action League, Inc., year ended December 31, 1981.

working toward a goal of zero rate of growth by the end of the century".[189] The book went so far as to call for "real population *control* both in North America and throughout the world" (emphasis in the original), saying that "ultimately this implies that the community and society as a whole, and not only the parents, must have a say about the number of children a couple may have."[190]

The National Academy of Sciences and the Population Council are sharing a grant of $12.5 million from the U.S. Agency for International Development for 1979–1988 to develop "government policies and programs . . . that will encourage lower fertility".[191]

National Alliance for Optional Parenthood (NAOP), 2010 Massachusetts Avenue, N.W., Washington, D.C. 20036.

Prior to its disbandment in 1982, the aim of the organization was to "call attention to the pressures . . . encouraging people to become parents" and to counter them with "better opportunities . . . to make informed choices".[192] It published numerous tracts, including the well-known "Am I Parent Material?", which is prolific in public schools and depicts the great disadvantages of having children. NAOP, formerly called the National Organization of Non-Parents, also operated a speakers' bureau, conducted "research" and a "media relations effort", and distributed quantities of materials for "clinical" counseling. Its board of directors and advisory council included such population activists as Paul Ehrlich, Stewart R. Mott, millionaire benefactor of the antinatalist movement, and Edward Pohlman, author of *How to Kill Population*.[193]

National Family Planning and Reproductive Health Association, 122 C Street, N.W., Washington, D.C. 20001.

This is one of the family-planning advocacy groups funded by the U.S. government. It monitors legislative and public administrative action concerning birth control and reports to its members (private and public family planning agencies) so they can more effectively lobby for their programs.[194] The association invites "distinguished champions of the family planning and reproductive health field", such as Russell Hemenway, executive director of the National Committee for an Effective Congress, to take part in its meetings.[195]

---

[189] Committee on Resources and Man of the Division of Earth Sciences, National Academy of Sciences–National Research Council, *Resources and Man* (San Francisco: W. H. Freeman and Co., 1969), p. 11.

[190] Ibid.

[191] U.S. AID, Activity Data Sheet, FY 1984.

[192] National Alliance for Optional Parenthood, "Dear Friend" letter, undated, distributed in 1981.

[193] Ibid.; The Population Crisis Committee, op. cit., p. 4.

[194] The Population Crisis Committee, op. cit., p. 5.

[195] *NFPRHA Annual Report*, July 1980–June 30, 1981.

It reported that half its income in 1982–1983 was derived from federal government grants.[196]

The Pathfinder Fund, 9 Galen Street, Watertown, Massachusetts 02172.

The Pathfinder Fund was founded in 1957 by the wealthy activist Clarence Gamble, whose history as a worker to promote birth control among the poor stemmed back to 1929. Gamble's gift to the North Carolina Department of Health made it the world's first government-operated birth-control program.[197] The Pathfinder Fund, one of the most militant, well financed, and pervasive organizations, focuses on the developing world, with programs of population limitation in more than fifty countries. An advocacy group, it acts as a "prodder and facilitator . . . to develop local concern for population issues"[198] and finds that "adolescent populations are advantageous groups with whom to work because their attitudes have not been so strongly shaped . . . "[199] It provides funds for contraceptives, abortions, and sterilizations, trains workers for these purposes, and has even operated its own village programs in Indonesia, where the village system exerts powerful peer pressure.[200] Prominently involved in the aggressive and controversial program in Iran, and in Nicaragua before the revolution,[201] it has aggressively promoted programs in Africa despite the admitted "resistance" in the continent.[202] In 1967 the Pathfinder Fund began to receive federal grants and by 1983 the government was financing 90 percent of its activities.[203] Because of the Pathfinder's close association with AID, from whom it had received $65 million by September 1982, it seems likely that many foreign citizens and governments regard it as an agency of the U.S. government. Like other population agencies, Pathfinder combines birth control, which encounters indifference or resistance, with other services such as infant care and inoculations, which are in short supply in less-developed countries. Since the offerings in combination attract more clients, and thus enhance the acceptance of birth control, critics charge that such practices are likely to amount to subtle (or not so subtle) coercion.[204]

---

[196] National Family Planning and Reproductive Health Association, Inc., Form 990, Return of Organization Exempt from Income Tax, year ending June 30, 1983.

[197] The Population Reference Bureau, *World Population Growth and Response,* op. cit., p. 251.

[198] The Pathfinder Fund, *Annual Report, Fiscal Year 1980,* p. 6.

[199] Ibid., p. 5.

[200] Ibid., p. 97; *The Pathfinder Fund,* official organization brochure, 1980; Pathfinder, Return of Organization Exempt from Income Tax for years 1974 to 1978.

[201] The Population Reference Bureau, *World Population Growth and Response,* op. cit., pp. 170, 151.

[202] The Pathfinder Fund, *Annual Report, Fiscal Year 1980,* p. 26.

[203] U.S. Agency for International Development, Activity Data Sheet FY 1984; The Pathfinder Fund, *Annual Report, Fiscal Year 1983.*

[204] Robert G. Marshall, "AID's Carrot Is a Big Stick", *A.L.L. About Issues,* September 1984, pp. 6–9.

Planned Parenthood.

The oldest and largest of the population control organizations, it has several groupings and headquarters, including Family Planning International Assistance (see above).

Planned Parenthood Federation of America (PPF), also called *Planned Parenthood World Population,* 810 Seventh avenue, New York, New York 10019, and 1220 19th Street, N.W., Suite 303, Washington, D.C. 20036.

PPF succeeded the National Birth Control League, under which Margaret Sanger organized her first birth-control clinic in 1916,[205] and itself spawned the Alan Guttmacher Institute, discussed above. Now a national federation of about 200 local "affiliates" operating almost a thousand clinics throughout the United States, it provides services and acts as an advocacy group.

Planned Parenthood clinics provide contraceptives, abortions, sterilizations, and training for physicians and others in these activities. But its primary goal has been promotion by the public health-and-welfare organizations at all levels of government. In keeping with its tradition, the organization's main interest is in the "low-income" groups, the young, and those it picks for "genetic counseling" and "genetic screening".[206]

The organization has pledged to "sustain the long-term trend in the nation's birthrate towards a zero rate of natural population increase" and, to this end, to act "as the nation's foremost agent of social change in the area of reproductive health".[207] It is one of the major birth-control and abortion advocates funded by the government, and takes pride in its "ability to command authority in the councils where national decisions are made",[208] maintaining "hotlines" for political information, and employing numerous professional political lobbyists.

The organization has taken the lead in securing government-funded birth control for schoolchildren, abortion-on-demand without spousal or parental knowledge, and free access to sterilization, in pursuit of which it uses political lobbying, public relations, and frequent litigation. It piloted the court battles in 1982 and 1983 to prevent the government from requir-

---

[205] Alan F. Guttmacher, "The Planned Parenthood Federation of America, Inc., General Program", op. cit.

[206] *Planned Births, the Future of the Family and the Quality of American Life* (Planned Parenthood et al., June 1977), Table 1, "Proposed 1979–1981 Program for Improving Fertility Regulation".

[207] *A Five Year Plan: 1976–1980 for the Planned Parenthood Federation of America, Inc.,* approved by the PPFA membership, October 22, 1975, Seattle, Washington (reprinted by U.S. Coalition for Life), pp. 3, 4.

[208] Ibid., p. 4.

ing federally funded clinics to notify parents after giving prescription contraceptives to minors.[209]

Planned Parenthood policy holds that breaking the law is an appropriate and effective way of inducing the kinds of social change which the organization desires. As a recent policy statement by the organization has put it,

Family planning associations and other non-governmental organizations should not use the absence of law or the existence of an unfavourable law as an excuse for inaction; action outside the law, and even in violation of it, is part of the process of stimulating change.[210]

Over the years the organization's leaders have become masters of the art of "coalition building" in promoting public fertility regulation.[211] For example, between 1954 and 1964, Planned Parenthood's National Medical Committee, under the direction of Mary S. Calderone (later founder and director of the Sex Information and Education Council of the U.S., Inc.), applied steady pressure on the American Medical Association (AMA) to adopt a policy on population control. Though there was "little interest" shown by the AMA membership, Calderone persuaded the AMA Board to appoint a "Committee on Human Reproduction", with herself as a member, which brought in the "Policy on Population Control" that was accepted by the AMA House of Delegates at its 1964 convention. The policy stated that "an intelligent recognition of the problems that relate to human reproduction, including the need for population control, is more than a matter of responsible parenthood; it is a matter of responsible medical practice".[212]

For years, one of the most dedicated officers of Planned Parenthood was Frederick S. Jaffe, who appeared regularly before congressional committees to plead for government family planning. In 1970 *Family Planning Perspectives* published Jaffe's list of thirty-three "Proposed Measures to Reduce U.S. Fertility", among them—"fertility control agents in water supply", measures to "encourage increased homosexuality", a "substantial marriage tax", "discouragement of private home ownership", "permits for children",

[209] Planned Parenthood Federation of America, *Federation Declaration of Principles & Purposes: A Planning Document for 1979–1981; Planned Parenthood v. Danforth,* 428 U.S. 52, 1976; *Planned Parenthood Association of Utah v. Schweiker,* No. 82-2334, slip op. (D.C. Cir. February 18, 1983); *Memphis Association for Planned Parenthood v. Schweiker,* No. 83-2060 (W.D. Tenn.), pending 1983; *Planned Parenthood Federation of America, Inc., et al. v. Schweiker,* No. 83-1232, No. 83-1239 (Court of Appeals, D.C. Cir., pending 1983).

[210] *The Human Right to Family Planning,* Report of the Working Group on the Promotion of Family Planning as a Basic Human Right to the Members' Assembly and the Central Council of the International Planned Parenthood Federation (IPPF, 1984), pp. 28–29.

[211] *A Five Year Plan,* op. cit., p. 9.

[212] Mary S. Calderone, "The National Medical Committee in the Decade 1954 to 1964", in Calderone, ed., *Manual of Family Planning and Contraceptive Practice,* op. cit., pp. 96–106.

"compulsory abortion", and "compulsory sterilization of all who have two children".[213]

Planned Parenthood avidly champions sex education in the public schools, and openly looks on the schools as referral agents for its clinics.[214] With school children as their aim, they turn out explicit sex books, films—*About Sex* features nude intercourse—and pamphlets—*Abortion Eve* pictures a pregnant Virgin Mary with the face of Alfred E. Newman saying, "What, Me Worry?"[215]

The organization urges the practice of picking teenagers to act as "outreach" agents, and employing them as public relation agents and sex counselors in the schools.[216]

Critics of the organization are quickly stigmatized as "zealots" in pursuit of an "unholy alliance of religion and politics" with an eye to a "religious dictatorship", dooming the country to a return of "the Dark Ages . . . the Inquisition".[217]

The federation's expenditures in 1983 amounted to $200 million, the bulk from government sources with only about one-fifth derived from private contributions,[218] although over the years it has benefited from the munificence of a number of financial angels. Stewart R. Mott, heir to the General Motors fortune, a lavish donor, has given millions of dollars to Planned Parenthood, the Population Council, the Population Crisis Committee, the Population Reference Bureau, and other groups,[219] and is a director of some of them, including Planned Parenthood. Planned Parenthood also has the privilege of being one of the seven agencies permitted by

[213] *Family Planning Perspectives,* Special Supplement–U.S. Population Growth and Family Planning: A Review of the Literature, vol. 2, no. 4, October 1970, ff. p. 24.

[214] See contract for the preparation of California State Department of Education, *Education for Human Sexuality: A Resource Book and Instructional Guide to Sex Education for Kindergarten Through Grade Twelve,* Contract No. 9968, Agreement No. 8853, dated September 1, 1979, between the Los Angeles Regional Family Planning Council and the State Department of Education. This contract specified that a major purpose of the school sex instruction was to encourage "appropriate referral processes" to establish "linkages" between the schools and "health" (i.e., birth control) programs and agencies. The resulting curriculum provided for close cooperation between the schools and local Planned Parenthood clinics, as shown in chapter 5. The Los Angeles Regional Family Planning Council is an umbrella agency for Planned Parenthood and other birth-control providers.

[215] Planned Parenthood Federation of America, Inc., "Getting It Together: On Stage Teen Counseling," vol. 8, no. 1, October 1977; *Hearings* of U.S. Senate Committee on Labor and Human Relations, March 31, 1981; Planned Parenthood–Santa Cruz County, *Sex Education: Teacher's Guide and Resource Manual,* 1979.

[216] Planned Parenthood Federation of America, Inc., "Getting It Together . . . " op. cit.

[217] Planned Parenthood Federation of America, Inc., fundraising letter signed by Faye Wattleton, president, undated, mailed in 1981.

[218] Planned Parenthood Federation of America, Inc., *Serving Human Needs, Preserving Human Rights,* 1983 Annual Report.

[219] *Washington Post,* August 10, 1975.

the U.S. Office of Personnel Management to solicit on-the-job contributions from U.S. federal employees and military personnel.[220]

International Planned Parenthood Federation (IPPF), Regent's College, Inner Circle, Regent's Park, London, NW1 4NS, England.

As its name indicates, it is the international federation of Planned Parenthood and other birth-control organizations in some one hundred countries. Created in 1952, the federation specializes in population control at the village level, employing villagers as local recruiters and distributors. Governments provide the bulk of IPPF income, with the United States as chief donor until 1985. In that year the United States withdrew its support because of IPPF support of abortion. IPPF income in 1986 was $53 million.[221] Since 1980 the organization has been giving money to China for its strenuous population-control program,[222] which includes forced abortions.[223]

International Planned Parenthood Federation/Western Hemisphere Region, 105 Madison Avenue, New York, New York 10016.

The western hemisphere arm of Planned Parenthood, it was established in 1953, with generous help from Hugh Moore, to promote population control in Latin America and the Caribbean, and has outposts in more than forty countries.[224] Three-fourths of its $10 million income in 1986 came from the U.S. Agency for International Development, which redirected to this organization and others the amounts withdrawn from IPPF in London. The latter donated $2 million to IPPF/Western Hemisphere.[225]

The Population Council, One Dag Hammarskjöld Plaza, New York, New York 10017.

Established in 1952 by John D. Rockefeller III, a dedicated population activist, the Population Council has played a leading role in the history of the movement. It has figured prominently in establishing population control programs in virtu-

---

[220] Planned Parenthood Federation of America, Inc., *Strengthening America Through Individual Choice: Financial Information, 1980.*

[221] The Population Crisis Committee, op. cit., p. 3; International Planned Parenthood Federation, *Report to Donors: 1980: Programme Development and Financial Statements, 1979–1981* (London: October 1980), pp. 30–64; International Planned Parenthood Federation, *Annual Report,* 1986.

[222] Ibid.

[223] *Country Reports on Human Rights Practices for 1983,* report submitted to U.S. House Committee on Foreign Affairs and U.S. Senate Committee on Foreign Relations by the Department of State, 98th Congress, 2d Session, Joint Committee Print, February 1984, p. 746.

[224] International Planned Parenthood Federation/Western Hemisphere Region, Inc., *Annual Report 1983.*

[225] American Life Lobby, "Their Eyes Gleam with Population Control" (Stafford, Virginia, 1982); International Planned Parenthood Federation, *Annual Report,* 1986.

ally all countries where they exist.[226] A number of the programs, for example, the ones in India and Indonesia, are famous for the force of their operations. Some— such as those in Iran and Nicaragua—became so controversial as to suggest they may have been factors in the nations' present anti-U.S. fervor.[227]

The Population Council abundantly finances university research and publishes books, pamphlets, and journals, such as *Studies in Family Planning* and *Population and Development Review,* which deal with experiments in population control throughout the world. The council has for years led the research on the effects of incentives in population control. A grant from the U.S. Agency for International Development for the period 1979–1988 is financing its research "leading to the development of government policies and programs . . . that will encourage lower fertility".[228] In 1986 the Population Council received almost half of its annual budget of $23 million directly from the U.S. government and additional amounts from agencies supported by the government.[229]

Population Crisis Committee (PCC) *and the Draper Fund,* 1120 19th Street, N.W., Washington, D.C. 20036.

Established in 1965 by Hugh Moore and General William Draper, the fund is one of the major population-control advocacy organizations and has succeeded in incorporating population control into development aid programs operated by the United States and United Nations throughout the world. Its lavish advertising campaigns, featuring prominent citizens, have broadcast the population-crisis message and won over the support of the major media. Friendly, intimate contacts with influential diplomats and high-level policymakers, in the UN and in many of its member nations, have furthered its objectives, which it protects by monitoring legislation and policy.

A measure of its success can be gleaned from a PCC statement in 1982 that speaks of

> higher-level personal contacts between PCC leaders and top Administration officials—contacts which included in 1980 and 1981 the Vice President [George Bush], senior Presidential aides, the Secretaries of State and Defense and their key advisors, the Director of the Central Intelligence Agency, the National Security Advisor and a host of lesser Presidential appointees in a position to influence the new Administration's attitudes toward international population programs.

[226] Population Reference Bureau, Inc., *World Population Growth and Response,* op. cit.

[227] See discussion in chapter 4. Also see *Intercom,* vol. 8, no. 3, March 1980, p. 5.

[228] U.S. Agency for International Development, Activity Data Sheet FY 1984.

[229] The Population Council, *Annual Report* for 1983; U.S. Agency for International Development, Activity Data Sheet FY 1984; New York Department of State, Annual Report–Charitable Organization, The Population Council, for year ended December 31, 1983.

The importance of these contacts was illustrated in December, 1981, when a surprise OMB proposal to eliminate population assistance funds from the 1983 federal budget (encouraged by a few individuals in the White House and State Department) met with united and active opposition from most senior Administration officials, including the Vice President. PCC mobilized population supporters across the country ... but Administration insiders credit the intervention of top White House and State Department officials with the reversal of a potentially disastrous proposal.[230]

Population Crisis Committee expenditures in 1981 amounted to $2.6 million, derived from foundations, corporations, individuals, and the United Nations (which in turn has received a large part of its population funds from the U.S. government).[231] The committee's officers and directors have included former Senators Joseph Tydings and Robert Taft, Jr., Robin Chandler Duke, General Maxwell Taylor, General William Westmoreland, Dr. Russell Peterson (president of the National Audubon Society), Congressman Paul McCloskey, and other prominent persons.[232]

Population Information Program, The Johns Hopkins University, 624 North Broadway, Baltimore, Maryland 21205.

Another of the prestigious government-supported, university-based programs, and formerly at George Washington University, it has been one of the Johns Hopkins population programs since 1978. It concentrates on disseminating timely information on population, fertility control, and government programs throughout the world, and publishes the bimonthly *Population Reports,* containing reviews of research in English, French, Spanish, Portuguese, and Arabic. For years it has been financed by the U.S. Agency for International Development with sums ranging from $1 million to $2 million annually.[233]

The Population Institute/Population Action Council (PAC), 110 Maryland Avenue, N.E., Washington, D.C. 20002.

The Population Institute, together with its subsidiary, the Population Action Council, is aggressive in propagandizing the notion that "overpopulation is a time bomb that threatens everyone's future" and that the world's leaders and people must be persuaded by the "most sophisticated educational, motivational mass

---

[230] The Population Crisis Committee/Draper Fund, *Report of Activities 1980–81,* p. 6.

[231] The Population Crisis Committee, op. cit., p. 6, and *Report of Activities 1980–81;* UN Fund for Population Activities, *1981 Report.*

[232] Population Crisis Committee/Draper World Population Fund, Form 990, Return of Organization Exempt from Income Tax, 1982.

[233] The Population Crisis Committee, "Private Organizations, etc.", op. cit., p. 6; Agency for International Development, Activity Data Sheet FY 1984.

communications" to "defuse the human explosion".[234] It promulgates its message through television, direct mail, and publishing—such as *Popline* and *International Dateline,* a newsletter for broadcasters—and lobbies vigorously for more government spending on foreign population programs. In its own words,

PAC coordinators enlist leaders in ... law, business, religion, education, labor, science, banking and medicine ... to become acquainted with the population issue and to speak out at both the local and national levels. PAC director Werner Fornos reasons that 'no policy maker can long withstand this kind of positive clamor for solutions from the people back home'.[235]

The Population Institute has pledged to "create an environment in which men and women perceive their traditional roles differently".[236] It has produced an "Educators Who Care Program", which solicits classroom teachers to join in "working together to solve the world population crisis", to "include discussions of world overpopulation in your classroom material", to "motivate your students to do research on world overpopulation", to lobby congressmen, write "Letters to the Editor", and urge others "to become involved" in the struggle.[237] Contributions to the Population Institute/Population Action Council are tax deductible and the organizations are tax exempt, as is generally the case for organizations in the population network; these privileges confer great financial benefits in addition to the direct government grants which they receive. PAC claims that it "neither receives nor seeks funding from the United States Government",[238] but it receives support from the UN Fund for Population Activities, which in turn has been subsidized by the U.S. government,[239] and from the Population Institute, which receives both U.S. and UN grants.[240] And the materials PAC distributes to "Educators Who Care" are supplied by the Population Reference Bureau, again substantially financed by the U.S. government.[241]

In preparation for the 1984 International Conference on Population in Mexico, the Population Institute participated in all of the preparatory meetings, briefed 5,000 "media leaders" on the dangers of "overpopulation", and trained thirty-five journalism students to "report on population issues".[242] It presented awards for "Excellence in Population Reporting" to the *Los Angeles Times,* the *Christian*

---

[234] The Population Institute, "Decade of Hope", report for 1981, pp. 1–2.
[235] Ibid., p. 2.
[236] Ibid., introduction.
[237] Population Action Council, "The Educators Who Care Program", 1981.
[238] Ibid.
[239] UN Fund for Population Activities, *1981 Report* and *Summary of Allocations, 1984.*
[240] Ibid.; "Decade of Hope", the Population Institute, op. cit.
[241] *Intercom,* March 1982.
[242] "The Cutting Edge", The Population Institute Annual Report, 1983–1984; The Population Institute, "Dear Friend" letter, undated, 1984.

Science Monitor, the *Chicago Tribune,* and other newspapers.[243] Its director, Werner Fornos, bitterly protested the Reagan administration's policy statement to the conference, and the institute gave a $963 luncheon in honor of the Chinese delegates to the conference. Guests at the luncheon reported that the Chinese discussed their methods of enforcing the one-child-family rule.[244]

In common with other population-control groups, the institute makes its appeals to and through prominent persons. Its advisory council in 1983–84 included Isaac Asimov, Joan Baez, Norman Borlaug, Paul Ehrlich, John Galbraith, Clare Booth Luce, Robert S. McNamara, Mary Tyler Moore, Gunnar Myrdal, Linus Pauling, and Rafael Salas (director of the UN Fund for Population Activities), among others.[245] Stewart Mott and Mary Dent Crisp have served as officers of PAC.

Population Reference Bureau, 777 14th Street, N.W., Washington, D.C. 20005.

Established by Guy Irving Burch in 1929, the bureau is one of the oldest population agencies. Burch, the son of a wealthy rancher, became passionately concerned in his youth about overpopulation by the poor. Devoting his life to the antinatalist cause, Burch was one of the early and most fervent participants in the eugenics movement. He believed and taught and wrote that the world needed "a vital revolution, a change in attitudes concerning the quantity and quality of people themselves".[246] A tireless worker and prolific author, he wrote a column for *Eugenics* and contributed to Margaret Sanger's *Birth Control Review* and other journals.[247] Among his numerous activities was a study, undertaken with Clarence Gamble, of the fertility of college graduates, out of concern "that educated people were not replacing themselves".[248]

Even during the Depression, when low birthrates harbingered "de-population", Burch warned about "population pressures".[249] During this period, due to financial difficulties, he found work as a paid lobbyist for the predecessor to Planned Parenthood.[250] During the World War II peace negotiations, Burch submitted his plan to solve all world problems through compulsory sterilization of "all persons who are inadequate, either biologically or socially". His bureau has received U.S. government support from the start, with office space provided by the Library of Congress in the 1930s.[251]Today the bureau advertises its "stance of non-

---

[243] "The Cutting Edge", op. cit., pp. 10–11.

[244] "Pro Choice?" The *Washington Times,* August 10, 1984; representative John E. Porter, letter to the editor, The *Washington Times,* August 23, 1984.

[245] "The Cutting Edge", op. cit.

[246] Population Reference Bureau, Inc., *Annual Report for the Year Ended December 31, 1978,* p. 3.

[247] Ibid., p. 9.

[248] Ibid., p. 3.

[249] Ibid., p. 9.

[250] Ibid.

[251] Ibid.

advocacy", but takes credit for coining the term "population explosion".[252] It publishes the *Population Bulletin,* a bimonthly report; *Population Today* (formerly *Intercom*), a monthly newsletter in English and Spanish; *Interchange,* a quarterly review of population education; an annual *Population Data Sheet,* with data for 162 countries; *Population Education Sources and Resources;* and other materials. It gives workshops for schoolteachers and provides them with appealing library materials on the urgency of the population problem.

Bureau school materials sound the usual tocsins—"pressures put on food production by population",[253] the "reduced reserves of the world's minerals",[254] and the "insults" to the planet that stem from all those people in the world.[255] Together with the Population Institute, it has dreamed up a game for schoolchildren in which they simulate physically the "overcrowding" and lack of food produced by "exponential growth" of population.[256]

The bureau actively works for federal funding of "population education" in elementary and secondary schools under the terms of the Population Education Act of 1978,[257]which funding, of course, stimulates demand for its materials. The bureau's 1986 income amounted to $2.3 million, of which almost $1 million came directly from the U.S. government.[258]

Population Resource Center, 622 Third Avenue, New York, New York 10017.

The center is devoted to encouraging foundations, corporations, and individuals to contribute to population programs. Its seminars instill in potential contributors the notion that population is detrimental to their vital economic and political interests, and it briefs foundation trustees and others on how to give most advantageously.[259]

Population Services International, 1013 15th St., N.W., Washington, D.C. 20005.

The agency specializes in subsidized advertising, promotion, and provision of contraceptives, sterilizations, and abortions. Using marketing techniques such as direct mail, it operates in Bangladesh, Mexico, Kenya, Sri Lanka, Colombia, and other countries, as well as the United States where it concentrates on sales to male

[252] Ibid., pp. 3, 11.

[253] Population Reference Bureau, Inc., "Population and Resources: What About Tomorrow?" undated, distributed late 1970s.

[254] Ibid.

[255] Population Reference Bureau, Inc., *Interchange,* vol. 9, no. 1, May 1980.

[256] Carol C. Fletcher, "Food for Thought", reprinted from the July 1976 edition of *Intercom,* published by the Population Reference Bureau. "Food for Thought" was jointly produced by PRB and the Population Institute.

[257] Population Reference Bureau, Inc., *Interchange,* vol. 9, no. 2, September 1980.

[258] Population Reference Bureau, Inc., *1986 Annual Report.*

[259] The Population Crisis Committee, op. cit., p. 6.

teenagers. Its 1983 income of $3 million came almost entirely from U.S. government sources.[260]

The Rockefeller Foundation, 1133 Avenue of the Americas, New York, New York 10036.

One of the greatest of the private foundations active in the population field, it reflects the devotion of the Rockefeller family to the worldwide movement. The foundation supports research in contraceptive technology, reproductive biology, and on the socioeconomic factors that influence human reproduction. The foundation publishes *RF Illustrated,* which illuminates its motives by posing provocative questions—"Why do the poor have so many children?"—and making flat pronouncements—"The rate of population growth is...impeding efforts at social and economic development".[261]

The foundation finances population research worldwide in universities and makes large grants to the Population Council, another Rockefeller creation. Theodore Hesburgh, priest and former president of the University of Notre Dame, served as a trustee of the foundation for many years and as chairman of its Board of Trustees from 1977 to 1982. Cyrus Vance, secretary of state in the Carter administration, served as a trustee for nine years, including two as chairman of the board. In 1986 the foundation made grants of $6.3 million for various population programs.[262]

The Sierra Club, 730 Polk Street, San Francisco, California 94109.

Along with other environmental organizations, the Sierra Club has for years urged a public antinatalist policy on the public and Congress. The club's *Bulletin* regularly stresses the population problem; and it works with the Population Reference Bureau to bring population education to the schools, replete with workshops for teachers, and simulation games for children on the problems of "overcrowding" and world hunger.[263]

In January 1981, under the leadership of the National Audubon Society, the Sierra Club joined with fifty-nine other groups—most of the environmental and some of the population organizations—to call for a public policy of "coordinated planning toward the goal of population stabilization", and for hearings on Richard L. Ottinger's bill H.R. 907, previously introduced as H.R. 5062, to declare a national policy goal of population stabilization.[264] The participants included

---

[260] *Report from PSI,* November 1979; Population Services International, *Report on Examination of Financial Statements, Years Ended December 31, 1980 and 1979;* Population Services International, *Annual Report—Charitable Organization,* to New York Department of State, year ended 1983.

[261] *RF Illustrated,* vol. 2, no. 2, March 1975.

[262] The Rockefeller Foundation, *Annual Report, 1986.*

[263] Sierra Club, "Dear Teacher" letter dated April 13, 1977, and enclosures.

[264] *Intercom,* vol. 9, no. 2, February 1981; Zero Population Growth, "Action Alert", July 31, 1980 and February 2, 1981.

Environmental Action, the Environmental Fund, the National Parks and Conservation Association, the National Wildlife Federation, the Natural Resources Defense Council, the National Audubon Society, Defenders of Wildlife, the Izaak Walton League, Zero Population Growth, the Population Crisis Committee, the Population Reference Bureau, the American Public Health Association, the Los Angeles Regional Family Planning Council, the National Alliance for Optional Parenthood, the National Family Planning and Reproductive Health Association, the Population Action Council, and on and on.

Between 1978 and 1981 the Sierra Club is reported to have received almost $1 million from various agencies of the U.S. government.[265]

Trilateral Commission, 345 East 46th Street, New York, New York 10017.

The Trilateral Commission was organized by David Rockefeller in 1973 to analyze the problems facing North America, Western Europe, and Japan. Membership on the commission has included former-President Jimmy Carter and many in his administration — Vice-president Walter Mondale, Secretary of State Cyrus Vance, Secretary of Defense Harold Brown, Presidential Assistant Zbigniew Brzezinski, Deputy Secretary of State Warren Christopher — among others. Vice-president George Bush was a member for a time but later resigned.

Commission reports have taken the position that "the economic officials of . . . the largest countries must begin to think in terms of managing a single *world* economy, in addition to managing *international* economic relations among countries"[266] (emphasis in the original). In view of its predilection toward centralized management, it is not surprising that it also believes that "population planning should be an integral part of social and economic development".[267] The commission has been vexed by the problems attributed to the "rapidly growing population", and has called on the developed countries to increase their aid "substantially", including, of course, "family planning", to the less-developed countries.[268] The commission has suggested that "grants can properly be subject to conditions to achieve their stated objectives" and "recipient countries whose sense of national sovereignty is offended by such conditions can decline the foreign assistance".[269] These conditions, as we have seen, have already been imposed in Sections 102 and 104(d) of the U.S. International Development and Food Assistance Act — i.e., countries

---

[265] *Conservative Digest,* vol. 8, no. 4, April 1982, p. 17.

[266] *The Reform of International Institutions: A Report of the Trilateral Task Force on International Institutions to the Trilateral Commission* (New York: The Trilateral Commission, 1976), p. 22.

[267] *Reducing Malnutrition in Developing Countries: Increasing Rice Production in South and Southeast Asia: Report of the Trilateral North-South Food Task Force to the Trilateral Commission* (New York: Trilateral Commission, 1978), p. xi.

[268] *Towards a Renovated International System: A Report of the Trilateral Integrators Task Force to the Trilateral Commission* (New York: Trilateral Commission, 1977), p. 28.

[269] Ibid.

receiving American aid must take steps to curb their population growth—but the commission continues to harp on the "intractable" problems posed by "rapid growth of population".[270]

Worldwatch Institute, 1776 Massachusetts Avenue, N.W., Washington, D.C. 20036.

The institute was created by the Rockefeller Brothers Fund to "alert policymakers and the general public to emerging global trends in the availability and management of resources—both human and natural".[271] Under the leadership of the prominent activist Lester R. Brown, Worldwatch focuses the attention of the press on the population "crisis" through the annual publication of ten to twelve *Worldwatch Papers* and one or two books announcing the imminence of various population-induced calamities. The "research" is supported by the United Nations, the Rockefeller Brothers Fund, the Rockefeller Foundation, the Ford Foundation, and other agencies.[272]

Zero Population Growth (ZPG), 1346 Connecticut Avenue, N.W., Washington, D.C. 20036.

ZPG is a registered lobbying organization committed to halting population growth in the United States by implementing a comprehensive government policy. Its tax-deductible ZPG Foundation has the job of infiltrating "educational" materials for population control into all grade-levels of the public schools. It has worked closely with Planned Parenthood in publishing proposals for a national population policy and for government funding of antinatalist drives.[273]

Endless as this list may appear, it is by no means complete. In its 1981 *Directory of the Population-Related Community in the Washington D. C. Area* (Fourth Edition), the Population Reference Bureau listed ninety-two private (but mostly publicly funded) agencies, sixteen professional associations, twelve United Nations agencies, and fifty-seven agencies of the U.S. government. Not only the population organizations themselves but many private charities and much of the scientific establishment (heavily subsidized by the government) have been enlisted to give the drive to limit births a formidable strength. Table 7-1 lists some, but by no means all, categories of government spending for population control in the United States for the years 1982 and 1985. The table excludes some important categories of spending, such as the amounts spent on population education, sex education, and publishing, for which no estimates are available.

Among the international agencies promoting population control, none is more

[270] Toshio Komoto, speaking before the Trilateral Commission meeting, Tokyo, April 4–6, 1982.

[271] *Worldwatch Institute,* informational brochure, distributed 1981.

[272] Ibid.; the Population Crisis Committee, op. cit., p. 8.

[273] The Population Crisis Committee, op. cit., p. 8; *Planned Births, the Future of the Family and the Quality of American Life,* op. cit.

important than the United Nations Fund for Population Activities, under its enthusiastic director Rafael M. Salas. The long-classified document NSSM 200 discloses that the U.S. Department of State and its Agency for International Development "played an important role in establishing the United Nations Fund for Population Activities (UNFPA) to spearhead a multilateral effort in population as a complement to the bilateral actions of AID and other donor countries".[274] Created in 1967, the fund has grown steadily. With expenditures of $122.7 million in 1983, the UNFPA program was second only to AID itself.[275] With one-fourth of its funds coming directly from the United States, and much of the rest in response to American pressure on other countries, according to AID statements,[276] UNFPA assists almost 2,000 projects designed to curb population growth in all continents.

Since 1979 UNFPA has assisted a virulent program of population control in Mainland China to train workers, collect data, and produce contraceptive and abortion equipment. By the end of 1984 UNFPA had poured $54 million into the Chinese program, not including the Chinese share of UNFPA's regional projects in Asia.[277] While vivid accounts were seeping out on the harsh realities of the new one-child-per-family program—compulsory abortion and infanticide[278]—UNFPA's *1981 Report* glowed with high praise: "exceptionally high implementation rate", "high commitment", "remarkably efficient financial reporting".[279] The friendly approval was in general echoed by the population network: Patricia Harris, Health and Human Services Administration secretary for the Carter administration, signed a cooperative research agreement in family planning with representatives of the Chinese government;[280] the Population Reference Bureau listed the Chinese program as an example of "well-designed family planning programs";[281] Lester Brown of Worldwatch found it a promising model in "Popu-

[274] U.S. Government Document NSSM 200, "Implications of Worldwide Population Growth for U.S. Security and Overseas Interests", December 10, 1974, declassified on December 31, 1980, p. 121.

[275] UN Fund for Population Activities, *1983 Report*.

[276] Agency for International Development, "Rationale for AID Support of Population Programs", January 1982, p. 24.

[277] UN Fund for Population Activities, *Reports* for 1980, 1981, 1982, 1983, and *Summary of Allocations*, 1984.

[278] Christopher S. Wren, "Chinese Region Showing Resistance to National Goals for Birth Control", *New York Times*, May 16, 1982, p. 29; Michele Vink, "Abortion and Birth Control in Canton, China", *Wall Street Journal*, November 30, 1981; Henry P. David, "China's Population Policy: Glimpses and a 'Minisurvey'", *Intercom*, September/October 1982, pp. 3–4. The U.S. Department of State officially confirmed the reports of forced abortions in late pregnancy on page 743 of its *Country Reports on Human Rights Practices for 1983*, submitted to the House Committee on Foreign Affairs and the Senate Committee on Foreign Relations, February 1984.

[279] UNFPA, *1981 Report*, p. 52.

[280] Reported in *Intercom*, July 1980, p. 4.

[281] *Intercom*, March/April 1983, p. 7.

Table 7-1
U.S. Public Expenditures on Some Types of
Population Control and Population Research, 1982 and 1985
(millions of dollars)

	1982	1985
Federal government expenditures on contraceptives		
Title X, Public Health Services Act	118	133
Title XIX, Medicaid	94	137
Social services block grant	46	40
Maternal and child health block grant	17	23
State government expenditures on contraceptives	53	64
Federal government expenditures on sterilizations	50*	60
State government expenditures on sterilizations	5**	4
Federal government expenditures on abortions	1	—
State government expenditures on abortions	67	66
Total for domestic population control	451	527
Federal expenditures for population research	150	198
U.S. Agency for International Development expenditures on foreign population control	211	290
Total for domestic and foreign population control and research	812	1015

SOURCE: Expenditures on contraceptives, sterilizations, and abortions from Barry Nestor and Rachel Benson Gold, "Public Funding of Contraceptive, Sterilization and Abortion Services, 1982," *Family Planning Perspectives*, vol. 16, no. 3, May/June 1984, pp. 128–133, and Rachel Benson Gold and Jennifer Macias. "Public Funding of Contraceptive, Sterilization and Abortion Services, 1985," *Family Planning Perspectives*, vol. 18, no. 6, November/December 1986, pp. 259–264; research expenditures from U.S. Department of Health and Human Services, National Institutes of Health, *Inventory and Analysis of Federal Population Research*, Fiscal Years, 1983 and 1985; AID expenditures from *Budget of the U.S. Government*, fiscal year 1984 and fiscal year 1987.
*Medicaid
**Public expenditures other than Medicaid

lation Policies for a New Economic Era";[282]International Planned Parenthood wondered if it could serve as a "Third World Model";[283] and the Planned Parenthood Federation of Korea launched its own one-child-per-family drive.[284] Finally, however, the United States withdrew its support of UNFPA in 1986 and 1987.

The UN Fund for Population Activities excellently illustrates the labyrinthine financial connections of the world population network. Deriving its income from the United States and other governments, it provides support to numerous "nongovernmental organizations", including the Population Council, the Population Action Council, Worldwatch, the Population Crisis Committee and Draper

[282] Lester Brown, Worldwatch Paper #53.

[283] International Planned Parenthood Federation, *People*, vol. 10, no. 1, 1983, p. 24.

[284] International Planned Parenthood Federation, *People*, vol. 10, no. 2, 1983, p. 28.

Fund, and the Centre for Population Activities.[285] These organizations in turn make grants to each other and to still other organizations. Chart 7-1 shows a few of the annual inflows and outflows during the early 1980s.

There is no dodging such a multiplicity of facts—the common thread in the activities is far more convoluted than simply providing "access to the means of family planning". The design is intricate. And it is intensely promotional. It ties the power and prestige of government to the imagination and zeal of private interests. Its methods are relentless: paying people to frustrate their fertility and to solicit others to thwart theirs; combining birth control in "integrated" programs with goods, such as life-saving infant health care, that are desperately needed by poor people—combinations that slip into conditions and, finally, become forceful pressures.

Above all, when private promotion of birth control is steeled by the muscle of government, individual choice disperses. A powerful leverage is exerted by U.S. foreign-aid law (see Chapter 4) under the terms of Sections 102 and 104(d) of the International Development and Food Assistance Act, whereby countries receiving American aid must take steps to curb their population growth. It insures that population-control groups, at the expense of the American taxpayer, find a friendly reception in countries receiving U.S. aid. They can demonstrate their spirit of cooperation, at the expense of the American taxpayer, by welcoming International Planned Parenthood, the Population Council, the Pathfinder Fund, the Association for Voluntary Sterilization, and other stars of the movement. The costs imposed on humbler citizens must seem a small price to pay to the government elites receiving the foreign aid.

Though the eugenic bents of the population activists are less blatant now than in the days of Margaret Sanger and Guy Irving Burch, they still exist, though screened by euphemisms: "needs of the poor", "genetic counseling", "outreach". And the inheritors of this bounty? They are pictured in the publicity flyers—the dark-skinned young people living in poor neighborhoods. The work—selective and imperious—is increasing in intensity at home, though subsidized birth-control services are rampant; and abroad, where the programs target the same groups.

The story of the population-control movement—its history and organization and leaders—is a story of the growth and deployment of great power. Massive amounts of money and powerful political influence are involved. In the United States alone, a constituency of 3,100 publicly subsidized birth control agencies with 40,000 workers has emerged.[286] Universities and research agencies, with thousands of workers, receive hundreds of millions of dollars annually for their work in population control, often justified on the slippery grounds that it serves to "counteract pronatalist influences". For, as Julian Simon has pointed out, where are

---

[285] UNFPA, *1981 Report.*
[286] Alan Guttmacher Institute, *Informing Social Change,* op. cit., p. 39.

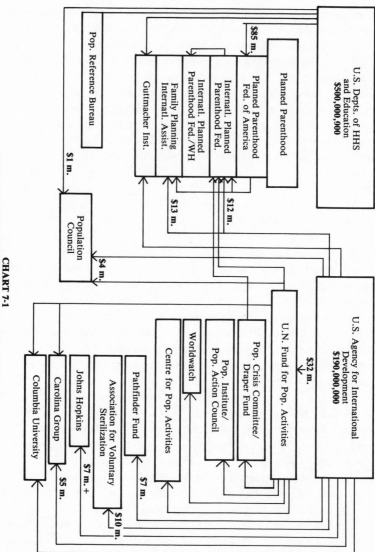

CHART 7-1
ESTIMATED FLOWS OF U.S. POPULATION FUNDS, 1981

Source: See discussion in text.

the organizations persuading people to have more children, when even the Catholic church is silent?[287]

The question, of course, is whether public entanglement with a private ideology can ever, even under ideal circumstances, be neutral. Obviously not in this case. We have as proof of our own government, which has for years now subsidized the visionary concepts of an elite, a set of people who are prejudiced against other people, and who are unrestrained in their reach for power.

[287] Julian L. Simon, *The Ultimate Resource* (Princeton: Princeton University Press, 1981), p. 301.

CHAPTER EIGHT

GOVERNMENT FAMILY PLANNING NOW
AND IN THE FUTURE

When President Carter, in his farewell speech, called on the nation to continue to "tackle ... with courage and foresight" the problem of "overpopulation",[1] he was only echoing a conviction that had dominated U.S. policy for the last decade and a half, especially during his administration.

The government's encroachment in the reproductive process, a most intimate area of private choice, has gone far indeed. If this summary were to stand alone, without the evidence and documentation of the foregoing pages, the reader would find it hard to believe.

But the reality remains: the government's family-planning roots have dug deep, with a tangle of branches entwined in public programs. The intricate complex of power and money, fed by an annual flow of hundreds of millions of dollars in federal grants, not only supports the population programs, but finances the political pressures that ensure their continuance. A host of new research, itself the result of pressure, drums into the public a steady beat for grants, and more grants, and still more grants.

President Johnson's original request—that all families have "access" to birth control to inform their free decisions—has long since been superseded by a "motivation" agenda for fewer children, a euphemism for psychological and economic pressures so heavy as to amount to *coercion*. The word is harsh, unpalatable to democratic ears, yet it is the honest word to describe the "village system" embraced by the U.S. Agency for Development; it is the honest word to portray the school sex education and adolescent pregnancy programs adopted by the Department of Health and Human Services for use in the United States.

The justification for the extent of government involvement in reproductive decisions rests on the contention that the severity of overpopulation in an over-crowded earth demands that people, especially poor people, be educated to control their fertility. The teaching speaks metaphorically of the earth as a "spaceship", or "lifeboat". We are, the tale continues, spilling over the edges, and an accretion of more people will sink us all. Put only slightly less dramatically, but as apocryphally, unless the government moves in, human attempts to achieve peace, prosperity, and justice will be doomed.

---

[1] Jimmy Carter, "Farewell Address: Major Issues Facing the Nation", *Vital Speeches of the Day*, vol. 47, no. 8, February 1, 1981, p. 227.

The advocates of government family planning have their own set of justifications, thinly disguised to avoid arousing resistance to population control. Sex education, for instance, will overcome "ignorance" and "fears and anxieties", and the adolescent pregnancy programs will in turn "reduce teenage pregnancy and prevent abortion". Not reported in the headlines, but frankly admitted in the programs, is the truth: the limitation of population. Equally absent from the news are the results of the government programs—no improvement in the psychological or physical health of the young and no reduction in pregnancy or abortion. Nor, ironically, is there any proof that they have reduced fertility. What the programs have achieved, and to a frightening degree, is the power and influence of the clique advocating government family planning, which it well understands is an essential intermediate step toward comprehensive population control.[2]

The population planners begin with the peremptory judgment that human beings, especially the poor and the minorities, are incapable of procreating rationally. It follows, then, that the administrators of the government programs assume extraordinary powers. "Outreach" and "motivation" programs are ideally fit for education in sex and population. They are adapted, after all, to reach the malleable young, at the most tender ages, to instruct them to fear something called "overpopulation", and to train them to find sensual pleasure in nonprocreative ways—delayed marriages, barren marriages, no marriages. For the adolescents, government-paid counselors are, in the words of their own literature, "actively involved" in extending contraception, abortion, and sterilization services with no regard for spousal or parental feelings, or even informed consent.

The details described in chapters past—the assault of sex teachings, and life-limiting services on our own people and those abroad—are, according to influential and highly placed American officials, only a prelude. Even more coercive measures are likely to be "necessary" in the days to come.

As frightening as it is to watch the government assiduously at work reducing the number of people, the deeper danger lies in the frank, explicit aspiration to "improve the quality of the biological product". "Genetic screening" and "genetic counseling", accompanied by selective abortion and sterilization, are gaining ground, a haunting historical reminder.

As for the economic claims of the population controllers, they (the lifeboat metaphor among them) disintegrate under examination. Resources, far from being limited, are abounding. No more than 1 to 3 percent of the earth's ice-free land area is occupied by human beings, less than one-ninth is used for agricultural

[2] A Republican Study Committee *Fact Sheet* of 1981 reported that the relationship between federally supported private groups such as Planned Parenthood and the federal administration had become so intimate that federal administrative agencies were promoting the private groups' programs by issuing federal family-planning regulations in direct contravention of laws passed by Congress. See Republican Study Committee, *Fact Sheet,* "Family Planning Reauthorization: Block Grant or Categorical?" (Washington: U.S. House of Representatives, 1981).

purposes. Eight times, and perhaps as much as twenty-two times, the world's present population could support itself at the present standard of living, using present technology; and this leaves half the earth's land surface open to wildlife and conservation areas. The ubiquitous and overworked visitor from Mars would be astonished to discover that the earth planet, with its resources barely touched, its yawning spaces, and its human fertility rapidly declining, is in the throes of a panic about overpopulation.

Pollution and environmental degradation, charged to the depredations of the population, are more properly due to a lack of political will. Nor have theoretical models and empirical studies produced real evidence that economic problems are traceable to population growth. Above all, the cherished notion advanced by the population programmers—of a hapless humanity, out of control, breeding itself into misery—is a far cry from the truth. Families throughout the world have balanced their childbearing to their fluctuating economic circumstances. They have, after all, the best of reasons—they must bear the costs of their mistakes.

The claim that the poor lack "access" to family-planning services is equally vulnerable. If they lack "access" and want more birth control, why do the government programs exert such tremendous pressure? Why all the "motivation" and "outreach"? Why the strenuous work to overcome what the planners themselves describe as "resistance" to the services?

If, in fact, the real problem had ever been the inability of the poor to buy family-planning services, an economically efficient voluntary solution was available. Those who want the poor to have more birth control than they are willing or able to buy could simply give it to them by supporting birth-control clinics as private charities. This would preserve everyone's freedom of choice—those who pay for the services and those who receive them. It would avoid coercion—on the taxpayer, who is neutral to or repelled by the programs, or on the recipient, who resists them but is outflanked by his dependence on public economic assistance.

Those who insist on the intrusions of government have so stubbornly rejected this free option as to suggest, along with other evidence, that, from the start, they have set their eyes on a good deal more than "access"—something vaguely referred to as "needs" that annually swallow hundreds of millions of public dollars.[3] And their simultaneous insistence on outreach and motivation suggests that the unmet needs are not those of the resisting poor for more birth control, but of their own for further control over the lives of people.

The government family planners aspire not only to exert more control over those whom they ostensibly serve—the young and the poor and the minorities— but also over those who are forced to support the programs by taxation. As an example, the largest private operator of subsidized birth-control clinics, Planned

[3] Faye Wattleton, President, Planned Parenthood Federation of America, Testimony before the U.S. Senate Committee on Labor and Human Resources, March 16, 1981.

Parenthood, receives only about one-fifth of its support from private voluntary contributions, and part of even that comes from government payroll-deduction drives among public employees and military personnel. Put succinctly, the government antinatalists have reached the point where they can press their indoctrination and their services on targeted groups of citizens while taxing them for the privilege.

Then there is the argument that the needs of the individual are secondary to those of society, which must be protected from the excessive births of selected groups. But it falters in face of the facts: society thinks otherwise—it has been obviously unwilling voluntarily to support the effort. And if the argument claims that public birth control is properly a public good, it certainly cannot be made on the usual grounds of economic theory. Unlike military defense and other activities commonly recognized as being public goods, birth control is not collectively consumed (at least not yet, despite a suggestion by one Planned Parenthood official that fertility control agents be put in the water supply).[4] Moreover, it contradicts another major contention—that birth control is a "private matter" —which if so, blows apart the case for its public adoption. The one possible basis in economics is that private reproduction has external effects on third parties, a very old argument that has been used variously and at various times to justify public action to influence private reproductive choice. And ironically, it has usually served the pronatalist policies (or at least policy statements) of governments who feared a future barren of enough children to grow and serve the public interest.

It cannot be disputed, certainly not in these pages, that private reproductive decisions affect third parties, but only if the results are proved to be negative could they possibly justify an antinatalist public policy. A considerable body of evidence advises that parents, especially in the modern industrial society, experience such high economic costs and so few benefits from raising children that they end up having too few children for the good of society. The tendency is reinforced by modern social programs, which ostensibly transfer to society part of the costs of children but in fact separate children from their parents and load them instead with the cost of a growing public bureaucracy. The rapid decline of fertility—below replacement levels for years in industrialized countries; in the United States the school-age population has been dropping by more than a half-million children a year—makes the population scare a venture in irrationality.

The awesome increase in social wealth in the past century indicates that children have grown up to make a positive, not a negative, contribution to society. And this, never mind the antinatalist prejudice against them, includes the offspring of the poor and the minorities. A well-known tenet of economic theory holds that

[4] Frederick S. Jaffe, Memorandum to Bernard Berelson, *Family Planning Perspectives,* Special Supplement, vol. 2, no. 4, October 1970, ff. p. 24.

the productivity of any economic agent is enhanced by larger quantities of other productive agents, i.e., larger numbers of ordinary workers enable the specially skilled to produce at higher levels.

Another pet assumption of the population controllers concerns the costs of public assistance to the poor. Costs, to begin with, have been enormously exaggerated, as have the vaunted "savings" of the family-planning programs. Nor, on net balance and despite all the pressures, have the programs reduced fertility. Fertility had been declining precipitously for some time, and if contemporary reasoning about such matters is correct, would have continued to fall as a result of social and economic forces, regardless of the government birth-control programs.

But the vitalizing inspiration for government birth control is, and always has been, eugenic. The slick, professional booklets of the likes of Planned Parenthood and the Guttmacher Institute are profusely illustrated with pictures of pot-bellied, dusky women surrounded by hordes of children living in slums here and abroad. To explore the rationale of the eugenics movement—scientific racism—would fill another volume. In a nutshell, eugenic policies do not solve social problems, they eliminate people. Both history and reason reveal that eugenic manipulation—the redefinition of the social purpose and reallocation of power—are nothing short of revolutionary. And revolution is precisely the word used by the more articulate population activists.

The tenor of any eugenics movement, of course, depends on the background of its leadership. If, say, the poor and the minorities were drawing up the agenda, who would be targeted? The beguiling speculation pinpoints the fact that eugenics requires people—the social and political leadership—to make judgments about the value of other people and, even more significantly, refuses to invest other people with human rights if they fall short of manmade qualifications. In a word, eugenics requires humanity to pass a test. The reigning leaders, picked, or self-appointed, make up the test, administer it, and decide who graduates. The view is fundamentally opposed to the basic documents of the United States, which deem all human beings of equal value in the eyes of their divine Creator, who endows them with rights as his inalienable gift.

The government family-planning programs implicitly, but fundamentally and necessarily, assume that government can, in its wisdom, correct the "mistakes" of private actions, a faulty assumption all the way around. Individual families have always faced real cost restraints on their behavior, including reproduction, unlike government planners who do not risk their own resources in their projects but shift the costs of their mistakes to others. And the ideology of population control is peculiarly versatile in alibiing the failures of the economic policy of modern governments. From urban unemployment to slow growth, government planners can lay the blame, not on the failed plans, but on "overpopulation".

And, even should the plans work, it is in the very nature of economic planning to expand in scope. Public intervention in the market process, the natural activity of exchange, changes both prices and the quantities that are exchanged. These changes in turn affect other, related markets—those that supply inputs for the one in which the original intervention took place and those that take its output, as well as those in which complementary goods and substitute goods are exchanged. The planners, for example, trying to control an "energy shortage" or an agricultural price, find themselves, willy-nilly, intervening in an ever-widening network of exchange relationships connected to the original one, and almost always for the worse. Even those who intend only limited intrusions find themselves drawn deeper and deeper into a mesh of controls.

For example: when Congress first enacted the minimum wage it probably foresaw no further public controls of the market process. But when, inevitably, there was a surplus of labor due to the artificially high price, pressures came about to provide public jobs for the unemployed, which meant new taxes, which in turn reduced consumer purchasing power and thus demand in other parts of the economy. The resulting unemployment in these sectors created pressures for still more government jobs financed by increases in the money stock. Since production and output were not rising but only shifting from the private to the public sector, the additions to the money stock generated inflation. The inflation, in turn, stimulated demands for still further increases in statutory wages—and so on, in endless repetition. Obviously, many other economic forces were also at work. This is not to assign sole blame for unemployment and inflation on the minimum wage, but to show that economic life is an intricately interrelated complex of human activities, affecting and connecting with one another by means of synapses, known as prices, including the price of human labor, known as the wage. (Incidentally, the directors of the comprehensively planned economies, such as the Soviet Union, understand these relationships very well, taking pains to set the price of labor so low as to generate a labor shortage, which is also inefficient but has certain benefits for the planners.)

Since the legal practice of holding some wages high enough to generate unemployment has persisted, so has unemployment, which especially affects the young minorities in the inner cities. Families who might enjoy a comfortable income if their teenagers could work are denied it, young people delay marriage, and there is an increasing proportion of illegitimate births. Yet again, pressures mount for public assistance, leading the government into still another realm of interventions, which have profound effects on work incentives and family stability. Each new attempt at correcting the results of a previous intervention leads further into the quagmire.

Given the frustration over the results of meddling—the continuous inner-city unemployment—it was hardly surprising to find Carter administration economists frankly looking forward to the time when there would be fewer people in those groups most susceptible to the effects of the minimum wage.[5] Birth control is now the final solution to poverty. And this because of the innate myopia of planners, who cannot see the failures of their plans; ergo, it must be the fault of the people who are in fact the victims of those failures. What the planners actually do is to blunder, like clumsy giants, into the intricately poised and infinitely complex network of market communications, so that messages become garbled and contact is broken at essential points. And the awkward attempts at repair only exacerbate the damage.

Inexorably, the planners will, sooner or later, find population control "necessary" — either as an attempt to correct for their mistakes, as in the case of inner-city poverty, or to predict and control consumption and labor in their comprehensive economic plans, as in the Soviet Union.

Beyond this, it is, of course, to their own interest to maximize the scope of their programs. It is childish to imagine that government administrators have no interest in their own incomes, prestige, and advancement. And all of these are enhanced in proportion to the size of the projects. Planners do not make profits by reducing costs relative to sales made to voluntary buyers, but receive incomes proportional to the costs they incur in the process of producing goods, which they then distribute "free" to recipients whom they select. Since birth control is now within the purview of government, it is obviously in the best interest of the publicly subsidized birth-control industry to provide as many contraceptives, sterilizations, abortions, and "counseling" in favor of these as possible. To expect them to do otherwise would be to expect them to act against their own economic interests.

Inevitably then, a government that sets out to do nothing more than to provide free, voluntary "access" to family-planning services is only warming up the motor. The fact that Planned Parenthood clinics receive their public grants based on the size of their patient load guarantees that they will maximize the load by every means possible, by seeking entry to the schools to recruit customers and access to all those who depend on government for economic assistance — welfare mothers, the disabled, the recipients of special education — everyone, in a word, who is in a client status relative to the government social welfare establishment and can therefore be expected to cooperate. Campaigns accompany the increase in services, promising the public great tax "savings". The birth-control programs work exactly as economic theory predicts of a program of cost-plus payments to producers: they maximize the cost and the volume of output of the services, irrespective of consumer preferences.

The real problem of government family planning is not one of families out of control, but of planners out of control.

The population-control movement is informed by a social philosophy that

[5] *Economic Report of the President, 1980* (Washington: U.S. Government Printing Office, 1980), pp. 134–136.

holds that there is no universal, unchanging standard of goodness, truth, and justice. Rather, the movement embraces the view that values must shift to accommodate the changing technology and the changing "needs" of society. Change, as interpreted by the few disciples who understand it, is the only reality. In contrast to the philosophical view that imposes the same, acknowledged, traditional standards of value and behavior on rulers and ruled alike, protecting the weak against the caprice of the powerful, the population-control movement grants special privileges to its elite. Its leaders are the chosen ones who interpret the meaning of technological and social changes; they are the enlightened few who dictate what changes in beliefs and behavior are suitable to the new conditions; and they are the hierarchy who impose the new standards on their subjects. They are, in the words of Planned Parenthood, the "change agents", the vanguard of society's trek toward the new future.

The leadership is fundamentally different from that of societies adhering to a belief in eternal standards. In the latter, though the people may or may not have democratic liberties, they share a commonly understood standard by which to judge their leaders as just or unjust. But in the new society, which rejects the very notion of an immutable standard, there can be no judgment. The people not only lack power, they lack even a measuring-rod by which to condemn the tyranny of their leaders. It is a society in which only the "best minds" can proclaim the new values, and in which the social engineers devise the conditioning processes to implement them. Although the people may be invited to participate in the "values clarification" process, they have no independent standard against which to measure its outcome other than those preordained by the "best minds", a Catch-22 inanity. "Values clarification" is a sop in one respect, but in another it helps the conditioning process by adding peer pressure on the populace to impose the prescribed values of the elite.

Barring any drastic changes, the hard vise on our population will continue to tighten. The movement has gained momentum in the centers of power; it has captured the subsidized and politicized educational and research systems with its rationalizations; it has its own publishing and advertising outlets; and it has won prodigious public funding and reciprocal political support. Within the past fifteen years, the idea that matters concerning reproduction are properly within the public domain has swept throughout the federal and state bureaucracies. In the epitome of doublethink, the public takeover has brandished the slogan *private choice.*

Even if abortion were to be acknowledged as a homicidal act as it was before 1973, and therefore restricted, the population-control movement would barely feel the effects, if at all. The ideology of public intrusion into the private reproductive choice has been entrenched too deeply to be rooted up by a single legislative or constitutional act, no matter the gravity of the issue.

Unless it is prohibited, abortion will become in fact, even if not by law, increasingly compulsory in numerous cases where the bureaucratic elite hands down its judgment—too young, too poor, unsuited to carry on the race. Sterilization will be even more aggressively promoted, especially if the attempts to limit abortion are successful, and "genetic screening" will ensure that, together, sterilization and abortion reach the targeted groups. Infanticide, already tacitly accepted for babies born with Down's syndrome and other conditions,[6] will seep into the mores of society.

The bastions of education, the universities, will continue to swallow and purvey the rationalizations of population control that come combined with financial sweets for research, as they face the drops in enrollment that a declining birth rate promises. The currency of belief in government population control will be enshrined by the educated classes and permeate the popular information networks—the newspapers, magazines, television, and radio.

In order for population planning to be complete, fully to assuage the desires of its proponents, the control cannot be limited to numbers or even quality, but must extend to the age structure. Death control must follow upon birth control as the night the day. The care of the "terminally" ill in hospices and other facilities slips easily from the alleviation of discomfort to the "merciful" acceleration of the dying process.[7]

The movement to encourage and assist suicide, already in progress, will gain momentum,[8] and the legalized killing of "imperfect" babies and disabled adults by withdrawing their food and water, increasingly frequent in the 1980s, will accelerate. Exotic treatments such as organ transfers to advance medical knowledge (and medical reputations), will be justified on cost-benefit bases, as abortion is now and with similar biases. The important—by virtue of their incomes, political connections, or value to research—will be treated; those who are not—the poor, the politically undistinguished, the routine medical cases—will be classified as "terminal" and sent to hospices for expeditious therapy.

In line with its successful strategy in promoting its antinatalist aims, the bureaucracy will define the language, such as "terminal", to expedite its plans. Since it is impossible to predict the time of death with accuracy, the decision to

---

[6] Dennis J. Horan et al., *Death, Dying, and Euthanasia* (Chicago: Americans United for Life, 1980): Americans United for Life, *Proceedings*, International Conference on Infanticide and the Handicapped Newborn, December 6, 1980; Effie A. Quay, *And Now Infanticide*, 2nd ed. (Thaxton, Virginia: Sun Life, 1980); "Death Drugs for Some Spina Bifida Babies", *Medical Tribune*, May 10, 1978; Mary Tedeschi, "Infanticide & Its Apologists", *Commentary*, vol. 78, no. 5, November 1984, pp. 31–35.

[7] *Concern for Dying*, published by Concern for Dying (formerly the Euthanasia Educational Council), vol. 5, no. 3, Summer 1979; "No Legal Reprisals Follow Recent Acts to Hasten Death", p. 5; and "Hospice: A New Dimension in Care for the Dying", p. 1.

[8] *Concern for Dying*, vol. 7, no. 2, Spring 1981, "Conference to Weigh Suicide for the Terminally Ill"; *Hemlock Quarterly* (published by the Hemlock Society, P.O. Box 66218, Los Angeles), various issues.

label a patient "terminal" is necessarily left to the discretion of the professional. Current trends toward death instruction and counseling will accelerate, making these new public "services" as common as birth control, and with the same official justification—to "dispel the ignorance and myths"—this time around in respect to death.[9]

The new and large discretionary powers that must be exercised by the public bureaucracy are obvious. Not so obvious is that, in the nature of all systems of social and economic planning, these powers have to be producer-oriented, unlike the market economy of voluntary exchange which, by its nature, is consumer-oriented—sellers must please consumers in order to make sales and profits. In the publicly planned economy, on the other hand, the plans seek to ease the flow of production—by guaranteeing the availability of inputs and by providing for the ready allocation of output. The producers make their plans with an eye to their own rewards and the needs of the productive process, as they understand them.

Population control, a concomitant of social and economic planning, cannot avoid being promulgated from the point of view of the planners, and as they perceive to be in the best interests of society, about which they have firm convictions. It is precisely this sense of rightness, this lack of self-doubt, that makes it virtually impossible for them to conceive of any position other than their own, and cements their governance in oppressive and rigid rules. The messianic mentality that is determined to better mankind, no matter the cost to the individual, enforces the most intolerant and intolerable tyrannies.

In contrast, participants in the market economy have no illusions of self-righteous unselfishness; they are frankly working to better themselves and their families. They suffer the besetting attitude, not of self-righteousness, but of guilt because of their "selfishness". This fuels the view that the rationalizations of the market economy are uninspiring compared with the vaunted ideologies of socialism.

But the guilt born of self-seeking, essential to the market economy, has its benefits—a salutary humility, for one. It discourages the illusions of grandeur endemic among those who believe they have a mission to act for the good of others; and it deters them from saddling the populace with the terrible oppressions of the collectivist regimes hallowed by phrases like "for the good of society" or "for the good of future generations." The guilty awareness of selfishness characteristic of participants in the market economy also breeds charity, a compensatory desire to share, to help the less fortunate. Collectivist planning, on the other hand, discourages charity; that, after all, would be to admit that the plans are fallible, the system itself has failed, which is intolerable. Those who fall short under socialism are, in the eyes of the planners, not unfortunate or pitiable but reprehensible: they need to be reformed, not helped. It is no accident that the government family

<hr/>

[9] "Abortion Scrap Over: Now It's Euthanasia", *Hemlock Quarterly*, Issue 14, January 1984, p. 1.

planners only pay lip service to assisting their clients toward their personal goals while they set about making them "responsible".

If this picture of the future seems improbable, recall how much of it has already come about. The talk of "facts" about the world population "explosion" is universally accepted. The notion of a duty to "stop at two", or better yet, one child or none, commands wide respect. The right and duty of government to intrude in reproductive choice is accepted as a given. All methods of limiting births—contraception, sterilization, and abortion—are legal, extensively practiced, and accepted. Infanticide is gaining ground for the "defective" newborn. Suicide is becoming permissible, at times even encouraged. Above all, the idea that human life has meaning only insofar as it contributes to the welfare of society has gained dominance over the eternal significance of the individual human life, which is essentially religious in its origin.

Only a radical operation on our fundamental policy could reverse this accelerating trend, probably announced by a political event—an upset election, or a series of them—in which the prevailing philosophy of social planning is thoroughly repudiated. And the disavowal must be total—encompassing the religious, political, social, and economic thinking that has ravaged our traditions and values. It must renounce the nineteenth-century dogmas that deny to human life its divine creation and divine purpose. It must challenge the concept of social and economic "progress" taking place by historical necessity, when assisted by "social engineering". It must reject the modern view of the individual and society, in which the individual is "meaningful" only insofar as he "contributes" to the society, as judged by the leaders. It must eradicate the autocratic presumption that an elite leadership can know an individual's interests better than he can know them himself. It must overturn the notion that a selfless bureaucracy is infallible in correcting the "abuses" of the private sector. And it must renounce the belief that the highest good is reached in physical perfection and sensual pleasure.

Above all, it must reject the dogma that denies an absolute, unchanging good, understood and honored by all and substitutes a progression of changing values adapted to the "needs" of the day by a social clique. And, finally, it must stop the government from subsidizing, and the educational system from indoctrinating the people in all of these dogmas.

It is a long hard list of challenges to a new ideology that has caught humanity in a spiraling movement toward complete social and economic control. Paramount to its fulfillment is population control, most especially powerful for being unexamined, uncriticized, and even largely unperceived. Its systematic support by the media, education, and research is so adroitly managed by the social welfare apparatus that the reins are hardly felt, making it all the more effective.

Those who believe in the desirability of these developments should rejoice that they have been taking place with such rapidity and with so little opposition or even awareness. Those who believe that man is now creating himself, "actualizing" himself, at last freeing himself from ancient superstitions that no longer apply in the modern technological age, have every reason to rejoice. They are riding the crest of a mighty wave that began more than a century ago with the ideas of Malthus, Darwin, Marx, Spencer, Galton, and Pearson.

Those, however, who believe in the enduring truths need not despair. They may be in the position of those who viewed with similar pity and sadness the last splendid fires of other dying civilizations. They may be the remnant that will preserve the true achievements of a civilization bent on self-immolation.

INDEX